M A R K   D A N N E R ' s

THE MASSACRE AT EL MOZOTE

"*The Massacre at El Mozote* is a compelling and terrifying tale in its own terms—and it is also a powerful indictment of our national capacity to betray our own noblest ideals when we claim the right to decide the destiny of other countries."
—Arthur Schlesinger, Jr.

"Mark Danner, in an account of such careful and dispassionate clarity as to finally retrieve what had threatened to become lost history, lifts away each of the systematic prevarications and useful polarizations that had come to obscure something terrible that happened in El Salvador, and to the United States."
—Joan Didion

"A brilliant work of research, reportage, and moral discrimination. An outstanding contribution to our knowledge of the destructive forces in the world and an eloquent offering of remembrance to the sufferings of the victims."
—Elizabeth Hardwick

"Mark Danner's study of the El Mozote massacre proves that he is a reporter of dazzling ability. I admire his remarkable powers of narration and synthesis, and the consistently fair, balanced, and humane tone he was able to maintain in his description of these atrocious events."
—Louis Begley

MARK DANNER

THE MASSACRE AT EL MOZOTE

Mark Danner was born in Utica, New York, on November 10, 1958. He was educated at Utica Free Academy and then at Harvard College, from which he was graduated in June 1981, with a degree in Modern Literatures and Aesthetics. In September 1981, he joined the staff of the *New York Review of Books*. In 1984, he became senior editor of *Harper's Magazine* and, two years later, an editor of *The New York Times Magazine*. He joined the *New Yorker* as a staff writer in April 1990. His three-part series on Haiti won the 1990 National Magazine Award for Reporting. His book about Haiti, *Beyond the Mountains: The Legacy of Duvalier*, is forthcoming from Knopf.

THE MASSACRE
AT EL MOZOTE

THE MASSACRE AT EL MOZOTE

A Parable of the Cold War

MARK DANNER

VINTAGE BOOKS

A DIVISION OF RANDOM HOUSE, INC., NEW YORK

Grateful acknowledgment is made to the following for permission to reprint previously published material:

Alma Guillermoprieto: "Salvadoran Peasants Describe Mass Killing; Woman Tells of Children's Death" by Alma Guillermoprieto (*The Washington Post,* January 27, 1982). Reprinted by permission of the author.

The New York Times Company: "Massacre of Hundreds Reported in Salvador Village" by Raymond Bonner (*The New York Times,* January 27, 1982), copyright © 1982 by The New York Times Company. Reprinted by permission.

The Wall Street Journal: "The Media's War" (*The Wall Street Journal,* February 10, 1982), "The Americas: The War's Over, But El Salvador Still Fights Propaganda Battle" by David Asman (*The Wall Street Journal,* February 25, 1993), "On Credulity" (*The Wall Street Journal,* March 19, 1993), copyright © 1982, 1993 by Dow Jones & Company, Inc. Reprinted by permission of *The Wall Street Journal.* All rights reserved.

Photos on pages 6, 8, 15, 51, and 157 courtesy of Stephen Ferry/Matrix. Photos on pages 29, 56, 100, 103, 134, 145, 148, and 162 courtesy of Susan Meiselas/Magnum. Photo on page 121 courtesy of Michel Philippot/Sygma.

Library of Congress Cataloging-in-Publication Data
Danner, Mark, 1958–
The massacre at El Mozote : a parable of the Cold War / by Mark Danner.—1st ed.
p.   cm.
"A Vintage original"—T.p. verso.
ISBN 0-679-75525-X
1. El Salvador—Politics and government—1979–   2. Massacres—El Salvador—El Mozote.   3. El Mozote (El Salvador)—History.
I. Title.
F1488.3.D36   1994
972.84'33—dc20   94-2637
CIP

Book design by Holly McNeely
Maps copyright © 1994 by Mike Reagan;
first published in The New Yorker

Manufactured in the United States of America
79B86

FOR SHEILA

CONTENTS

A NOTE ON THE TEXT

The reader will find the sources of many of the
quotations, as well as some suggestions for further reading, in the Notes section. Many of the
documents quoted in the text—the government
cables, newspaper articles, and Congressional
testimony—are printed in the Documents section.

THE MASSACRE
AT EL MOZOTE

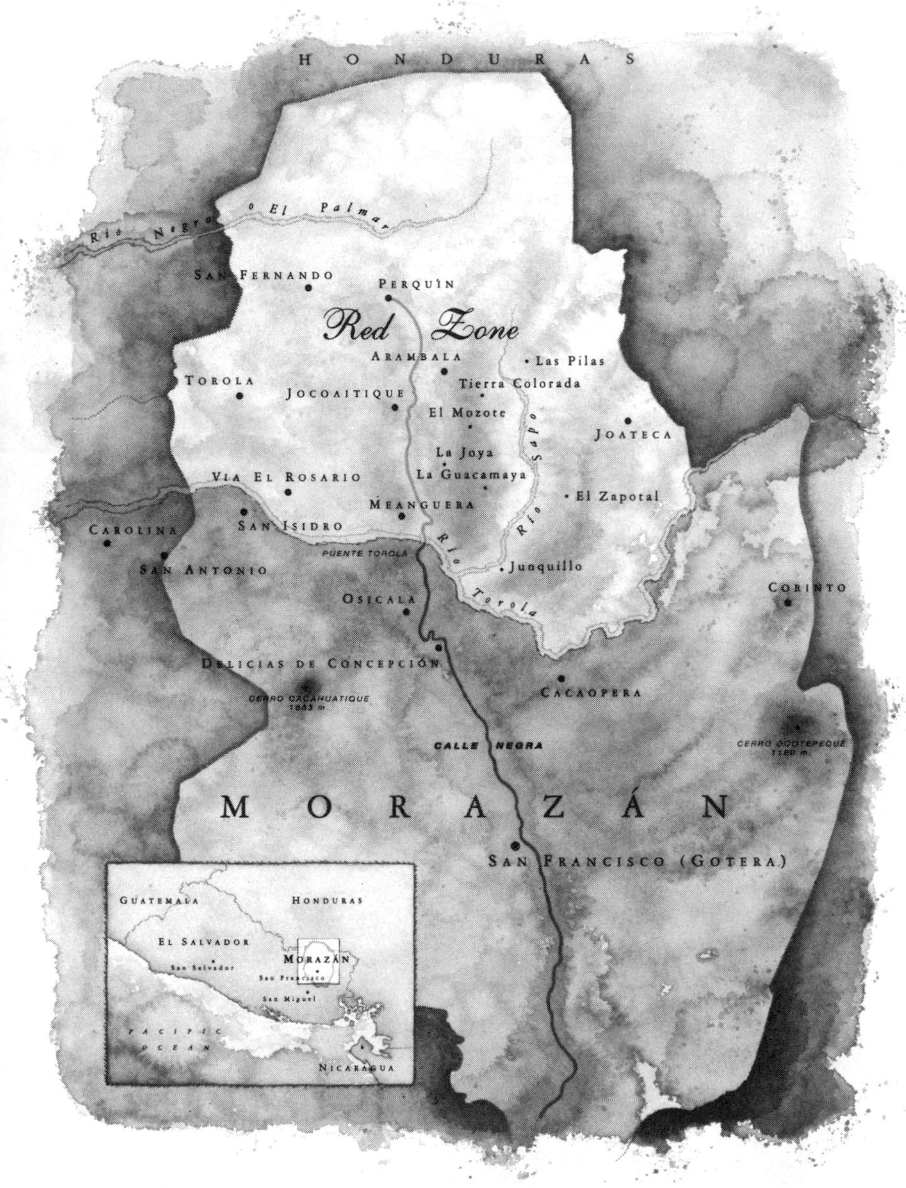

The Red Zone, Northern Morazán, 1981

CHAPTER 1

Prologue: The Exhumation

Heading up into the mountains of Morazán, in the bright, clear air near the Honduran border, you cross the Torola River, the wooden slats of the one-lane bridge clattering beneath your wheels, and enter what was the fiercest of El Salvador's *zonas rojas*—or "red zones," as the military officers knew them during a decade of civil war—and after climbing for some time you take leave of the worn blacktop to follow for several miles a bone-jarring dirt track that hugs a mountainside, and soon you will find, among ruined towns and long-abandoned villages that are coming slowly, painfully back to life, a tiny hamlet, by now little more than a scattering of ruins, that is being rapidly reclaimed by the earth, its broken adobe walls cracking and crumbling and giving way before an onslaught of weeds, which are fueled by the rain that beats down each afternoon and by the fog that settles heavily at night in the valleys. Nearby, in the long-depopulated villages, you can see stirrings of life: even in Arambala, a mile or so away, with its broad grassy plaza bordered by collapsed buildings and dominated, where once a fine church stood, by a shell-pocked bell tower and a jagged adobe arch looming against the sky—even here, a boy leads a brown cow by a rope, a man

3

in a billed cap and blue jeans trudges along bearing lengths of lumber on his shoulder, three little girls stand on tiptoe at a porch railing, waving and giggling at a passing car.

But follow the stony dirt track, which turns and twists through the woodland, and in a few minutes you enter a large clearing, and here all is quiet. No one has returned to El Mozote. Empty as it is, shot through with sunlight, the place remains—as a young guerrilla who had patrolled here during the war told me with a shiver—*espantoso*: spooky, scary, dreadful. After a moment's gaze, half a dozen battered structures—roofless, doorless, windowless, half engulfed by underbrush—resolve themselves into a semblance of pattern: four ruins off to the right must have marked the main street, and a fifth the beginning of a side lane, while an open area opposite looks to have been a common, though no church can be seen—only a ragged knoll, a sort of earthen platform nearly invisible beneath a great tangle of weeds and brush.

Into this quiet clearing, in mid-October 1992, a convoy of four-wheel drives and pickup trucks rumbled, disgorging into the center of El Mozote a score of outsiders. Some of these men and women—most of them young, and casually dressed in T-shirts and jeans and work pants—began dumping out into the dust a glinting clutter of machetes, picks, and hoes. Others gathered around the hillock, consulted clipboards and notebooks and maps, poked around in the man-high brush. Finally, they took up machetes and began to hack at the weeds, being careful not to pull any, lest the movement of the roots disturb what lay beneath. Chopping and hacking in the morning sun, they uncovered, bit by bit, a mass of red-brown soil, and before long they had revealed an earthen mound protruding several feet from the ground, like a lopsided bluff, and barely contained at its base by a low stone wall.

They pounded stakes into the ground and marked off the mound with bright-yellow tape; they stretched lengths of twine this way and that to divide it into quadrangles; they brought out tape measures and rulers and levels to record its dimensions and map its contours. And then they began to dig. At first, they loosened the earth with hoes, took it up in shovels, dumped it into plastic pails, and poured it onto a screen large enough to require several people to shake it back and forth. As they dug deeper, they exchanged these tools for smaller, more precise ones: hand shovels, trowels, brushes, dustpans, screens. Slowly, painstakingly, they dug and sifted, making their way through the several feet of earth and crumbled adobe—remnants of a building's walls—and, by the end of the second day, reaching wood-beam splinters and tile shards, many now blackened by fire, that had formed the building's roof. Then, late on the afternoon of the third day, as they crouched low over the ground and stroked with tiny brushes to draw away bits of reddish dust, darkened forms began to emerge from the earth, taking shape in the soil like fossils embedded in stone; and soon they knew that they had begun to find, in the northeast corner of the ruined sacristy of the church of Santa Catarina of El Mozote, the skulls of those who had once worshiped there. Here and there, the skulls had been crushed by the falling brick, and eleven years' sleep in the acidic soil had stained them a sickly coffee-brown. But there could be no doubt about what they were; and by the next afternoon, the workers had uncovered twenty-five of them, and all but two were the skulls of children.

Later that afternoon, the leaders of the team—four young experts from the Argentine Forensic Anthropology Team,[1] who had gained a worldwide reputation for having exhumed sites of massacres in Guatemala and Bolivia and Panama and Iraq, as well as in their own country—piled into their white four-wheel-

"Late on the afternoon of the third day, as they stroked the tiny brushes to draw away bits of reddish dust, darkened forms began to emerge from the earth. Soon they knew that they had begun to find, in the ruined sacristy of the church of Santa Catarina of El Mozote, the skulls of those who had once worshipped there."

drive vehicle and followed the bumpy, stony road out of El Mozote (The Thistle). Slowly, they drove through Arambala, waving to the smiling little girls standing on their porch, and out onto the *calle negra*—the "black road"—which traced its way up the spine of the red zone, stretching north from the city of San Francisco Gotera to the mountain town of Perquín, not far from the Honduran border. At the black road, the Argentines turned left, as they did each evening, heading down to Gotera, but this time, after driving past the rough hillsides planted with patches of sorghum and corn and maguey—this last a cactus-like, thorny bush that looks like tousled dark-green hair—after passing the low-slung wood-plank buildings that housed the boot factory and the craft factory and the other shops the exiles had brought back with them from the Honduran refugee camps two years before, they came to a stop in front of a small house, a hut really, made of scrap wood and sheet metal and set among the banana trees some fifteen yards from the road. They got out of the car, climbed through the barbed wire—a kind of gate had been fashioned from a forked tree trunk—and called out, and before long there appeared at the door a middle-aged woman, heavyset, with high cheekbones, strong features, and a powerful air of dignity. In some excitement, the Argentines told her what they had found that day. The woman listened silently, and when they had finished she paused, then spoke.

"*¿No les dije?*" she asked. ("Didn't I tell you?") "*Si sólo se oía aquella gran gritazón.*" ("If only you could have heard that enormous screaming.")

For eleven years, Rufina Amaya Márquez had served the world as the most eloquent witness of what had happened at El Mozote, but though she had told her story again and again, much of the world had refused to believe her. In the polarized and brutal world of wartime El Salvador, the newspapers and radio stations

For twelve years, Rufina Amaya told anyone who would listen
about what happened at El Mozote, but the United States
Government refused to believe her.

simply ignored what Rufina had to say, as they habitually ignored unpalatable accounts of how the government was prosecuting the war against the leftist rebels. As for those who were meant to know about what happened at El Mozote—the Salvadoran rebels and those peasants who might be sympathetic to them—word-of-mouth would carry the message of El Mozote quite efficiently enough.

In the United States, however, Rufina's account of what had happened at El Mozote appeared on the front pages of the *Washington Post* and *The New York Times*, at the very moment when members of Congress were bitterly debating whether they should cut off aid to a Salvadoran regime so desperate that it had apparently resorted to the most savage methods of war. El Mozote seemed to epitomize those methods, and in Washington the story heralded what became perhaps the classic debate of the late Cold War: between those who argued that, given the geopolitical stakes in Central America, the United States had no choice but to go on supporting a "friendly" regime, however disreputable it might seem, because the alternative—the possibility of another Communist victory in the region—was clearly worse, and those who insisted that the country must be willing to wash its hands of what had become a morally corrupting struggle. Rufina's story came to Washington just when the country's paramount Cold War national-security concerns were clashing—as loudly and unambiguously as they ever would during four decades—with its professed high-minded respect for human rights.

In the United States, the free press was not to be denied: El Mozote was reported; Rufina's story was told; the angry debate in Congress intensified. But then the Republican Administration, burdened as it was with the heavy duties of national security, denied that any credible evidence existed that a massacre had taken place; and the Democratic Congress, after denouncing, yet again, the murderous abuses of the Salvadoran regime, in the end accepted the Administration's "certification" that its ally was nonetheless making a "significant effort to comply with internationally recognized human rights." The flow of aid went on, and soon increased.

By early 1992, when a peace agreement between the government and the guerrillas was finally signed, Americans had spent more than four billion dollars funding a civil war that had lasted twelve years and left seventy-five thousand Salvadorans dead. By then, of course, the bitter fight over El Mozote had largely been forgotten; Washington had turned its gaze to other places and other things. For most Americans, El Salvador had long since slipped back into obscurity. But El Mozote may well have been the largest massacre in modern Latin-American history. That in the United States it came to be known, that it was exposed to the light and then allowed to fall back into the dark, makes the story of El Mozote—how it came to happen and how it came to be denied—a central parable of the Cold War.

C H A P T E R 2

Surviving in the Red Zone

In the weeks that followed the discovery of the skulls of the children, as each day's work at El Mozote yielded up a fresh harvest, the initial numbers came to seem small. But in San Salvador, five hours by road to the west, where President Alfredo Cristiani and the generals and the guerrillas-turned-politicians were struggling with one another about how to put in place, or not put in place, a purge of the officer corps, which was proving to be the most difficult provision of the ten-month-old peace accord[1]—struggling, that is, over what kind of "reconciliation" would come to pass in El Salvador after more than a decade of savage war—the first skulls of the children were enough to provoke a poisonous controversy. Those twenty-three skulls, and the nearly one hundred more that were uncovered in the succeeding days, were accommodated by the nascent Salvadoran body politic in two ways. Members of human-rights groups (those members, that is, who had survived the war), along with the politicians of the left (many of whom had been guerrillas shortly before), hailed the discovery as definitive evidence that a *matanza*—a great killing—had taken place in Morazán, and that what they had been saying for eleven years had at last been proved true.

Members of the government, on the other hand, and various military officers found themselves forced to concede that *something* had indeed happened in Morazán, but they insisted that the situation was more complicated than it appeared. Dr. Juan Mateu Llort, the director of El Salvador's Institute of Forensic Medicine, declared that the skulls themselves proved nothing, for "there were an abundance of armed children in the guerrillas." *El Diario de Hoy*, an influential right-wing daily, published a reconstruction according to which guerrillas had "barricaded themselves in what seemed to have been a religious center and from there opened fire on the troops, making the deaths of children, women and old people possible." President Cristiani's government, already under attack for stalling in the dismissal of senior officers, maintained its position that no records existed of any Army operation in Morazán in early December of 1981.[2]

And yet on the ninth day of that month any reader of *La Prensa Gráfica*, one of San Salvador's major dailies, could have learned that "all the highways with access to Gotera and the other towns in the Department of Morazán are under strict military control. . . . No vehicles or individuals are permitted to enter the zones of conflict in order to avoid accidents or misunderstandings. . . . Neither was the entry of journalists or individuals permitted." The Department of Morazán had been sealed off from the rest of the country. Four thousand men, drawn from the security forces—the National Guard and the Treasury Police—and from regular units of the Salvadoran Army, were hard at work. The area north of the Torola River, the heart of the red zone, was alive with the thud of mortars, the clatter of small-arms fire, and the intermittent roar of helicopters. Two days before, *Operación Rescate*—Operation Rescue—had begun.

Many of the towns and villages were already empty; during and after Army operations of the previous spring and fall, thousands of peasants had left their homes and begun a long trek over the mountains to the Honduran border and the refugee camps beyond. Of those who remained, many made it a practice, at the first sign of any Army approach, to leave their villages and hide in the caves and ravines and gullies that honeycombed the mountainous region. But El Mozote was crowded; in the days before Operation Rescue, people from the outlying areas had flooded into the hamlet.

"Many people were passing by the house, saying, 'Come on, let's go to El Mozote,' " an old peasant named Sebastiano Luna told me as he stood behind the yellow tape, watching the experts bent low over the brown earth of the sacristy of Santa Catarina. Between their feet lay an expanse of dark rubble, a miniature landscape of hills and ridges and valleys in every shade of brown. It took a moment or two to distinguish, among the dirty-brown hillocks, the skulls and parts of skulls, each marked with a bit of red tape and a number; and, beneath the skulls and skull fragments and the earthen rubble, scores of small brown bundles, heaped one on top of another, twisted together, the material so impregnated with blood and soil that it could no longer be recognized as clothing.

Amid the rubble in the northeast corner of the tiny room that had been called *el convento* (though it was really a kind of combined sacristy and parish house, in which an itinerant priest, when he visited the hamlet, would vest himself, and sometimes, perhaps, stay the night), a dark-haired young woman in denim overalls was kneeling. Leaning forward, she placed a tape measure against the rubble and called out coordinates in the softly accented Spanish of Argentina, while a few feet away another young woman placed a ruler against her notebook and inscribed a red dot, locating #59 amid the other dots that by now clustered and ran together on the page. Now the woman in overalls bent down and gently drew toward her a small bundle, slowly smoothing out the creases and folds, disentangling and unwrapping, exposing at last what appeared to be a cluster of tiny brown twigs. Finally, she began, with almost agonizing gentleness, extracting the brown bits and placing them on a sheet of cardboard.

"Left tibia, fragments only," she sang out in a low monotone.

"Vertebrae, one, two, three . . . six of them . . .

"Tibia, left, I think . . .

"Metacarpals . . ."

Nearby, sitting on the stone foundation, a man in a billed cap wrote rapidly on a clipboard. After some minutes, #59 began to take shape on the bit of cardboard, incomplete but recognizable: a tiny skeleton, perhaps a foot-and-a-half long.

Now she began to disentangle the bits of ruined fabric:

"Shirt, light in color, fragmented, with buttons . . .

"Belt of brown leather, metal buckle . . .

"Pants, light in color, with patches of blue and green color in the posterior part . . .

"In the pants pocket . . . ah . . . um . . ."

The strong voice took an odd slide downward and stopped. Over her shoulder, I saw her staring at something in her palm, then heard her swear in a low voice: *"¡Hijo de puta!"* She turned and opened her hand to reveal a tiny figure: a little horse of bright-orange plastic. #59 had been a lucky child, had had a family prosperous enough to provide a lucky toy.

After a moment, the anthropologist Mercedes Doretti said, "Ordinarily, we could use this for identification. I mean, even after eleven years, any mother would recognize this as her kid's, you know?" She looked back at #59 and then at the brown rubble. "But here, here they killed all the mothers, too."

. . .

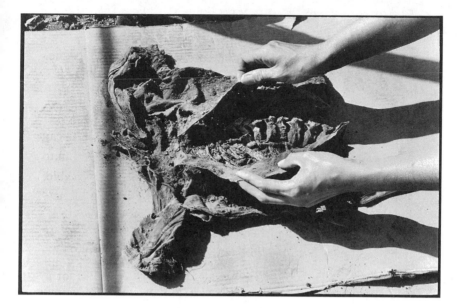

By the fourth day, investigators had found the remains of
twenty-five inhabitants of El Mozote—all but two
of them children.

Behind the yellow tape, Sebastiano Luna and his wife, Alba Ignacia del Cid, stood silent amid a knot of peasants, watching. They had walked from their small house, several miles outside El Mozote, where the dirt track joins the black road. Eleven years before, in early December 1981, scores of people were passing by their house, pulling their children along by the hand, laboring under the weight of their belongings. "Come with us!" they had called out to the old couple. "Come with us to El Mozote!"

The afternoon before, the people of El Mozote had gathered, some fifty yards from the church, in front of the general store of Marcos Díaz. (Today that building is easy to identify, for one can still make out, in the dusty adobe ruin, the division between the living quarters and the shop—though it is harder to appreciate now that the house had been the hamlet's grandest, that Díaz had been the richest man in town.) Marcos Díaz had summoned the townspeople, neighbors and customers all, and when they had assembled—perhaps a couple of hundred campesinos milling about in the dusty street, the men in caps and straw hats and the women in bright-colored skirts, holding children in their arms— he addressed them from his doorway. He had just come up the mountain from his regular buying trip to San Miguel, Marcos Díaz said, and as he was waiting at the checkpoint in Gotera, at the entrance to the red zone, an officer in the town had greeted him—Marcos Díaz, an important man, had friends among the officers—and then pulled him aside for a little talk. Díaz would do well to stock up, the officer said, for soon the Army would launch a large operation in Morazán, and "nothing and no one" would be permitted to enter or leave the zone. But his friend Díaz needn't worry, the officer assured him. The people of El Mozote would have no problems—provided they stayed where they were.

In the street that day, these words of Marcos Díaz's set off a debate. Some townspeople wanted to head for the mountains immediately, for the war had lately been coming closer to the hamlet; only the week before, a plane had dropped two bombs near El Mozote, damaging its one-room school, and though no one had been hurt, the people had been terrified. "A lot of people wanted to leave—there was a lot of fear," Rufina Amaya told me when I visited her in November 1992. "And a few people did leave. My godfather left, with his family. My children were crying. They said, 'Mamá, let's go.' " But Marcos Díaz, a man of influence, had put his prestige on the line, and he insisted that his neighbors would be safe only if they stayed in their homes—that if they left the hamlet, they and their families risked being caught up in the operation; the officer had been quite explicit. "That was the lie," Rufina Amaya told me. "That was the betrayal. Otherwise, people would have left." In the end, Marcos Díaz's prestige decided the issue. Though the debate went on that afternoon and into the following morning, most of the people of El Mozote finally accepted his assurances.

They had seen soldiers before, after all; soldiers often passed through on patrol and sometimes bought supplies in El Mozote. Only the month before, soldiers had come during an operation and occupied El Chingo and La Cruz, two hills overlooking the town, and though the people of El Mozote could hear mortars and scattered shooting in the distance, the soldiers had not bothered them. In the crazy-quilt map of northern Morazán in 1981, where villages "belonged" to the government or to the guerrillas or to neither or both, where the officers saw the towns and hamlets in varying shades of pink and red, El Mozote had not been known as a guerrilla town. "The Army spent a lot of time around here," Rufina told me. "We all sold them food. If the soldiers were looking to find guerrillas, that was fine with us, because we didn't have anything to do with them. And the guerrillas knew about our relations with the Army."

The guerrillas knew, the soldiers knew: northern Morazán during the early eighties was a very small world, in which identity, or the perception of identity, often meant the difference between living and dying. That El Mozote in late 1981 was not a guerrilla town is a fact central to Rufina's story and lies at the heart of the mystery of what happened there; and though it is a fact— one that almost everyone from the zone affirms—it seems to have nonetheless been a slightly more complicated fact than Rufina makes out. As in many other communities in northern Morazán, the people of El Mozote were struggling to keep their balance in the middle of the perilously shifting ground of a brutal war— were working hard to remain on friendly terms with the soldiers while fearing to alienate the guerrillas. Joaquín Villalobos, who was the leading *comandante* of the People's Revolutionary Army (or E.R.P.), the dominant guerrilla group in Morazán, told me flatly during an interview in his headquarters in San Salvador that the people of El Mozote "would not support us"—only to concede twenty minutes later that his fighters had, at least on some occasions, bought supplies in the hamlet. "They had the lowest level of relationship with us—only the very slightest commercial one," Villalobos said. Licho, a rebel commander who had grown up in Jocoaitique, a few miles from El Mozote, acknowledged to me during an interview in Perquín that in the late seventies "some from El Mozote had been our supporters," but that long before 1981 these supporters "had come along with us, they were with us." He added quickly, "The people who were still in El Mozote were afraid of us."

But the reason, apparently, was not only their fear—the frank terror that many villagers in the zone felt about exposing themselves to Army retribution—but their ideology. The guerrillas' support in Morazán had grown largely in soil made fertile by the work of liberation theology—by the teachings of left-leaning Catholic priests—but El Mozote had been uniquely unreceptive to such blandishments, for the hamlet was known throughout the zone as a stronghold of the Protestant evangelical movement. People had begun to convert as early as the mid-sixties,[3] and by 1980 it is likely that half or more of the people in El Mozote considered themselves born-again Christians; the evangelicals had their own chapel and their own pastor, and they were known—as were born-again Christians throughout Central America—for their anti-Communism. "Everyone knew there were many evangelicals in El Mozote, and these people wouldn't support us," Licho told me. "Sometimes they sold us things, yes, but they didn't want anything to do with us."

So, unlike many other hamlets of Morazán, El Mozote was a place where the guerrillas had learned not to look for recruits; instead, a delicate coexistence had been forged—an unstated agreement by both parties to look the other way. The guerrillas passed by El Mozote only at night and, when they did, Rufina says, "the people would hear the dogs barking and they'd be afraid." She remembers seeing guerrillas only once in daylight: a few ragged young people, unarmed and wearing civilian clothes, had come into the hamlet and tried to hold a meeting in the tiny church of Santa Catarina. Rufina didn't attend, nor did most of the other townspeople. "I remember people saying, 'Don't get involved. Let's just live and work and not get involved.' People just didn't want anything to do with it. I had four children to look after. You're worrying about feeding your family, and you try not to pay attention to these other things."

And so when Marcos Díaz brought his news from Gotera, when he conveyed the strong words of the officer and presented the choice as one of leaving the town and risking "getting involved" in the operation or of staying put and remaining safe, there was never much doubt about what the people of El Mozote would in the end decide. That very afternoon, at Marcos Díaz's urging, people began fanning out from the hamlet into the outlying districts to spread the word that one and all should come to El Mozote, and quickly, for only there would they be protected. Marcos Díaz helped matters along by letting it be known that he would offer on credit as much food and other supplies as the newcomers needed. "He told them to spread the word that we would all eat here," Rufina says, "that we would all be safe."

Peasants poured into the hamlet, occupying every bit of space. "All the rooms in Marcos Díaz's house were filled with people. Every house had people staying there from outside." Even the plaza in front of the church was crowded with people, for the few houses could not accommodate them all.

" 'Come to El Mozote'—that's what everyone was saying," the old peasant Sebastiano Luna told me. He and Alba Ignacia del Cid had stood in front of their house, had watched the people pass. But they had decided not to go. "I had half an idea something bad might happen," Sebastiano said. "So I told her"— nodding to his wife—" 'You, you go if you want to. I'm staying.' " "And I," said Alba, "I said, 'No, no, I won't go without you, because they'll ask me where my husband is. They'll say he's not here because he's a guerrilla and then they'll kill me. Either we both go or we both stay.' " So Sebastiano and Alba hid in the mountains above their house. They saw soldiers pass by, and saw a helicopter hover and descend. And later they saw thick columns of smoke rising from El Mozote, and smelled the odor of what seemed like tons of roasting meat.

CHAPTER 3

Monterrosa's Mission

Four miles south of El Mozote, outside the hamlet of La Guacamaya, the guerrillas of the People's Revolutionary Army also
awaited the soldiers. From their agents in the capital, they knew
that large shipments of American munitions had been arriving
at Ilopango Airport, and that truckloads of troops had begun
moving along the Pan-American Highway toward Morazán. On
December 1st, Jonás, the most powerful *comandante* in the zone,
had pulled aside Santiago, the director of the E.R.P.'s clandestine
Radio Venceremos, and informed him that "an operation of great
breadth, named *Yunque y Martillo*"—Hammer and Anvil—was
being planned. Santiago recalls that "intelligence sources within
the Army itself" had passed on a report of a key meeting at the
High Command.[1] According to the source's reconstruction, the
Minister of Defense, Colonel José Guillermo García, declared to
his officers that Operation Rescue must "wrest the offensive from
the FMLN"—the guerrilla umbrella group, of which the E.R.P.
was one of five members. His Vice-Minister, Colonel Francisco
Adolfo Castillo, added that the troops "must advance no matter
what the cost until we reach the command post and Radio Venceremos." Then Lieutenant Colonel Domingo Monterrosa Bar-

rios, the dynamic commander of the elite Atlacatl Battalion, broke in, agreeing wholeheartedly that "so long as we don't finish off this Radio Venceremos, we'll always have a scorpion up our ass." Colonel Monterrosa, who at the time was the most celebrated field commander in the Salvadoran Army, was well known to have an obsession with Radio Venceremos.

He was not alone: the station, which specialized in ideological propaganda, acerbic commentary, and pointed ridicule of the government, infuriated most officers, for its every broadcast reminded the world of the Army's impotence in much of Morazán. Even worse, the radio managed to be funny. "They actually acted out this daytime serial, like a soap opera, with Ambassador Hinton in it,"[2] a United States defense attaché of the time recalls. "They'd call the Ambassador 'this gringo who is marrying a Salvadoran woman' "— Deane Hinton was about to marry a woman from one of the country's wealthy families—"and at the end they'd say, 'Tune in again tomorrow.' And you couldn't do anything about it. Most people at the Embassy, including the Ambassador, wanted to hear it." The mortified Salvadoran officers maintained that the broadcasts originated in Nicaragua or Honduras.

Colonel Monterrosa was mortified by Radio Venceremos as well, but, unlike his colleagues, he had determined, in his rage and frustration, to do something about it. For Monterrosa, as American military advisers had come to recognize, was a very different kind of Salvadoran officer. By late 1981, with Congress and the American public having shown themselves resolutely opposed to dispatching American combat forces to Central America, it had become quite clear that the only way to prevent "another Nicaragua" was somehow to "reform" the Salvadoran Army. "We were on our last legs," an American military adviser who was in the country at the time told me. "We had to reform or we were going to lose. And it wasn't because the guerrillas were so good; it was because the Army was so bad." Salvadoran troops were sent into the field virtually untrained, soldiers rarely left the barracks after five o'clock in the afternoon, and officers rarely left the barracks at all. "The institution simply did not support people being good commanders," this adviser said. "I mean, who ever got relieved? You could surrender with eighty-five men and nothing at all would happen to you."

As the Americans soon realized, however, "reform" meant remaking an officer corps that had developed its own very special criteria for advancement and reward. These had to do not with military competence but with politics: with showing unstinting loyalty to "the institution" and, above all, to one's military-academy class—one's *tanda*, as it was called. A hundred teen-age boys might enter the Gerardo Barrios Military Academy,[3] and from their number perhaps twenty toughened, hardened men would emerge four years later; throughout the next quarter century, these men would be promoted together, would become rich together, and would gradually gain power together. If among them there proved to be embarrassing incompetents, not to mention murderers and rapists and thieves, then these men were shielded by their classmates, and defended ferociously. Finally, perhaps two decades after graduation, one or two from the *tanda*—those who had stood out early on as *presidenciables*, as destined to become leaders of the country—would lobby within the officer corps to become the President of El Salvador.

Monterrosa had graduated in 1963, and though the records show him fourth in his class of nineteen, it is a testament to the respect he inspired that many officers now remember him as first. In the academy, he was a magnetic figure, charismatic from the start. Short, with the simple face and large nose of a Salvadoran peasant, he walked with the peasant's long, loping stride, which made his distinctly nonmartial figure recognizable from far off.

General Adolfo Blandón, a former chief of staff, who was in his last year in the academy when Monterrosa was in his first, recalls that the young man "established himself immediately as the best in his class—the top rank in studies, physical conditioning, knowledge of the concepts of war."

Normally, of course, such prestige, such respect from his colleagues, would brand him *presidenciable*. But, unlike his fellows, Monterrosa was, as Blandón puts it, "that rare thing: a pure, one-hundred-percent soldier, a natural leader, a born military man with the rare quality of being able to instill loyalty in his men."

In the years after his graduation, Monterrosa taught at the academy, took courses from the Americans in Panama, traveled to Taiwan to study anti-Communist counter-insurgency tactics, and served in the paratroops as part of El Salvador's first free-fall team. After the controversial elections of 1972, in which a hard-line faction of the military stole the ballot from what looked to be a winning Christian Democratic ticket, led by San Salvador's Mayor José Napoleón Duarte, Monterrosa grew close to the new military President, Colonel Arturo Molina.

In the Army at this time, the key focus was on politics, and the struggle over El Salvador's stunted political development increasingly split the country,[4] and the officer corps. By the late seventies, after Molina had given place to General Carlos Humberto Romero, in another dubious election, the situation had become even more polarized. On the far left, several tiny guerrilla groups were kidnapping businessmen, robbing banks, and, on occasion, assassinating prominent rightist leaders. Activists on the moderate left, having been denied an electoral path to the Presidential Palace by the Army's habitual ballot tampering, joined populist forces in organizing vast demonstrations, and managed to bring hundreds of thousands of people into the streets. The security forces generally responded to these demonstrations with unflinching violence, shooting down scores, and sometimes hundreds, of Salvadorans.

Within the Salvadoran officer corps, the country's political crisis had reopened a political fault line that had spread apart periodically throughout the century. Back in 1960, a faction of "progressive" officers had staged a coup, but it had been quickly reversed by a conservative counter-coup; in 1972, when Duarte's victory was stolen by conservative officers, the progressives attempted another, with the same result. Finally, in October of 1979, with at least tacit American support, a group of young "reformists" who called themselves the *juventud militar*—the "military youth"—overthrew General Romero and set in his place a "progressive" junta, which included politicians of the left. As had happened two decades before, however, the conservatives in the Army almost immediately regained the upper hand, and now, under cover of a more internationally acceptable "reformist" government, they felt free to combat the "Communist agitation" in their own particular way—by intensifying the "dirty war" against the left.

The most visible signs of the "dirty war"[5] were mutilated corpses that each morning littered the streets of El Salvador's cities. Sometimes the bodies were headless, or faceless, their features having been obliterated with a shotgun blast or an application of battery acid; sometimes limbs were missing, or hands or feet chopped off, or eyes gouged out; women's genitals were torn and bloody, bespeaking repeated rape; men's were often found severed and stuffed into their mouths. And cut into the flesh of a corpse's back or chest was likely to be the signature of one or another of the "death squads" that had done the work, the most notorious of which were the Union of White Warriors and the Maximiliano Hernández Martínez Brigade.

The latter was named for a general who had taken over the country in 1931, during a time of rising leftist agitation among the peasantry, and had responded the following year with a campaign of repression so ferocious that it came to be known simply as *la matanza*.[6] Throughout the western part of the country, where an abortive rebellion had been centered, members of the National Guard, along with civilian irregulars, lined peasants up against a wall and shot them. Before the purge was over, they had murdered well over ten thousand people. (Some estimates put the number at four times that.) The reasoning behind the repression was quite simple: where the "infection" of rebellion had taken hold it must be rooted out, ruthlessly and thoroughly. And the technique proved extremely effective; a half-century later, when the infection raged once again in Salvador, those areas where the killing had been rampant five decades before remained remarkably quiescent.

Now rightist officers who proudly counted themselves heirs of Martínez determined to root out this new leftist infection with equal thoroughness. Drawing on money from wealthy businessmen who had moved to Miami to avoid kidnapping or assassination, and benefiting from the theoretical guidance of ideological compatriots in neighboring Guatemala, the officers organized and unleashed an efficient campaign of terror in the cities—a campaign that intensified dramatically after the "progressive" coup of October 1979. By the end of the year, monthly estimates of the dead ranged as high as eight hundred.

Against the urban infrastructure of the left—the network of political organizers, labor leaders, human-rights workers, teachers, and activists of all progressive stripes which had put together the enormous demonstrations of the late seventies—this technique proved devastating. "These people weren't organized militarily, which is what made them so easy to kill," William Stanley, a professor of political science at the University of New Mexico, told me in an interview in San Salvador. As the repression went on, month after month, it became less and less discriminating. "By the end, the killing basically outran the intelligence capability of the Army and the security services, and they began killing according to very crude profiles," Stanley said. "I remember, for example, hearing that a big pile of corpses was discovered one morning, and almost all of them turned out to be young women wearing jeans and tennis shoes. Apparently, one of the intelligence people had decided that this 'profile'—you know, young women who dressed in that way—made it easy to separate out 'leftists,' and so that became one of the profiles that they used to round up so-called subversives."

With some exceptions, intelligence officers in the various security services and in the Army brigades organized the death squads, recruiting National Guardsmen, Treasury Police, and regular soldiers who were interested in "moonlighting" for extra money, and supplying them with lists of the names of people who were to be picked up and brought back for interrogation and torture. Some civilians were certainly involved, particularly on the funding end, but there can be no doubt that the "dirty war" was basically organized and directed by Salvadoran Army officers—and no doubt, either, that the American Embassy was well aware of it. "There was no secret about who was doing the killing," Howard Lane, the public-affairs officer in the Embassy from 1980 to 1982, told me in an interview. "I mean, you formed that view within forty-eight hours after arriving in the country, and there was no secret at all about it—except, maybe, in the

White House." In public, the fiction was resolutely maintained that the identity of the killers was a mystery—that the corpses were the work of "rightist vigilantes." This campaign of lies was designed in part to accommodate the squeamishness of the Administration in Washington, which had to deal with growing concern in Congress about "human rights violations," particularly after several notorious cases, including the murder, in March of 1980, of Archbishop Oscar Romero while he said Mass; the rape and murder, the following December, of four American churchwomen; and the assassination, in January of 1981, of the head of the Salvadoran land-reform agency and two of his American advisers.

On the evening of December 1, 1981, Santiago, the director of Radio Venceremos, after learning from Jonás, the *comandante*, about the coming operation, set out on foot from the guerrilla base at La Guacamaya, four miles south of El Mozote. As darkness fell, Santiago hiked east over the hills and through the gullies, crossed the Río Sapo, and climbed down into a heavily forested ravine at El Zapotal. Here, dug into a rock niche half a dozen feet underground, was the "studio" of Radio Venceremos, which consisted of a small transmitter, an unwieldy gasoline generator, assorted tape recorders, microphones, and other paraphernalia, and a flexible antenna that snaked its way up through a forest of brush. Santiago gathered his handful of young staff members, and soon news of the coming operation was broadcast throughout the zone.

Back in La Guacamaya, in a rough encampment in the open air, perhaps two hundred young men and women, outfitted in a motley combination of peasant clothing and camouflage garb (the latter having been mostly captured, or stolen, or purchased, from the Salvadoran Army), were making preparations. Some cleaned

Santiago, director of Radio Venceremos, broadcast news of the coming military operation throughout the zone.

their weapons—mostly old M-1s and Mausers, along with a few captured German G-3s and American M-16s. Many of the women bent over smooth flat stones, grinding corn, making the meal that would serve as the company's fuel during the days ahead—for, confronted with the arrival of thousands of troops, the guerrillas of the E.R.P. were preparing not to fight but to flee.

Mobility and quickness had always been central to the guerrillas' strength,[7] along with their familiarity with the mountain terrain. Like El Salvador's other radical groups, the People's Revolutionary Army had been the brainchild of young urban intellectuals, who had founded the organization in Mexico City in 1972, funded it during the mid-seventies largely by robbing banks and by seizing and ransoming wealthy businessmen, and battled among themselves for its leadership, using high-toned abstract arguments of the left—which more than once deteriorated into violent schisms. (The most notorious of these conflicts came in 1974, when Villalobos and other ERP leaders charged that one of their number, the celebrated poet Roqué Dalton, was a counter-revolutionary and a CIA agent, and, after a perfunctory trial, executed him.)

In the northern mountains, the guerrilla movement took root somewhat later. "The revolutionary process started in Morazán around 1977 or '78 with the consciousness-raising of Christian 'base communities' led by radical priests," said Licho, the rebel commander, whose parents were campesinos living on the other side of the black road from El Mozote. "We young people would get together and read the Bible and apply it to our own situation, and gradually we became more politically aware." When the young men came of age, the guerrilla leaders often urged them to join the Army—they had urged Licho to do so—in order to receive military training and gain firsthand knowledge of the enemy while providing useful intelligence until they could return to their home provinces to take up arms. (This widespread infiltration of their ranks soon engendered near-panic among many Salvadoran officers. In a lengthy confidential cable to the State Department in early 1980, U.S. Ambassador Frank Devine noted the officers' "fears that the new recruits may include elements of . . . leftist organizations whose purpose is to infiltrate the rank and file . . . and ultimately to destroy the military from within.")

By 1980, small groups of young guerrillas were operating throughout northern Morazán, drawing food and support from sympathetic peasants, and launching raids from time to time against the National Guard posts in the towns. They would attack suddenly, kill a few Guardsmen and capture their weapons, then fade back into the bush. After the posts had been reinforced, the Guardsmen responded, as they had done for years, by beating or killing peasants they suspected of having been "infected" with Communist sympathies. This quickened the flow of able-bodied men and women into the mountains. Soon some villages were inhabited almost entirely by old people and mothers and their children. Some towns the Guardsmen abandoned completely—in effect, ceding them to the control of the guerrillas. And the people abandoned other towns, either fleeing to the refugee camps beyond the Honduran border or joining the guerrillas, and thus forming, as time went on, a quasi-permanent baggage train of *masas*, or civilian supporters. "The people who supported us moved around as our rear guard, providing food and other help," Licho told me. "In some areas, our supporters were in the majority, in others not." The distinction between combatants and noncombatants, never very clear in this guerrilla war, was growing cloudier still.

The Salvadoran High Command had become increasingly alarmed by the situation in Morazán. "The military view the situation in the countryside as critical," Ambassador Devine wrote in the same 1980 cable. "Many feel there are 'liberated' areas where they dare not operate due to the concentration of leftist-terrorist strength." When they pleased, the guerrillas could concentrate their forces, attack the towns, and rout the isolated posts, holding them until Government reinforcements arrived.

In January of 1981, the FMLN proclaimed a "final offensive"— the badly equipped guerrillas hoped to provoke a popular insurrection, as the Sandinistas had done in Nicaragua eighteen months before, and to do it in the days just before Ronald Reagan took power in Washington—but the people did not rise up, and the offensive ended in a costly defeat. After the collapse, hundreds of fighters streamed out of the cities and headed for the mountains. Having failed to overthrow the government, and having seen many of their civilian sympathizers liquidated in the past months by death squads, the guerrillas decided to focus their forces on a full-scale rural insurgency rooted in the northern mountains.

Soon soldiers dared cross the Torola only in force, and small garrisons in the towns were regularly routed. By November, General Fred F. Woerner, whom a worried Pentagon had sent to assess the Salvadoran war, was concluding in a secret report[8] that the situation on the ground had so deteriorated that a primary aim of the Salvadoran Army had now become to "prevent the establishment of an insurgent 'liberated' zone in the Department of Morazán, which could lead to international recognition of the insurgents as a belligerent force." This was no idle fear; only three months before, France and Mexico had recognized the FMLN as "a representative political force." If the guerrillas were not dislodged from Morazán, the Salvadoran officers feared, they would risk seeing their country split in two.

. . .

On December 1, 1981, after Radio Venceremos broadcast word that the Army was coming, people throughout northern Morazán began talking among themselves, arguing, and coming to decisions about what to do next. During the next few days, many families left their homes and climbed up into the caves and gullies around their villages, in some cases leaving the father or elder son behind to watch the house, for in past operations the soldiers had sometimes burned houses left unoccupied, declaring that they must belong to guerrillas. Others made ready to flee the zone. At La Guacamaya, hundreds of people gathered outside the guerrilla camp, having packed up what tortillas and beans they had, and gathered their children, ready for the hard trek ahead.

On Monday, December 7th, the young men and women of Radio Venceremos began doing what they had practiced many times: rapidly dismantling the components, loading the generator aboard a mule, and hoisting the transmitter, the antenna, and the other equipment on one another's backs. Then they hiked off to join the fighters at La Guacamaya.

Around this time, according to Joaquín Villalobos, representatives of the guerrillas approached El Mozote and attempted to warn the campesinos there. "We always had rearguard people, political people, behind the lines," he says. "So when the fighting was beginning in the south they advised people in the north to leave the zone." But the people in El Mozote had already made their decision. "Because they had little relation to us, and because they were evangelical, they decided they had little to fear from the Army," Villalobos says. More likely, they had decided, after listening to the words of Marcos Díaz, that the danger would be greater outside the hamlet than within.

"We told them what might happen," Licho says. "But they didn't believe that the Army would do anything to them." Perhaps they regarded the guerrillas' warnings—those who heard them, that is (Rufina, for one, heard nothing)—as attempts at recruitment. As the people of El Mozote well knew, in the view of the Salvadoran Army, to go with the guerrillas was to be a guerrilla.

By Tuesday morning, December 8th—even as, a few miles to the north, the last groups of peasants were straggling into El Mozote, dumping their belongings wherever they could find space in the overcrowded hamlet—the guerrillas at La Guacamaya could hear the sounds of battle, of mortars and small-arms fire, coming, it seemed, from all directions; they knew by now that perhaps four thousand soldiers had entered the zone, that troops had crossed the Torola and were moving toward them from the south, that others were approaching the Sapo from the east. The only way clear had seemed to be to the north, toward the Honduran border; but, even as the Radio Venceremos announcers were putting out their last broadcast, urging the people of the zone to join the guerrilla columns, the guerrillas heard the helicopters approach and saw them pass overhead, carrying the troops of Domingo Monterrosa's Atlacatl Battalion northward, to the mountain town of Perquín.

CHAPTER 4

Hammer and Anvil

To reach Perquín from El Mozote, you turn right on the black road and begin to climb. Soon the grade grows steeper, the tropical brush gives place to mountain pine, and the air lightens and grows fresh. Here and there, a bit of sorghum or corn or maguey pokes out from among the trees, but, increasingly, from the red soil of the mountainside only great white rocks grow. The overpowering fragrance of freshly cut pine announces the hamlet of La Tejera and its sawmill, a low building of unstripped logs surrounded by stacks of new planks. Finally, a sign announces Perquín; the road tilts sharply upward and becomes a street of large cobblestones; and, after a few moments' jolting, the traveler comes upon a dramatically uneven town square, which, despite blasted buildings and damaged streets, remains an oddly beautiful, vaguely otherworldly place. At its heart is a bizarre park, which accommodates many wildly slanting levels of green grass, like lopsided terraces on a cultivated but dilapidated hillside. Bordering the park are a yellow-painted clinic, a rough-hewn little hut, and a remarkable church crowned by a bulbous, vaguely Eastern-looking steeple and decorated on two of its walls by enormous murals: facing the park, calmly blessing his flock, appears the huge face of the martyred Archbishop Oscar Romero, assassinated while he was saying Mass; facing north, a brightly-colored map of the Americas and Europe, in which a colorful stream of riches—cars, refrigerators, motorboats—flows from New World to Old above the caption "Five Hundred Years of Pillage."

When Colonel Monterrosa set his helicopter down here in December of 1981, he found a town in government hands, but barely. Only four months earlier, in mid-August, the guerrillas had swept out of the surrounding hills and overwhelmed the local National Guard post, killing four men and capturing five. "There were many young ones, but some really old ones, too," children in Perquín told Alma Guillermoprieto, then a stringer for the *Washington Post*. "There were eight women. Some of them were in uniforms, but most of them wore raggedy clothes, like us. We knew some of them; they were from this town." The guerrillas had spent a week and a half digging defensive trenches, buying corn from the local cooperative, and marching about the streets shouting *"¡Pueblo libre!"* and other slogans. When the Air Force began bombing the city, ten days later, the guerrillas swiftly vanished, fading into the mountains and ravines they knew so well, and leaving behind the four dead men, buried in a bomb crater, and also the civilians who had been there all along—the civilians who, after playing host to the guerrillas for ten days, now gazed with all innocence into the faces of the National Guardsmen who had come to take the places of their dead comrades.

Colonel Monterrosa had thought long and hard about civilians and guerrilla war, about the necessity of counterinsurgency, about the frustrations of the odd and bloody conflict that the overextended Salvadoran Army had been fighting and losing. When the men of his Atlacatl Battalion touched down in Perquín that Tuesday morning in December, storming from helicopters in a crouch, gripping their helmets tightly against the backwash from the rotors, the officers had in their pockets lists of names to hand to the National Guardsmen who were waiting to receive them. While the Atlacatl captains mustered their troops, the Guardsmen marched off through the town and pounded on doors. They were big men, well fed, and they looked even bigger than they were, outfitted in high black boots[1] and uniforms of heavy greenish-brown cloth, with automatic rifles on their backs, and razor-sharp machetes hanging at their belts.

"In those days, if they came to your house to ask you to come with them to 'do something,' you'd end up dead," a Perquín man whom the Guardsmen visited that morning told me. When he heard the pounding and pulled open the door to find the Guardsmen there glowering down at him—they always glowered, for their business was, and had been since the early days of the century, to induce fear in the countryside and to stamp out rebellion from the moment it revealed itself as a lessening of fear in a campesino's eyes—this man could only try to control his terror as the Guardsmen stared for a moment, then barked, "Hey, we have work to do! Come with us and help us do it!" The man came outside, watched as one of the Guardsmen ran his finger down the list that Monterrosa's men had handed him, then looked up, exchanged glances with his partner, and murmured, *"Ya vamos dándole."* ("Now let's get started.") The Perquín man knew what that meant—the killing was to begin—and, in a panic, he began to protest, digging an identification card out of his pocket and begging the Guardsmen to look at it carefully. Finally, after a terrible few minutes, he succeeded in convincing these impassive men that the name on the list was not his—that one of the surnames was different.

Nonetheless, the Guardsmen hustled him along the streets with them, and as they moved through town they pounded on other doors and collected other frightened men. Those men numbered ten by the time they reached a field in front of the clinic, which was a blur of unaccustomed activity: helicopters landing and hovering and departing, and, amid the blast and the roar from the rotors, hundreds of men in green moving about, checking weapons, cinching the straps on their packs, and talking among themselves as officers marched back and forth shouting orders. By then, several hundred of the Atlacatl soldiers had stormed off the helicopters, most of them in olive green, and a few in camouflage garb above black jungle boots. On the shoulders of their uniforms they bore, in white or yellow, the figure of an Indian and the word "Atlacatl" (the name of a legendary Indian warrior who had led the fight against the conquistadores). To a practiced eye, they seemed a somewhat different breed from most Salvadoran soldiers—more businesslike, grimmer even—and their equipment was better: they had the latest American M-16s, plenty of M-60 machine guns, 90-millimeter recoilless rifles, and 60- and 81-millimeter mortars.

But it wasn't their equipment that made them "the elite, American-trained Atlacatl Battalion" (as press accounts invariably identified them). It was their aggressiveness, their willingness to "do the job": a willingness that the rest of the badly led and badly trained Army generally lacked. In part, perhaps, this aggressiveness was instilled by American trainers—Special Forces personnel, who, beginning in March, had been coming over from Southern Command, in Panama, to show the Salvadoran recruits how to shoot and how to seize positions. Mostly, though, it came from Monterrosa. Among senior field commanders who in many cases, as one lieutenant put it to me, "don't even own fatigues," Monterrosa seemed a soldier of the classic type: aggressive, charismatic, a man who liked nothing better than to get out in the field and fight alongside his troops. The Salvadoran grunts—mostly unlettered peasant boys, many of whom had been pulled from buses or off country roads and pressed into service, having received little training and less regard from their officers—loved Monterrosa for his willingness to get down in the dirt with them and fight. The press loved him, too: not only was he a natural story—the dynamic, gung-ho colonel—he was only too happy (in an officer corps distinctly hostile to the press) to invite reporters to come along with him in his helicopter. And, of course, the Americans loved him as well: Colonel John Cash, a United States military attaché, speaks of "a hotshot strategist like Monterrosa, whom I'd put up against any American hotshot."

By then, the Americans were growing desperate. For, as the war moved decisively to the countryside, the American government was no longer able to deny that it had a major problem on its hands. True, the Salvadorans had managed to "decapitate" the urban left, but this adversary had been largely unarmed; in the countryside, the guerrillas were shooting back, and the Salvadoran officers were showing themselves utterly incapable of fighting a war of rural counter-insurgency. Not only was the Army, with a total of thirteen thousand men facing perhaps a third that many guerrillas, terribly overstretched, but its officer corps was burdened by a byzantine political structure and a perverse system of anti-incentives. The most important commands from the military point of view were from the point of view of most Salvadoran officers the least desirable, and the result was that those posts tended to be assigned to the politically least powerful, and often least talented, members of the officer corps. "The guys in the real combat commands, these tended to be the total incompetents," Todd Greentree, who was a junior reporting officer in the

United States Embassy at the time, told me. "These guys would be sent out there to the end of the line, and they'd spend their days drinking in the *cuartel*."

Embassy officials recommended, cajoled, and finally urged reassignments, but changes, when they came at all, came only after enormous effort. The explanation was not just the superior political and economic power of the right wing of the officer corps but the fact that the *tanda* system, in which classmates, no matter what their failings, were fiercely protected, appeared nearly impervious to outside pressure—including pressure from the Americans, who were now pouring hundreds of millions of dollars into the country. As the officers understood only too quickly, the ultimate sanction that the Americans could brandish—turning off the aid spigot—threatened to hurt the Americans themselves as much as it would hurt the Salvadorans, since the American fear of a Communist El Salvador taking its place alongside Sandinista Nicaragua had become overriding. Even during the final months of the Carter Administration, this underlying reality became embarrassingly evident, when President Carter, after cutting off aid in response to the murder of the American churchwomen, rushed to restore it only a few weeks later, in the face of the rebels' "final offensive."

Ronald Reagan did not suffer from the same ambivalence. By the fall of 1981, Reagan had removed the outspoken American Ambassador, Robert White; had vowed, through Secretary of State Alexander Haig, to "draw the line" in El Salvador against Communist subversion in the hemisphere; had almost doubled economic aid for El Salvador, to a hundred and forty-four million dollars, and increased military aid, from twenty-six million dollars to more than thirty-five million; and, in November, had begun funding the Nicaraguan Contra fighters as a proxy force against the Sandinista government. By late 1981, the priorities of American policy in El Salvador had become unmistakable.[2]

The Americans had stepped forward to fund the war, but they were unwilling to fight it; it would be left to the Salvadorans to defeat the guerrillas. "The guerrilla always carries his *masas* into battle with him"[3] was a famous Army saying of the era, a piece of received wisdom from that darkest period of the Salvadoran civil war, and its author was Colonel Monterrosa himself. It was intended not only as a statement of fact but as a general affirmation of principle: in this bloody war, in the red zones, there was really no such thing as a civilian.

A large professional Army would have reoccupied territory and sent out aggressive patrols, all the while doing "political work" in the countryside to regain the loyalty of the people. Indeed, that was part of the rationale behind the search-and-destroy operations. "There are a lot of different names for counter-guerrilla fighting," Colonel Castillo, then the Vice-Minister of Defense, told me in an interview. "Whether they call it Hammer and Anvil, or the Piston, or something else, it's all the same idea—to try to expel the guerrillas from the zone—to kick them out of all those areas where they'd imposed a Marxist-Leninist system. After we managed to expel them, they would lose the support of all the people they had indoctrinated."

But in those days, Castillo conceded, the Army "didn't have enough equipment or forces to maintain operations there for a long enough time." The result was that the Army would enter a zone in force; the guerrillas, after a few minor engagements, would flee; and the soldiers, after killing a number of supposed "subversives" (civilians who may or may not have been guerrilla supporters but hadn't been quick enough, or smart enough, to get out of the way), would evacuate the zone, leaving a token force behind—which the guerrillas, when they flowed back in a few days later, would maul and expel.

The Army's tactic was not effective—few guerrillas were killed, nor was their civilian support eliminated—and it made for great frustration and, eventually, fear on the part of the Salvadoran High Command. "A mentality developed in those days," a senior Salvadoran officer told me. "The Army wasn't prepared for this kind of war, it wasn't trained for it. We were a small Army, not very well equipped, and we were just beginning to receive U.S. aid. We knew we were given this to confront the aggression to Salvadoran society from the Marxists, that we were now at the heart of the Cold War, right where these two great currents, from the Soviet Union and the United States, came smashing together. The result was you had an ideological overcharge here in this little country. And it didn't take much for a scenario to develop where you are either an enemy or a friend. If you are not with me you are against me, and if you are against me then I have to destroy you."

This mentality, and the desperation that lay at the root of it, set the stage for a particularly savage kind of war. "When I arrived here, in June of 1982, the Salvadoran officers used to brag to me that they didn't take prisoners," Colonel Cash, the military attaché, said. "They said, 'We don't want to dignify them by taking prisoners.' They wouldn't even *call* them prisoners, or guerrillas. They called them *terroristas—delincuentes terroristas.*" (General Blandón, the former chief of staff, told me bluntly, "Before 1983, we never took prisoners of war.") As the guerrillas were reduced to the status of terrorist delinquents, all civilians in certain zones were reduced to the status of *masas*, guerrilla supporters, and thus became legitimate targets. North of the Torola, for example, it was believed that the civilians and the guerrillas were all mixed together, and were indistinguishable.

By late 1980, the Army had begun the tactic that William Stanley, the political-science professor, refers to as "killing by zone." One of the first such operations took place in October, and began with a staff meeting in Perquín. "Colonel Castillo explained that it was necessary to stop the Communist revolution—that it was necessary to make an example of this place, so we wouldn't have the same problems in other parts of the country," an officer who had been present at the meeting told me. "He said we must take into account that the great majority of the people here are guerrillas. So the idea was to surround them all, to create this 'hammer and anvil' thing, push all the people down to Villa El Rosario, where a huge artillery barrage would be unleashed. The city would be totally destroyed. We were going to make an example of these people." In retrospect, the operation appears to be a less ambitious version of Operation Rescue, though centered on the other side of the black road. "The military formed a large circle, rear guard in the North, guard along the road, and thus they encircled the zone and closed in," Licho, the guerrilla commander, told me. "We fought for fifteen days, moving the population with us. We would put up a line of resistance with the population behind us, resist, then retreat. We would fight, then move them; fight, then move them. When we ran out of ammunition and supplies we took the young people with us to be combatants, crossed the river and left the others in El Rosario."

When the soldiers finally marched into El Rosario, they killed a number of those people, perhaps as many as forty. According to one account, an even larger massacre was averted partly because of disagreements among the middle-level officers involved—several of whom still counted themselves as members of the progressive "military youth" and were determined to resist the orders of the hard-liners. "There was going to be this great artillery barrage, along with sustained bombing," the former Captain Marcelo Cruz Cruz told me in an interview in Perquín. "When we made it to Villa Rosario, we found all the people had been crowded into the church. We had a discussion among all the officers to decide what to do, whether to follow the high command's decision to kill all the people. That would have been just one big massacre. Finally, Mena Sandoval"—Captain Francisco Emilio Mena Sandoval, another well-known "progressive"—"radioed the commanders, told them he had captured the town and they didn't have to bomb."

When they were able, the survivors fled, leaving behind a lovely ghost town occupied only by a crotchety old man and a handful of others. The soldiers proceeded to burn all the crops they could find, setting off the first of the major migrations from Morazán: peasants fled north over the Honduran border, to Colomancagua and the other camps, and south toward the displaced persons camps that had been set up outside San Francisco Gotera. The zone had begun to empty, to the Army's satisfaction. If the guerrillas were fish swimming in the sea of the people, as Mao had said, then the Army would do its best to drain the sea—"quitarle el agua al pez," as the officers put it: to take away the water from the fish.

"The soldiers would come in," said Nicholas Romero, an old man who stubbornly refused to leave Villa Rosario, "and they'd say, 'Well, anyone who's not a guerrilla has left.' So the rest of the people got out, because they didn't want to be accused of being guerrillas. Then the guerrillas would come, and they'd say everybody better leave because now we're going to attack the town. The only way I survived was when the guerrillas came I was nice to them, when the soldiers came I was nice to them; I just kept my tail between my legs, otherwise I'd have been dead long ago. I refused to leave—my umbilical cord is buried right here under the floor; I've never left—but I thought about suicide sometimes. It was terrible; all the time bombing and shooting and grenades. You'd be eating your soup and suddenly a bomb would land nearby and knock you to the floor. There was no money, no crops, no food. You couldn't even go beg for food in the next village because there were planes up there and every time they'd see people down here they'd shoot."

Despite the Army's success in taking away the water, however, the fish continued to multiply and grow stronger. In November of 1980, a month after the Villa El Rosario operation, the guerrillas began to receive the first of a number of shipments of small arms from the Sandinista regime in Nicaragua—"a mixture of FALS, M-16s, and Uzis," according to Stanley. After the collapse of the "final offensive," in January, the guerrillas also benefited from a fresh infusion of manpower, including not only the fighters who had fled the cities, but a number of important deserters from the Army, among them Captains Cruz Cruz and Mena Sandoval, the latter of whom had succeeded in seizing and holding for a time the Second Brigade in Santa Ana. When the rebellion collapsed, both officers joined the guerrillas, eventually making their way to the ERP *comandantes* in Morazán. It was the end of the "progressive" movement in the Salvadoran Army.

In front of the Perquín health clinic that Tuesday in early December, amid the backwash from the helicopters, the men of the Atlacatl mustered and made ready. The National Guardsmen, who by this time had collected the ten villagers, pushed their reluctant charges forward through the troops until they reached a tall, green-eyed officer in combat fatigues, who was striding about amid the commotion, pointing here and there and issuing orders. One of the Perquín men, who had served in the Army several years before, recognized the officer as Major Natividad de Jesús Cáceres Cabrera, a legendary figure: sixth in his academy class, a born-again Christian, a fanatical anti-Communist, and now the executive officer of the Atlacatl Battalion. (Later, his legend grew: as a colonel in command of Chalatenango in 1986, he forced all the residents of that substantial city to "express their desire for peace . . . their purity, their soul, and also their cleanliness" by painting the entire city white; and in 1989, on a Salvadoran highway, Cáceres ordered his men to block the convoy of the American Ambassador, William Walker, and, when the Ambassador refused to emerge and offer proof of his identity, threatened to blow up his limousine with antitank weapons. This last incident finally led the Defense Minister to relieve Cáceres of his command and send him to Chile as military attaché.)

On that Tuesday in front of the clinic in Perquín, Major Cáceres looked over the ten men and gestured to five captains who were organizing the companies under their command. "He put two of us with each company," one of the Perquín men told me, "and he said, 'We want you to come with us, to show us the area.' " They had been brought there to serve as guides for the Atlacatl.

Major Cáceres gathered the captains together, gave them pseudonyms to be used over the radio during the operation—he himself would be known as Charlie—and issued a few orders. Then the five companies of the Atlacatl moved out, down the mountainside. Everywhere, above the roar of the helicopters, could be heard the thud of mortars and the booming of artillery. "It was a huge operation," the guide from Perquín told me. "There were helicopters and planes and heavy equipment and troops all through the mountains, and they even had animals to cart along some of the guns and ammunition."

Though the guide didn't know it, he had become a part of Operation Rescue's "hammer and anvil." Even as the Atlacatl men set off south from Perquín, hundreds of other soldiers were moving steadily north. Having been deployed as a blocking force along the Torola and Sapo rivers, to the south and east, and along the black road, to the west, they were now tightening the circle. These units, the hammer of the operation, were meant to push all the guerrillas in the zone up toward the anvil of the Atlacatl and crush them against the best troops the Army had to offer. But, of course, the very size of the operation guaranteed the guerrillas would know of it far in advance and would have ample time to flee. As a lieutenant involved in the operation remarked to me, "you take troops from all over the country and move them up to Morazán in about ninety truckloads, right along the Pan-American Highway—I mean, you think somebody might notice?"

As Monterrosa's men circled the hills below Perquín, the guerrillas of the People's Revolutionary Army, far to the south, at La Guacamaya, completed their preparations. Confronted with a heavy force blocking the river to the south, and the Atlacatl moving down from the north, the guerrillas would break straight west, punching their way through the military's lines at the black road. That night, some of their train started the trek: long columns of peasants, their belongings, food, and young children bundled on their backs, trudged single file through the mountains, flowing in a vast nocturnal exodus that would carry them over the mountains to the Honduran border.

On the morning of Wednesday, December 9th, while thick mist still carpeted the valleys, the men of the Third Company of the Atlacatl rose in their encampment on a hill called El Gigante, broke camp, and circled back toward the black road. In the hamlet of La Tejera that afternoon, they seized three civilians, two youths and an old man of eighty or more, hustled them along to a field not far from the sawmill, and began interrogating them "very strongly, very brutally," according to the guide from Perquín. The officers accused the men of being guerrillas, demanded to be given the names of their comrades, to be told where they had hidden their weapons. When the men denied the charges, Major Cáceres declared that they would be executed; the killing, he said, would begin here. But then a farmer from the area came forward. The two youths worked for him, he told the Major, and he protested vigorously that they had nothing to do with the guerrillas. One of the guides vouched for them as well, and after a prolonged dispute the men were spared.

This argument over identity, over who was a guerrilla and who wasn't and what constituted evidence one way or the other, would recur during the next two days. Already in La Tejera, officers disagreed about whether the men should have been spared; according to the guide, Captain Walter Oswaldo Salazar, the company commander, reacted angrily when he was told of a comment from another officer that the local people should be treated with respect unless there was evidence that they were guerrillas. "Salazar said, 'No, these are all guerrillas,' " the guide said. "He said the soldiers could go ahead and kill any of them, or all of them." Later that day, according to the guide, Captain Salazar let slip his suspicion that the other officer was in fact a guerrilla himself, and vowed to assassinate him.

This wasn't simply paranoia. "We had tremendous infiltration in the Army at that time," the lieutenant involved in the operation told me. "We knew that certain sales of arms were going to these people, that information was being leaked—all our operations, all our movements, were being leaked." The overwhelming suspicion that this engendered, together with the growing panic among the officers about the deterioration in the government position, gave the hardest-line officers a decisive upper hand.

"The hard-core guys there really did believe that it was a virus, an infection," Todd Greentree said. "They'd always say 'a cancer'—you know, 'Communism is a cancer.' And so if you're a guerrilla they don't just kill you, they kill your cousin, you know, everybody in the family, to make sure the cancer is cut out."

These officers, of course, had Salvadoran history on their side. "They had a 'kill the seed' mentality," Professor Stanley told me. "After all, what happened in 1932? To this day, when someone wants to make a threat here, why do they invoke the name of Martínez?"—the author of the *matanza*. "Because he is an icon, that's why. The idea of going out to the zones and killing everyone is not a new idea. It's a proved idea."

Putting that proved idea into practice would become the mission of the Atlacatl Battalion. Hoping to ensure that at least one unit of the Salvadoran Army was adequately prepared to fight, the Americans sent Special Forces instructors in early 1981 to train the first recruits of the new Immediate Reaction Infantry Battalion (BIRI). Yet, as the American advisers well knew, the epithet of "elite, American-trained" that was hung on the Atlacatl by the press was a bit of a joke. "They had no specialized training," one of the original Special Forces trainers told me. "They had basic individualized training—you know, basic shooting, marksmanship, squad tactics. I mean, the difference was that the Salvadorans basically had no trained units in the country, so this was going to be a unit that would be trained."

Some officials in the Embassy and the Pentagon had wanted the entire unit to be trained in the United States—and, indeed, later in the year recruits for the second of the BIRIs, the Belloso, would be flown en masse to Fort Bragg, North Carolina. But the Atlacatl had something the Belloso didn't: it had Monterrosa.

"That the battalion wasn't sent to the United States but was trained by Monterrosa here was in large part a testament to his authority," a contemporary of Monterrosa's told me. "The High Command had been preparing him, grooming him. He had taken all the courses the Americans offered, including those for the paratroopers and the commandos. His ambition became very concrete around the time the Americans decided to direct a major counter-insurgency effort here. When the Atlacatl came along, he jumped at it."

From the beginning, Monterrosa worked to give his new force a *mística*—a mystique. "They shot animals and smeared the blood all over their faces, they slit open the animals' bellies and drank the blood," a lieutenant in another unit told me. "They were a hell of a raunchy unit. They had no discipline of fire, none at all. I mean, they saw something moving out there, they shot it—deer, pigs, whatever. You'd be out there in the field trying to sleep, and all night those assholes would keep shooting at things." According to one reporter, the men of the Atlacatl celebrated their graduation by collecting all the dead animals they could find off the roads—dogs, vultures, anything—boiling them together into a bloody soup, and chugging it down. Then they stood at rigid attention and sang, full-throated, the unit's theme song, *"Somos Guerreros"*:

> We are warriors!
> Warriors all!
> We are going forth to kill
> A mountain of terrorists!

By the fall of 1981, the Atlacatl was well on its way to building that mountain. The pattern of its operations had become well known: units of the regular Army and the security forces would

Soldiers of the Atlacatl Battalion, an elite Salvadoran Army unit trained by U.S. Special Forces instructors and commanded by Lt. Colonel Domingo Monterrosa.

move into place along the border of one of the red zones, walling it off, with the help, very often, of a natural barrier like a river or a mountain range. Then a blocking force would invade the zone, pushing before it everyone and everything living. Finally, the helicopters would sweep in, and the men of the Atlacatl would storm out, bombard all whom the trap had snared with artillery and mortar fire, and then with small arms.

One of the best known of these "search and destroy" operations had taken place in November in Cabanas Province. "The evacuation route for the civilian population to Honduras was blocked by the presence of Honduran soldiers along the banks of the Lempa River," Philippe Bourgeois, an American graduate student who became caught up in the Cabanas sweep, later told Congress.[4] "For the next fourteen days, I fled with the local population as we were subjected to aerial bombardment, artillery fire, helicopter strafing, and attack by Salvadoran foot soldiers. In retrospect, it appears as if the Salvadoran government troops had wanted to annihilate all living creatures, human and animal, within the confines of the thirty-square-mile area."

It was the strategy of "draining the sea," or, as Monterrosa was heard to describe it on occasion, of *La Limpieza*—The Cleanup. Those parts of El Salvador "infected" by Communism were being ruthlessly scrubbed; the cancer would be cut out, even if healthy flesh had to be lost, too. "El Mozote was in a place, in a zone, that was one hundred percent controlled by the guerrillas," one of the original American advisers with the Atlacatl told me. "You try to dry those areas up. You know you're not going to be able to work with the civilian population up there, you're never going to get a permanent base there. So you just decide to kill everybody. That'll scare everybody else out of the zone. It's done more out of frustration than anything else."

Joaquín Villalobos, the E.R.P. *comandante*, freely conceded to me in an interview that in a number of the most notorious operations, both before and after El Mozote, many of the civilians killed were in fact sympathetic to the guerrillas. "In San Vicente in 1982, for example, the massacre at El Calabozo that involved more than two hundred people," he said. "This was a situation where the Army was stronger, where our guerrilla force was too weak to protect our followers. We simply weren't able to provide those people sufficient military protection. It was the same in 1980 at the Sumpul River in Chalatenango, where a group of our sympathizers were fleeing, trying to cross the river." The guerrillas, benefiting from very good intelligence and excellent mobility, generally managed to escape from the zones ahead of the Army; it was their supporters, and any other civilians who happened to be there, who took the punishment.

In the case of many of the massacres during the early eighties, then, the Salvadoran Army was managing to do what it set out to do: killing Salvadorans who were sympathetic to the insurgents. However blatantly this behavior violated the rules of war—however infamous it was to murder men, women, and children en masse, without trial or investigation, simply because of the political sympathies of some of their number—the strategy did at least have *some* rationale. Even against this grim background, El Mozote stands out. "El Mozote was a town that was *not* militant," Villalobos said. "That's why what happened at El Mozote was special."

Sometime during the incident at La Tejera that Wednesday afternoon, word came over the radio that the First Company of the Atlacatl had engaged the guerrillas. "There was an exchange of fire, an armed confrontation," the guide says. But, like so much else in this story, the battle—its intensity, even its precise location—has become a matter of fierce dispute. From the start, the

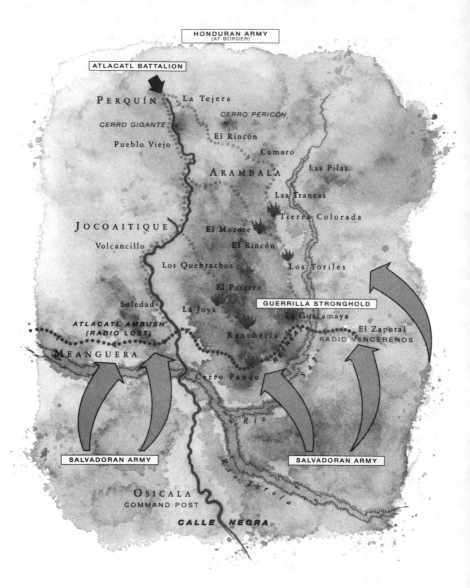

"Operation Rescue," December 1981

Salvadoran military claimed that the fighting took place at El Mozote itself. On December 17th—eight days later—a CIA officer cabled from San Salvador that "the heaviest fighting had occurred at El Mozote . . ."[5] where 30 to 35 insurgents and four Salvadoran soldiers were killed."

It is impossible to know for sure, but from the context of the cable it seems very probable that the CIA man's information came, one way or another, from the Salvadoran Army. The guide from Perquín, on the other hand, who was a few miles away and heard the report on the fighting as it came over the Atlacatl radio, places it "around Arambala. It was a little skirmish," he told me, "and it happened at El Portillón, near Arambala—a little over a mile from El Mozote."

Villalobos, who appears to remember the operation in great detail, also insists that the fighting took place at Arambala, which "was in effect our rear guard," he said. "Although most of the serious fighting took place south of us, along the Torola, there was a minor level of fighting, including maybe a little mortar fire, near Arambala." He went on to say, "It's normal when you displace a large force to leave small units to protect the retreat and keep up resistance." Guerrilla squads around Arambala, north of La Guacamaya, would have been in a perfect position to protect the flank of the main guerrilla force as it retreated west.

Santiago, who was still in La Guacamaya, readying his Radio Venceremos crew for that night's retreat, describes how "the pressure of the enemy was growing in his north-south advance." On that day, he writes in his memoirs, "the comrades of the Fourth Section took by assault a position of the Atlacatl Battalion and captured two rifles"—a plausible number in view of the four dead that the Salvadoran Army apparently acknowledged. But Santiago makes no mention of the "30 to 35 insurgents" killed

The town of Arambala in January 1982. Guerrillas insist
the skirmish with the Salvadoran army,
which official reports placed at El Mozote,
took place outside Arambala.

that are claimed in the CIA cable, and neither, so far as I know, does any other guerrilla memoir. This would have been a very large number of dead; the fact that no one mentions them, and the fact that, in the wake of this fighting, the guerrillas did indeed manage, as Santiago recounts, to "maintain the lines of fire and organize the movement to break the circle and make a joke of Monterrosa's hammer blow"—these two facts lead one to wonder whether the officers, in providing their reports to their own superiors (and possibly to the CIA), had created a victory at El Mozote from what was in fact a defeat at Arambala.

The officers would have been especially reluctant to admit a defeat at the hands of the Fourth Section. An elite guerrilla unit, it had been trained, in large part, by Captain Francisco Emilio Mena Sandoval, one of the Army officers who had deserted to the guerrillas the previous January. Salvadoran officers had developed a deep hatred for Mena Sandoval, regarding him and others like him as much more despicable forms of life than, say, Villalobos: in their eyes, the latter was merely a delinquent terrorist, whereas officers like Mena Sandoval were traitors. And, as it happened, the officers and men of the Atlacatl had a special reason not only to hate Mena Sandoval but to remember with the greatest distaste the town of Arambala and also the hamlet of El Mozote, just down the road.

It was near Arambala, eight months earlier, that the first unit of the brash new Atlacatl had ventured forth to show the guerrillas, and the rest of the Army, what it was made of; and it was there that, to the embarrassment of its officers and men, the highly touted new unit suffered a humiliating defeat—in large part because Captain Mena Sandoval had had the foresight to steal an Army radio when he came over to the guerrillas. Thanks to the radio and Mena Sandoval's knowledge of the enemy's codes, the rebels were able to keep one crucial step ahead of their opponents.

"We monitored the movements of their advance,"[6] writes Mena Sandoval in his memoirs. "They fell into the ambush we had set and responded only with a disorderly retreat. On the radio we could hear their frightened shouts. . . . We caused them a considerable number of casualties and recovered the first two M-16s to be taken from the Atlacatl Brigade."

Later in the same operation, Mena Sandoval writes, "the enemy directed various companies toward regrouping areas in Arambala, orienting its advance so that, for its first objective, it would reach the hamlet of El Mozote." But the rebels were able to fight this "war of position" one crucial step ahead of their opponents. "We defended one line on the outskirts of El Mozote, which the enemy was unable to take for many days. . . . Their cost in casualties kept growing, as did our morale. It had been twelve days of combat and we had almost no casualties."

Finally, after twenty-two days of intense fighting—the Army, says Mena Sandoval, had intended a "quick-strike operation" of perhaps seventy-two hours—the guerrillas slipped away across the black road under cover of night, taking two thousand civilians along with them. By proving their staying power while suffering very few casualties, they had won a significant political victory. As for the Atlacatl, news of its poor performance spread quickly through the Army. Soon officers and soldiers began passing on a little joke. The Atlacatl's designation as a BIRI, they said, stood not for Immediate Reaction Infantry Battalion, as everyone had thought, but for Immediate Retreat Infantry Battalion. This kind of needling would likely have assured that, eight months later, many officers and soldiers in the Atlacatl would have retained vivid memories of Arambala and El Mozote.

Now, after the initial engagement on Wednesday, according to the guide, "we heard by radio that the other company killed people there." Under the gaze of Major Cáceres, who was then with the First Company, the troops entered the town of Arambala, brought out the people who had remained there, and assembled them in the plaza. They led the women and children to the church and locked them inside. Then the troops ordered the men to lie face down on the ground, whereupon they bound them, blindfolded them, and began to beat them, demanding information about the guerrillas. A number of men—the guide believes as many as twenty (and his estimate agrees with the figure given in a detailed analysis of the operation in and around El Mozote by Tutela Legal,[7] the San Salvador Archbishopric's human-rights office in November 1991), though other estimates range as low as three—were taken from the assembly, led away, and executed.

In Arambala, the officers still relied on their lists to select who would die. However, by the following afternoon, Thursday, the lists had run out, and at some point—perhaps that day, perhaps late the day before—the officers made a decision about the direction the operation was to take. For, despite Rufina Amaya's bitter conviction that there had been a "betrayal," that the officer who had spoken to Marcos Díaz as he left Gotera was taking part in a nefarious plot to make sure that the people of El Mozote stayed in their homes to await the fate that had been planned for them, an equally likely explanation—and, in a way, a more horrible one—is that the officer was in fact trying to do his friend Díaz and the people of the hamlet a favor, for at that point nothing whatever may have been planned for them.

Whenever the officers made the decision, it is clear that by the time they reached El Mozote they had ordered a change in tactics. "They had lists from Perquín south to Arambala," the guide told me. "But farther down, there were no lists. Farther down, they killed everything down to the ground. Farther down was scorched earth."

Just after midnight on Wednesday, as the men of the Atlacatl settled down to sleep, a long column wound its way out of La Guacamaya and snaked slowly through the ravines and gullies, heading west toward the black road. The guerrillas and their entourage traveled quietly: the only sound in the tense darkness was that of hundreds of moving feet. The fighters came first, lugging their rifles and ammunition and whatever other supplies they could manage. Then came the civilian followers, loaded down with their bundles of clothing and sacks of tortillas and coffee, and nervously hushing their children. And at the rear came the men and women of Radio Venceremos, bent under the weight of the transmitter and the generator and the other equipment that formed the station's heart.

In the end, it was these burdens which betrayed them: the weight slowed them, so that, as they finally came within sight of the black road, struggling along in increasing panic, the darkness thinned and faded, dawn broke behind them, and they could see, as they gazed upward from their hiding place—a ravine full of prickly maguey—the men of the Atlacatl rising and stretching there on the highway. One soldier was swirling his poncho around him to free it of moisture, and the first rays of sunlight glinted off the droplets. The guerrillas had been caught, but turning back was out of the question; there was nothing for it but to run.

"Advance!" Jonás ordered. No one moved. "Advance, I say!"

A handful of guerrillas broke from their cover, zigzagging in a wild, desperate sprint toward the road, staggering under the weight of their equipment. A moment passed before they heard the shouts of the soldiers, and a moment more before the bullets started to come. They took cover and returned fire, then again ran, took cover, and fired; but they were badly exposed, and by the time they had managed to cross a hundred and fifty yards of open country three men had been hit. One of them, Toni, had been carrying the transmitter, and as he collapsed his precious burden slipped from his back and tumbled down, end over end, into another ravine. His comrades gathered around him. Toni was dying; the bullets kept coming; there could be no question of retrieving the transmitter. Monterrosa would have his war prize.

When the troop reassembled, Jonás ordered the Venceremos crew to head south, to the guerrilla base at Jucuarán. During the nightmarish week of forced night marches that followed, the now voiceless Santiago would turn on his shortwave to hear the triumphant voice of his adversary, coming to him from Monterrosa's own propaganda station, Radio Truth.[8] "Desert, Santiago," it said, "What are you doing out there? We have you surrounded, Jonás. We're going to finish you off. You've already lost . . ."

But that came later. The next evening, after they had spent a day and a night fleeing through the ravines, the Radio Venceremos crewmen were struggling up the slope of the great volcano that broods over Northern Morazán, when they paused to catch their breath. As they bent over, gazing back toward the mountains they had just fled, they could see, rising from the red zone over El Mozote, the great columns of black smoke.

CHAPTER 5

La Matanza

It was growing dark that Thursday afternoon, when the men of the Atlacatl trudged into El Mozote. They found the streets deserted. For the last two days, the thud of the mortars, the firecracker staccato of the small arms, and the roar of the aircraft had been coming steadily closer, and that morning helicopters and planes of the Salvadoran Air Force had strafed and bombed the area around the hamlet, terrifying the inhabitants. "Everything was closer every day, louder every day," Rufina Amaya told me, "and finally, by that day, the people were hiding in their houses."

The strafing ceased not long before the men of the Atlacatl entered the hamlet, dragging with them civilians they had found hiding along the way. Tired and impatient, the soldiers swarmed about the houses of El Mozote and pounded on the doors with the butts of their M-16s. *"¡Salgan!"* they shouted angrily. "Get out here! Get out here now!"

Hesitantly, the people came out into the twilight, frightened, bewildered, unsure of what was happening. The soldiers, cursing and yelling, pulled them forward, hustled them along with the butts of their rifles, herded everyone into the center of the street. Rufina and her husband, Domingo Claros, emerged with their four children: he was carrying three-year-old Marta Lilián and leading Cristino, nine years old, while Rufina had five-year-old María Dolores by the hand and carried at her breast María Isabel, eight months old. "They told us all to lie down in the street, *boca abajo*"—literally, "mouth down"—"and they began pushing some of us down," Rufina says. "As my husband was setting the little girl down, a soldier pushed him to the ground. The girl started to cry. By then, all the children were crying."

The entire town lay like that, perhaps four hundred people face down in the dirt, as darkness fell. Between the wailing of at least a hundred children and the shouting of the soldiers—hundreds had entered the hamlet by now—the din must have been unbearable. The soldiers marched up and down the lines of people, kicking one here and there, striking another with a rifle butt, and all the while keeping up a steady rain of shouted insults and demands. As Rufina tells it, a soldier would stop next to a man or a woman, kick the prone body, and bark out a question: Who were the guerrillas? Where were they? Where did they hide their guns? The men and women of El Mozote insisted that there were no guerrillas there, that they knew nothing of guerrillas or weapons. "If you want to find guerrillas," one woman shouted tearfully, raising her head from the ground, "go out there"—she waved toward the hills—"outside town. But here, here we're not guerrillas."

This only made the soldiers angrier. "All you sons of bitches are collaborators," an officer said. "You're going to have to pay for those bastards."

At one point, as Rufina tells it, the wealthy and influential Marcos Díaz, lying in the street beside his wife and their sons and daughters, raised his head. "Wait!" he pleaded. "They promised me nothing would happen to the people here. The officer told me so."

At that, the Atlacatl officer laughed and said, "No, motherfucker, you all have to pay. Now, get your face back in the ground." And he raised his black boot and pushed Marcos Díaz's head down into the dirt.

"They were very abusive," Rufina says. "We couldn't do anything. They had all these guns. We had to obey." Some of the soldiers took down names as others went along the lines demanding to see people's hands and pulling from their fingers any rings they saw, then ordering them to turn over their jewelry and crucifixes and anything else that might have some value.

The people of El Mozote lay there in the street, their faces in the dust, the children sobbing, for a long time. The soldiers yelled, strode back and forth, aimed their weapons at them. "We thought that they were going to kill us all—that we were sentenced to die right there," Rufina says.

But finally the soldiers ordered them to get up. As the people of El Mozote climbed unsteadily to their feet, the soldiers barked out an order: they were to go back into their houses, the soldiers said, and not let "even so much as their noses" poke out the door.

The people, terrified, grateful to be alive, hurried into their houses—crowded into them, for virtually every room in the hamlet held extra people. Now the wailing of children made the houses seem smaller still. No one slept. Outside, the men of the Atlacatl shouted and laughed and sang songs, punctuating the hilarity with celebratory bursts of gunfire. Rufina and her husband, packed into a house with two other families, struggled to calm their children. "They were hungry, and we had no food to give them," she says. "We were going to kill a chicken to feed them, but as soon as we lit a candle the soldiers yelled at us from the street to put out the light. Our children were scared, and hungry, and the littlest ones were messing all over themselves, and we couldn't even take them outside to clean them.''

So they huddled inside in the darkness, listening anxiously to the laughter, starting up each time it was cut by a burst of automatic fire, and all the while trying to soothe the children. "The saddest thing was that the children were crying and we could do nothing for them," Rufina says. Soon everything would be all right, their parents assured them—soon they would be safe.

Perhaps the parents began to believe it themselves. After the terror of that evening, after feeling the earth against their faces and the gun muzzles at their necks, Rufina and her husband prayed that they had seen the worst, that the soldiers would leave the next day. "We were thinking that because they hadn't killed us yet, maybe they wouldn't," Rufina says. After all, no one had really been harmed, and, even if the promises of Marcos Díaz's officer friend had been worthless—well, the people here had never had trouble with the Army. The people knew that they weren't guerrillas, and the soldiers, despite their angry shouting, must know it, too.

As the people of El Mozote huddled in their dark houses, down at Osicala, the base camp of the operation, south of the Torola River, the officers were taking stock. The first stage of the operation—the convergence of the Atlacatl companies on El Mozote, the capture of the hamlet and its people—had gone well.

"The first phase was over," the lieutenant involved in the operation told me. "All the unit commanders came to Osicala to talk it over. I was heading for the mess hall, and I bumped into"— he named a major who at that time was a key figure in military intelligence—"and he said to me, 'Look, we might need you tomorrow. Be ready.' " Then the major gave the younger officer a rundown of the situation. "He said, 'You know, the first phase is over, the units have gone through and done what they've had to do, and now it's just a question of going in there and interrogating those people'—you know, like P.O.W.s. I asked him if there had been any guerrillas there, and he said, 'No, they're gone. But we might need you tomorrow. We have people to interrogate. We have maybe six hundred people altogether.' "

That was a lot of people to interrogate. "If I had gone in there," the officer told me, "I would have expected to spend two or three days, considering all the people they had."

The two men stood there for four or five minutes while the major briefed the younger man on the sort of information they wanted to get out of the prisoners. "Basically, we were looking for the guerrillas' means of support—how they were getting their food, and so on. We'd stopped a lot of their communications, but we wanted to know their logistics, how they were getting their supplies, what their routes were, and so on. Especially, we wanted to know who it was they'd infiltrated"—into the Army itself—"and who was selling them arms. We had evidence that there was considerable selling of arms from the Army at that time—I mean, you could ask three and four times what a weapon was worth, and these people would pay it, and many of the soldiers couldn't resist that. There was selling of information as well. All our operations were being leaked. Everyone wanted to make a buck—that was the game."

Other officers passed by as the two men talked. That the first phase had been completed, that the Atlacatl had seized El Mozote and now held its population prisoner—that much was widely known among the officers at Osicala that night. "My impression was that the plan was to spend the next day interrogating these people," the lieutenant told me. "And apparently that was the major's impression as well. But the next day he never called me. And by that night everyone knew that something had happened."

While it was still dark, the soldiers came to Rufina's door and began pounding on it with the butts of their rifles. *"¡Salgan!"* they shouted once again. "Get out here!" The families were hustled outside. "We wanted to give our children food," Rufina says, "but they said, 'No, get out to the plaza.' "

All around, the people were emerging from the houses; the soldiers pushed them along roughly, and in the darkness they stumbled over the ground and bumped against one another. "Form lines!" the soldiers shouted. "Men and older boys over here! Women and children over there!"

Soon all the people of El Mozote were lined up in the plaza. The soldiers ordered them not to move. They stood for hours. The children, having had no food and no rest, sobbed and fussed; the mothers tried to quiet them. The soldiers, unlike the evening before, said little. "They just marched up and down the lines looking real mean and ugly, not saying anything," Rufina says. And so the sun rose on the people of El Mozote that Friday.

Around seven, they heard the sound of a helicopter approaching. As it hovered overhead, the soldiers began herding the people from the plaza. The men were ordered into the church, a small whitewashed building adjacent to the even smaller sacristy; the women and children were crowded into the house of Alfredo Márquez, a small building on the main street a few feet from the larger house of Marcos Díaz and directly opposite the church and the sacristy.

Looking out a window of the tightly crowded house—well over a hundred women and children had been forced into a space meant for perhaps a dozen—Rufina saw the helicopter touch down in the plaza and half a dozen officers climb out. She saw several of them, accompanied by soldiers of the Atlacatl, stride to the church, where the men were being held. The others came marching to the house where she was, and pushed through the door into the packed, noisy room.

"They had bayonets on their guns, and they used them to push the women back," Rufina says. "They said we were collaborators. They were angry. They kept asking us where our pistols were, where the men had hidden our guns, and when we kept saying, again and again, that we didn't have any, they'd push at us with the bayonets. Then they'd say, 'Shut up, old woman, what are you crying about?' They said they'd kill us if we didn't tell them."

After only a few minutes, the officers strode out, leaving soldiers to guard the door. Around this time, the helicopter lifted off, taking at least some of the officers along.

Now the women began to hear shouting from the church. "We could hear them yelling—the men," Rufina says. "They were screaming, 'No! No! Don't do this to us! Don't kill us!' "

When she heard the screams, Rufina, who together with her children had been sitting on a bench with her back to the front wall of the house—the wall facing the church—climbed up on the bench so that she could look out a small window high up in that wall. Through the window she saw soldiers leading groups of men from the little whitewashed church—blindfolded men whose hands were bound behind them. Each pair of soldiers led five or six men past the house of Alfredo Márquez and took them out of the hamlet in various directions. After a time, she saw her husband in one group, and as she watched, along with young Cristino, who had climbed up next to her, eager to see what was happening, they both saw him—Domingo Claros, twenty-nine-year-old woodcutter, husband of Rufina and father of Cristino, María Dolores, Marta Lilián, and María Isabel—bolt forward, together with another man, in a desperate effort to escape the soldiers. But there was nowhere to run. The men of the Atlacatl leveled their M-16s and brought both men down with short bursts of fire. Then the soldiers strode forward to where the men lay gasping on the ground, and, unsheathing their machetes, they bent over them, grasped their hair, jerked their heads back sharply, and beheaded them with strong blows to the backs of their necks.

"I got down from the bench and I hugged my children to me," Rufina says. "My son was crying and saying over and over, 'They killed my father.' I was crying. I knew then that they were all being taken away to be killed. I just hugged my children to me and cried."

While the officers had been questioning the women, other officers and soldiers were interrogating the men in the church. "Many of the men were bound, blindfolded, and forced to lie face down on the ground while they were interrogated," according to the Tutela Legal report (which was evidently compiled with the cooperation of at least one soldier who had been present). "The soldiers would step on their backs and pull their heads back by their hair until they screamed in pain." For all their brutality, however, the interrogations of the men appear to have been almost as perfunctory as those of the women. The officers devoted scarcely an hour to questioning the hundreds of supposed collaborators, which makes it difficult to believe that they really expected to acquire useful intelligence from the people of El Mozote.

At about eight o'clock, "various of the men who had been gathered in the church were lifted off the ground and decapitated with machetes by soldiers," according to the Tutela report. "The soldiers dragged the bodies and the heads of the decapitated victims to the convent of the church, where they were piled together." It must have been at this point that the women in the house across the street began to hear the men screaming. Decapitation is tiring work, and slow, and more than a hundred men were crammed into that small building. After the initial beheadings—it is unclear how many died inside the church—the soldiers began bringing the men out in groups, and it was from one of the first of the groups that Domingo Claros had attempted to escape.

While Rufina huddled with her children in the crowded house, mourning her husband, other women climbed up on the bench beside her and peered out the small window. From here, they, too, saw the soldiers taking groups of men from the church and marching them off in different directions.

Outside the hamlet, on a hill known as El Pinalito, the guides from Perquín waited in the company of several corporals—the officers had ordered them to stay there, lest they become confused with the townspeople during the operation—and throughout the morning the guides watched the soldiers pass. "I saw them marching along groups of maybe ten each," one guide told me. "They were all blindfolded, and they had their hands tied behind their backs. Then we would hear the shots, the bursts from the rifles." Out in the forest, the soldiers forced the men to the ground and ordered them to lie flat, with their faces against the earth, as they had lain, with their families, the evening before. Then the soldiers lowered their M-16s and fired bursts into each man's brain.

"All morning, you could hear the shots, the crying and the screaming," Rufina says. In the house of Alfredo Márquez, some of the children had become hysterical, and no one knew how to calm them. Cristino begged his mother tearfully to take them out of the house, lest they be killed, as he had seen his father killed. Rufina could do nothing but point helplessly to the guards and try to calm him. None of the women had any idea what would happen next. "We just cried and hugged one another."

Around midday, a group of soldiers came into the house. "Now it's your turn, women," one of the soldiers said. They were going to take the women out now in groups, the soldier explained, and then, he said, the women would be free to go to their homes, or down to Gotera, or wherever they liked.

With that, the soldiers began picking out, one by one, the younger women and the girls, and pulling them toward the door. "The girls would hang on to their mothers, and the soldiers would come in and just grab them from their mothers," Rufina says. "There was a lot of screaming and shouting. Everyone was screaming, 'No! No! Don't do this!' But the soldiers would hit the mothers with the butts of their rifles, and they would reach behind and grab the girls and pull them along with them."

From the house of Alfredo Márquez, the soldiers marched the group of young women and girls—some of them as young as ten years old—out of the hamlet and up onto the hills known as El Chingo and La Cruz. Before long, the women in the house could hear screams coming from the hills.

The guides, on El Pinalito, nearby, also heard the screaming. "We could hear the women being raped on the hills," the Perquín man told me. "And then, you know, the soldiers would pass by, coming from there, and they'd talk about it. You know, they were talking and joking, saying how much they liked the twelve-year-olds."

In the midst of this, one or perhaps two helicopters—accounts differ, as they do about many details of the story—touched down in the plaza in front of the church, and a number of officers climbed out. From his vantage point on the hill, the guide says, he recognized the distinctive figure of an officer he had seen several times before: Colonel Jaime Ernesto Flores Grijalba, the commander of the Third Brigade, in San Miguel, who was widely known as *El Gordo* (the Fat Man). Among the officers accompanying Colonel Flores was one famous figure, a small but charismatic man whom the soldiers of the Atlacatl proudly pointed out to the guide: Lieutenant Colonel Domingo Monterrosa, their beloved commander.

The officers, having been received at their helicopter by Major Cáceres and the company captains, were escorted to a house not far from the church, and disappeared inside. After some time, during which the killings went on around El Mozote—and also in the adjacent hamlet of Tierra Colorada, where patrolling Atlacatl troops had begun shooting people they found hiding in the houses—the officers strolled out onto the common, climbed back into their helicopter, and lifted off from El Mozote.

Around this time, the soldiers returned to the house of Alfredo Márquez. "I was still sitting on the bench with my kids," Rufina says. "When they came back, they began separating the women from their kids. They pulled the mothers away, leaving the children there crying. They took one group of women and then in a while they came back and took another. That was the saddest thing—little by little, the mothers disappeared, and the house became filled mostly with crying children."

Rufina found herself in one of the last groups. "It must have been five o'clock. There were maybe twenty of us. I was crying and struggling with the soldiers, because I had my baby on my chest. It took two soldiers to pull the baby from me. So when I came outside into the street, I was the last in the group. I was crying and miserable, and begging God to help me."

The soldiers marched the women down the main street. They passed the house of Marcos Díaz on the right and, on the left, that of Ambrosiano Claros, where Rufina and her family had spent the previous night. Ambrosiano Claros's house was in flames. "I saw other houses burning, and I saw blood on the ground. We turned the corner and walked toward the house of Israel Márquez. Then the woman at the head of the line—we were in single file—began to scream. She had looked through the door and seen the people in the house."

What the woman had seen was thick pools of blood covering the floor and, farther inside, piles of bloody corpses—the bodies of the women who only minutes before had been sitting in the house with them, waiting.

"The first woman screamed, 'There are dead people! They're killing people!' and everyone began screaming. All down the line, the women began resisting, hugging one another, begging the soldiers not to kill them. The soldiers were struggling with them, trying to push the first women into the house. One soldier said, 'Don't cry, women. Here comes the Devil to take you.' "

Rufina, still at the end of the line, fell to her knees. "I was crying and begging God to forgive my sins," she says. "Though I was almost at the feet of the soldiers, I wasn't begging them— I was begging God. Where I was kneeling, I was between a crab-apple and a pine tree. Maybe that was what saved me. In all the yelling and commotion, they didn't see me there. The soldier behind me had gone up front to help with the first women. They didn't see me when I crawled between the trees."

The crab-apple tree—which still stands, next to the ruin of Israel Márquez's house, as gnarled and twisted an old crab apple as one can imagine—was within about fifteen feet of the house. "I couldn't move, couldn't even cry," Rufina says. "I had to remain absolutely still and silent. The whole group was still out-side the house—the women grabbing one another and hugging one another and trying to resist. Finally, the soldiers pushed some of them into the house. I couldn't see inside, but I started hearing shots and screams."

Finally, when the screams and the gunfire had stopped, some of the soldiers went off. A few minutes later, they returned, pushing along the last group of women, and now Rufina heard the sequence—the cries of terror, the screaming, the begging, and the shooting—all over again. After a time, those sounds ceased. In the sudden silence, scattered shooting and fainter screams could be heard echoing from the hills. A few feet from where Rufina lay hidden behind the tree, nine or ten soldiers laid down their guns and collapsed wearily to the ground.

"Well, all these old bastards are dead," one said. "Go ahead and burn the house."

It was growing dark, and soon flames were rising from the house of Israel Márquez, highlighting the soldiers' faces and the trunk of the tree. It grew so hot that Rufina began to fear that the tree would catch and she would be forced to run. She had remained perfectly still, hardly daring to breathe, and her legs had begun to fall asleep. And the soldiers, still close enough to touch, remained where they were, smoking cigarettes and watching the fire.

"We'll just stay here and wait for the witches of Mozote to come out of that fire," one said.

The soldiers watched the fire and talked, and Rufina, frozen in her terror a few feet away, listened. "Well, we've killed all the old men and women," one said. "But there's still a lot of kids down there. You know, a lot of those kids are really good-looking, really cute. I wouldn't want to kill all of them. Maybe we can keep some of them, you know—take them with us."

"What are you talking about?" another soldier answered roughly. "We have to finish everyone, you know that. That's the colonel's order. This is an *operativo de tierra arrasada* here"—a scorched-earth operation—"and we have to kill the kids as well, or we'll get it ourselves."

"Listen, I don't want to kill kids," the first soldier said.

"Look," another said. "We have orders to finish everyone and we have to complete our orders. That's it."

At about this time, up on the hill known as El Pinalito, Captain Salazar was shrugging off a guide's timid plea for the children's lives. "If we don't kill them now," he said angrily, "they'll just grow up to be guerrillas. We have to take care of the job now."

Meanwhile, the soldiers sat and gazed at the burning house. Finally, one stood up. "Well, no witches came out," he said. "There are no witches. Let's go see what kind of food they have in that store."

With that, the other men got to their feet, picked up their rifles, and trudged off. A few minutes later, Rufina could hear, from the store of Marcos Díaz, "bottles clinking—you know, as if they were drinking sodas."

The fire was still burning furiously, but the big crab-apple tree, which some miracle had kept from igniting, shielded Rufina from the heat. Over the crackling of the fire she could still hear, coming from the hill called La Cruz, the screams of the girls. Now and again, she heard a burst of gunfire.

After a time, when the soldiers seemed to have finished drinking their sodas, Rufina heard crying and screaming begin from the house of Alfredo Márquez: the screaming of the children. "They were crying, 'Mommy! Mommy! They're hurting us! Help us! They're cutting us! They're choking us! Help us!'

"Then I heard one of my children crying. My son, Cristino, was crying, 'Mama Rufina, help me! They're killing me! They killed my sister! They're killing me! Help me!' I didn't know what to do. They were killing my children. I knew that if I went back there to help my children I would be cut to pieces. But I couldn't stand to hear it, I couldn't bear it. I was afraid that I would cry out, that I would scream, that I would go crazy. I couldn't stand it, and I prayed to God to help me. I promised God that if He helped me I would tell the world what happened here.

"Then I tied my hair up and tied my skirt between my legs and I crawled on my belly out from behind the tree. There were animals there, cows and a dog, and they saw me, and I was afraid they would make a noise, but God made them stay quiet as I crawled among them. I crawled across the road and under the barbed wire and into the maguey on the other side. I crawled a little farther through the thorns, and I dug a little hole with my hands and put my face in the hole so I could cry without anyone hearing. I could hear the children screaming still, and I lay there with my face against the earth and cried."

Rufina could not see the children; she could only hear their cries as the soldiers waded into them, slashing some with their machetes, crushing the skulls of others with the butts of their rifles. Many others—the youngest children, most below the age of twelve—the soldiers herded from the house of Alfredo Márquez across the street to the sacristy, pushing them, crying and screaming, into the dark tiny room. There the soldiers raised their M-16s and emptied their magazines into the roomful of children.

Not all the children of El Mozote died at the sacristy. A young man now known as Chepe Mozote told me that when the townspeople were forced to assemble on the plaza that evening he and his little brother had been left behind in their house, on the outskirts of the hamlet, near the school. By the next morning, Chepe had heard plenty of shooting, and his mother had not returned. "About six o'clock, around ten soldiers in camouflage uniforms came to the house," Chepe told me. "They asked me where my mother was. I told them she had gone to the plaza the night before. I asked them if I could see my mother, and they said I couldn't but I should come with them to the playing field"—near the school. "They said when we got there they would explain where my mother was."

Carrying his little brother, Chepe went with the soldiers and walked along with them as they searched house to house. "We found maybe fifteen kids," he says, "and then they took us all to the playing field. On the way, I heard shooting and I saw some dead bodies, maybe five old people." When they reached the playing field, "there were maybe thirty children," he says. "The soldiers were putting ropes on the trees. I was seven years old, and I didn't really understand what was happening until I saw one of the soldiers take a kid he had been carrying—the kid was maybe three years old—throw him in the air, and stab him with a bayonet.

"They slit some of the kids' throats, and many they hanged from the tree. All of us were crying now, but we were their prisoners—there was nothing we could do. The soldiers kept telling us, 'You are guerrillas and this is justice. This is justice.' Finally, there were only three of us left. I watched them hang my brother. He was two years old. I could see I was going to be killed soon, and I thought it would be better to die running, so I ran. I slipped through the soldiers and dived into the bushes. They fired into the bushes, but none of their bullets hit me."

Lying amid the maguey that night, Rufina Amaya heard the chorus of screams dwindle to a few voices, and listened as it grew weaker and weaker and finally ceased. She heard the officers order that fire be put to the house of Alfredo Márquez and the church and the sacristy, and from the maguey she saw the flames rise and then she heard faint cries start up again inside the buildings and the short bursts of gunfire finishing off a few wounded, who had been forced by the flames to reveal that they were still alive.

Soon the only sounds were those which trickled down from the hills—laughter, intermittent screams, a few shots. On La Cruz, soldiers were raping the young girls who were left. On El Chingo and El Pinalito, other soldiers busied themselves making camp. Down in the hamlet, a few troops walked about here and there, patrolling. Not far from the still burning house of Israel Márquez, two soldiers halted suddenly, and one of them pointed to the patch of maguey. He lowered his rifle and fired, and after a moment his companion fired, too. In the patch of brush, the stream of bullets sent a dark-green rain of maguey shreds fluttering to the earth. Then the soldiers charged forward and began poking among the weeds.

"She was right here," one said, pulling at some maguey. "I saw her, I know it."

Up on the hills, the soldiers listened to the shots, exchanged glances, and waited. Then they went on with what they had been doing: watching the flames rise from the burning houses and talking quietly among themselves, telling tales of the day's work.

They spoke wonderingly about the evangelicals, those people whose faith seemed to grant them a strange power.

"They said maybe some of the people believed in God so strongly that they just delivered themselves up, they didn't resist," the guide told me. "They said some of the people were singing even as they were killed."

There was one in particular the soldiers talked about that evening (she is mentioned in the Tutela Legal report as well): a girl on La Cruz whom they had raped many times during the course of the afternoon, and through it all, while the other women of

El Mozote had screamed and cried as if they had never had a man, this girl had sung hymns, strange evangelical songs, and she had kept right on singing, too, even after they had done what had to be done, and shot her in the chest. She had lain there on La Cruz with the blood flowing from her chest, and had kept on singing—a bit weaker than before, but still singing. And the soldiers, stupefied, had watched and pointed. Then they had grown tired of the game and shot her again, and she sang still, and their wonder began to turn to fear—until finally they had unsheathed their machetes and hacked through her neck, and at last the singing had stopped.

Now the soldiers argued about this. Some declared that the girl's strange power proved that God existed. And that brought them back to the killing of the children. "There were a lot of differences among the soldiers about whether this had been a good thing or whether they shouldn't have done it," the guide told me.

As the soldiers related it now, the guide said, there had been a disagreement outside the schoolhouse, where a number of children were being held. Some of the men had hesitated, saying they didn't want to kill the children, and the others had ridiculed them.

According to one account, a soldier had called the commanding officer. "Hey, Major!" he had shouted. "Someone says he won't kill children!"

"Which son of a bitch says that?" the Major had shouted back angrily, striding over. The Major had not hesitated to do what an officer does in such situations: show leadership. He'd pushed into the group of children, seized a little boy, thrown him in the air, and impaled him as he fell. That had put an end to the discussion.

Now, up on the hills, the soldiers talked and argued and

watched the burning houses, while the two men down below still searched among the maguey, cursing at the sharp thorns.

"I know she was here," the first soldier said. "I saw her. She was right here."

"No, no," his companion finally said. "There's no one here. You're just seeing the dead. You're seeing ghosts. The ghosts of the people you killed are frightening you." With that, the soldiers looked at each other, then turned and trotted back to the center of the hamlet. Amid the maguey, Rufina Amaya closed her eyes, remained motionless. After a time, she reached out a hand and began groping about in the weeds, slowly pulling the thorny strips to her, gathering them into a pile and heaping them over her body.

She lay there still when the stars began to disappear from the lightening sky. She heard sounds of movement from the hills, rising voices as the men woke, urinated, ate, prepared their equipment. Shots echoed here and there, interspersed with the barking and howling of dogs and the lowing of cows as the soldiers killed the animals one by one. From up on La Cruz came a burst of high-pitched screaming and begging, followed by a prolonged chorus of gunfire, and, at last, silence. And then the men of the Atlacatl, having completed the operation in El Mozote, moved out.

Hours earlier, when the chill of the night came on, Rufina Amaya had shivered, for the maguey had badly ripped her blouse and skirt. The thorns had torn the flesh of her arms and legs, but at the time she hadn't noticed. Now she could feel the cuts, swelling and throbbing, and the blood, dried and prickly, on her limbs. And as she lay sobbing amid the thorns, listening to the soldiers pass, her breasts ached with the milk that had gathered there to feed her youngest child.

. . .

Marching past the church, which was burning still, past the carcasses of cows and dogs, and out of El Mozote, the men of the Atlacatl did not see the dark shape in the maguey patch, the heap of dark-green leaves. Their minds were on their work, which on that Saturday morning in December lay ahead in the hamlet of Los Toriles.

In Los Toriles, "the soldiers pulled people from their houses and hustled them into the square," the guide told me, "and went down the line taking money and anything of value out of people's pockets. Then they just lined the people up against a wall and shot them with machine guns. The people fell like trees falling."

Even so, the killing in Los Toriles took much of the day. Some of the residents, having seen the columns of smoke rising the afternoon before from El Mozote, had fled their homes and hidden in caves above the hamlet. But most had stayed, wanting to protect their homes: they remembered that on a previous operation soldiers had set fire to houses they found empty, claiming that they belonged to guerrillas.

By afternoon, the streets of Los Toriles were filled with corpses. "It was so terrible that we had to jump over the dead so as not to step on them," the guide told me. "There were dogs and cows and other animals, and people of all ages, from newborn to very old. I saw them shoot an old woman, and they had to hold her up to shoot her. I was filled with pity. I wished we had gone out and fought guerrillas, because to see all those dead children filled me with sadness."

As night fell, the soldiers walked through the town setting fire to the houses. It was dark by the time they left Los Toriles, to march south toward the guerrilla stronghold of La Guacamaya.

They made camp in open country, rose at dawn, and, as they prepared to move out again, Captain Salazar motioned them over. The men of the Atlacatl gathered in a circle, sitting cross-legged on the ground as he stood and addressed them.

"*¡Señores!*" the Captain said angrily. "What we did yesterday, and the day before, this is called war. This is what war is. War is hell. And, goddammit, if I order you to kill your mother, that is just what you're going to do. Now, I don't want to hear that, afterward, while you're out drinking and bullshitting among yourselves, you're whining and complaining about this, about how terrible it was. I don't want to hear that. Because what we did yesterday, what we've been doing on this operation—this is war, gentlemen. This is what war is." And for perhaps half an hour the Captain went on speaking in his angry voice, and the men shifted uneasily.

"There had been a lot of talk about whether it was right," the guide said, "and this had clearly got back to the Captain." Finally, the tirade over, the men got to their feet. Soon they were marching south again.

Late that afternoon, they reached La Guacamaya. They found nothing there but dead animals; the guerrillas had long since departed. The soldiers spent two nights there, resting and cleaning their equipment. Helicopters landed, bringing Colonel Flores and other top officers, who met with the Atlacatl officers for "evaluation and coordination." The operation was now winding down.

"It was a walk-through by then, a joke," the lieutenant involved in the operation told me. "The guerrillas were long gone, and everybody knew it."

On the second morning, the men of the Atlacatl marched west, heading for the black road. On their way, they passed the hamlet of La Joya. "Everything was dead there—animals and people all mixed together," the guide said. "Vultures were everywhere. You couldn't stand to be there, because of the stink."

Above the hamlet, in the caves and ravines and wooded gullies, those who had managed to escape the troops shivered and waited, and tried to keep their children still. Some had left their homes before the soldiers came; others had managed to flee when men from the Atlacatl, on the day some of their comrades were "cleansing" El Mozote, stormed La Joya. "Suddenly, there was shooting and explosions all over," Andrea Márquez, who had been twenty years old at the time, said. "We didn't even see the soldiers at first. There were bullets flying everywhere. I grabbed my little girl—she was one and a half—and put her on my back, and we started crawling through the brush with bullets flying and explosions all around." She showed me an ugly scar from a shrapnel wound on her knee. "We crawled and then we ran and ran, and after a while my baby made sounds as if she were thirsty, and I pulled her around and then I saw there was a wound in her head, and I realized I was covered with blood."

No one else was around—the people had scattered at the soldiers' assault—and Andrea Márquez was too terrified to go back toward La Joya. Holding her child in her arms, she climbed higher into the mountains, found a cave, and tried to care for her daughter's wound with leaves and with water from a stream. Eight days later, she found a stick and dug a hole and buried her little girl. Then, delirious with grief and shock and terror, she wandered high into the northern mountains.

Months later, the surviving villagers, those few who remained in Morazán, began to murmur fearfully to one another that a witch had come to haunt the mountains—a savage woman, who could be glimpsed from time to time late at night by moonlight, naked but for her waist-length hair, as she crouched by a stream and stripped the flesh from a wriggling fish with long, sharp fingernails. The villagers were frightened of her, for they knew that it was after the *matanza*, the great killing of El Mozote, that the witch had come to haunt the mountains.

The First Reports

As the tide of soldiers ebbed from northern Morazán, the guerrillas flowed back in. "We knew there would be killing, but we never expected what we found," said Licho, who was with one of the first units to return. "It was desolation, total desolation—not a person alive, not an animal alive, not a house that hadn't been burned. There were bodies in the houses, bodies in the fields, bodies in the wells."

The guerrillas immediately sent reports of the killing to their commanders; but there was a problem. "The *comandancia* didn't believe us—they didn't believe the numbers," Licho said. "So we began to count. We sent units all over looking for bodies. A lot of them were not in the houses—they were lying out in the grass, in the fields, in the woods. We sent three reports up to the *comandancia*, and finally they sent other people down to the zone, because they still couldn't believe the numbers."

Survivors were straggling back from the caves and mountain gullies to find the plazas of their ruined villages so thick with vultures that, in the words of one man I talked with, "they seemed covered by a moving black carpet." People wept, mourned, and, when they could, buried their dead. Pedro Chicas, who had hid-en in a cave above La Joya, returned to the hamlet to find "everything burned, everything dead—corpses everywhere in the street," he said. "Everything was dead—cows, horses, chickens, pigs. We couldn't do anything with the badly charred people, but the others we buried."

As the survivors returned to the hamlets around El Mozote, people from the zone were making contact with representatives of Socorro Jurídico (which was then the human-rights organization of the Archbishopric of San Salvador). Roberto Cuéllar, a Socorro Jurídico official at the time, remembers hearing from "members of church groups, and just people there, you know, neighbors." Within days—it is unclear how many days: limited and sometimes conflicting memories make this sequence particularly difficult to reconstruct—Cuéllar telephoned the Reverend William L. Wipfler, who was the director of the human-rights office of the National Council of Churches, in New York. "Cuéllar said the Atlacatl Brigade had committed a massacre in a town called El Mozote and in another called La Joya, and that he thought there might be hundreds killed, and nothing had been cleaned up yet," Wipfler says. "Socorro had an eyewitness account—it had got two people into El Mozote."

Wipfler immediately sent a telegram to Ambassador Deane Hinton, asking "confirmation or otherwise" of "reliable reports received here [that] indicate that between December 10 and 13 joint military and security forces operation took place in Morazán Department which resulted in over 900 civilian deaths." He also telephoned officials at Amnesty International and other leading human-rights agencies in New York and Washington, and left a message for Raymond Bonner, at *The New York Times'* bureau in Mexico City. As Wipfler remembers it, Cuéllar's call came no later than December 20th and probably earlier. (The telegram to Hinton, sent under the name of the Reverend Eugene Stockwell, Wipfler's boss, has been dated December 15th, only four days after the massacre, but there is a possibility that it was actually sent later.)

On December 17th, an exhausted Santiago staggered into a guerrilla camp at Jucuarán—a town fifty miles south of La Guacamaya—along with the other Venceremos people, and there, he says, he found waiting for him a radio message from Morazán: "The Atlacatl Battalion massacred a thousand peasants in various hamlets and villages." If Santiago's memory of the date is accurate, then this number, arrived at less than a week after the killing, could only have been a very rough estimate; soldiers still occupied La Guacamaya and the area of El Mozote, and the guerrillas could have made no precise count. But after days of counting in some of the stinking hamlets, and the compilation, with the help of survivors, of partial lists of names, the *comandantes* had finally been forced to believe that many hundreds had died, and they had apparently settled on the round number of a thousand. And now they wanted Santiago and the others back, with a new transmitter that had been awaiting them in Jucuarán, so they could begin to make the world believe as well.

After five days of all-night marches, the small Venceremos crew trudged into the ravine at El Zapotal. It was noon on December 24th. On Christmas Eve, according to his memoirs, Santiago was able to take to the airwaves and tell the world that Radio Venceremos had been reborn—and to announce that during its two weeks of silence a great killing had taken place in northern Morazán. It was the inauguration of an ambitious propaganda campaign, which gathered steam steadily through December and January, and into February. The propaganda was based on truth, which is supposedly the most effective kind, but the Salvadoran government and, later, the American government would skillfully use the fact that it *was* propaganda—and particularly the fact that the number of dead seemed to increase with each broadcast—to undermine its truth.

On December 29th, the guerrillas stormed the Army detachments that had been left to occupy some of the hamlets in the zone, including at La Guacamaya and at or near El Mozote itself. "The attack on La Guacamaya became a major bloodbath," Villalobos, the guerrilla *comandante*, told me. "The lieutenant in charge knew he was in a hopeless position, but he refused to surrender—probably because he knew what had happened at El Mozote, and feared reprisals. We annihilated his position, and he died in combat. We buried him in his uniform to honor him."

The guerrillas took seven prisoners in the operation, and two of them were made use of a few days later in what Santiago calls the "information battle to denounce the genocide." Each prisoner described what he had seen in Cerro Pando, a village three miles south of El Mozote. "I expected to see dead, because we had talked to troops who had already been out and they said they had killed many guerrillas," a sergeant said. "Then we looked in the houses . . . and I realized that it wasn't the way they said, because I saw dead children, and the mother was hugging one of her children—I think it was her youngest son."

Santiago himself now visited El Mozote with his "mobile unit," and broadcast a description of the devastation, saying that "it looks as if a cyclone had passed through"; that from the ruins of the sacristy came "a penetrating odor that indicated that beneath . . . were to be found who knows how many cadavers of the people of El Mozote"; and that in the shattered building he could see "macabre scenes, hunks of human hair, and fingers amid the rubble."

Late in December, the FMLN got in touch with Raymond Bonner, of the *Times*, and informed him that his long-standing request to visit guerrilla-held territory would be approved; he would be welcome to come to Morazán in early January. Also around that time, a guerrilla patrol stumbled upon some campesinos cowering in a ravine, and discovered among them a near-hysterical woman of thirty-eight, whose legs and arms and face were scored with cuts. The peasants said that they had come upon her near a river—found her crouched there nearly naked, her limbs and body smeared with blood and covered with thorns. "I could hardly speak," Rufina Amaya recalls. "I talked and cried, talked and cried—couldn't eat, couldn't drink, just babbled and cried and talked to God."

Now the guerrillas had found her, and they rejoiced when they realized who she was. "They were all happy that there was at least one survivor," Rufina says. "They all came up around me and hugged me. I didn't know what was going on, who they were, what they wanted." She was taken to El Zapotal and interviewed, and before long the voice of Rufina Amaya, telling in careful detail the story of what had happened in El Mozote, was broadcast throughout El Salvador.

On December 31st, the General Command of the Morazán front of the FMLN issued "a call to the International Red Cross, the O.A.S. Human Rights Commission, and the international press to verify the genocide of more than nine hundred Salvadorans" in El Mozote and the surrounding hamlets. "We ask these organizations to be the eyes of the world's conscience," the *comandantes* said.

That night, at the same time that Radio Venceremos was broadcasting a Mass "in memory of the thousand massacred," El Salvador's provisional President, José Napoleón Duarte, felt obliged to take to the airwaves and deny the accusations personally. The entire massacre story, he said, was "a guerrilla trick" meant to smear his government at the very moment when the United States Congress was considering aid to El Salvador.

Duarte was right in at least one respect: though the El Mozote controversy appeared to center on what had happened in a handful of hamlets in a remote region of El Salvador, the real point of focus had shifted to Washington—and, in particular, to Congress, which was perceived as the weak spot in the armor of the Salvadoran government. It was Congress that voted the money that paid for the American guns and helicopters and military advisers; and in recent years, as the atrocities had grown ever more frequent, Congress had done so with increasing reluctance. Two days before Duarte's speech, Reagan had signed Congress's amendment of the Foreign Assistance Act of 1961, which required the President to "certify" that the Salvadoran government "is making a concerted and significant effort to comply with internationally recognized human rights" and "is achieving substantial control over all elements of its own armed forces, so as to bring to an end the indiscriminate torture and murder of Salvadoran citizens by these forces." If such a certification was not delivered to Congress by January 29th, and convincingly defended, all funds and assistance for El Salvador would be immediately suspended.

Now all sides prepared for the debate over certification, which would provide concerned congressmen, church leaders, heads of human-rights groups, and others with a new opportunity to document the abuses committed by the Salvadoran government in prosecuting the war. Administration officials, meanwhile, both in Washington and in the Embassy in San Salvador, prepared to defend the government and demonstrate that, despite appearances to the contrary—which were thanks largely, they would imply, to blatantly biased journalists and overly credulous human-rights zealots—the Salvadorans were improving in their respect for human rights. Many of these officials viewed the certification requirement with singular contempt.

"If Congress felt so strongly about human-rights abuses, it

could have simply cut off aid," Elliott Abrams, who had just been sworn in as Assistant Secretary of State for Human Rights and Humanitarian Affairs, told me. "But Congress didn't cut off aid, because it didn't want to risk being blamed, if the guerrillas won as a result, for 'losing' El Salvador. Instead, they required certification—which is to say, they agreed to fund the war while reserving the right to call us Fascists." Deane Hinton, the United States Ambassador at the time, later told an interviewer that he viewed certification "as a way for the Congress . . . to be for and against something at the same time." Congressmen, he said, "didn't want to take the responsibility to deny resources to the government of El Salvador and on the other hand they didn't want to endorse it, so they created a certification procedure and made the rest of us jump through the hoop, and the President had to certify it." The entire certification procedure, Hinton said, "is a political cop-out by a lot of congressmen."[1]

At the root of this "political cop-out," in the unspoken view of many Administration officials, was a simple truth: that when it came down to either supporting the Salvadoran government, however unseemly its methods, or allowing a victory by the guerrillas, the choice was clear—and the only difference between the people in the Administration and the hypocrites in Congress was that the Reagan officials were not afraid to say it straight out. Abrams told me, "I used to say to people, 'I mean, I can see arguing for an FMLN victory on political grounds or economic grounds—but on human-rights grounds? I mean, that's crazy.' " Abrams stood the human-rights argument on its head, contending that to argue for an aid cutoff was, in effect, to argue for a guerrilla victory, and that at the end of the day, however badly the Salvadoran government behaved, those collective atrocities could never approach the general disaster for human rights that an FMLN victory would represent.

Whatever one can say about the logic of this view—and its premise that the guerrillas, had they managed to attain power, would have acted anywhere near as violently and savagely against their own people as the Salvadoran Army had already done— Abrams's position certainly did not produce the extended moral self-lacerations, and the abrupt shifts in policy, of the Carter Administration. In part, no doubt, this was because it was just that—a position; for, by the winter of 1981, it had become clear to all, including the Salvadoran officer corps, that for the Americans in El Salvador "national security" came first. Abrams's argument appears to have been aimed at persuading those— Democrats most prominently—who, however much they deplored human-rights abuses in El Salvador, nonetheless worried about taking the blame for any advance of Communism in the hemisphere. The day after the certification was delivered to Congress, the State Department sent out a cable, over Secretary of State Haig's name, urging American diplomats to describe the El Salvador policy as "a grit-your-teeth policy: to support a reformist junta, with a lot of bad eggs in and around it, in order to avoid a Somoza-Sandinista choice. For critics to narrow their focus to the teeth-gritting without considering the policy's larger aims is shallow and unfair." For those who "can't take" the current Salvadoran government, Haig wrote, "the honest response is not to say the junta is—surprise—beset and flawed, but rather to make the case that it's acceptable to the United States if El Salvador goes the Cuban way."

It was against this background that Ambassador Hinton and the State Department began receiving reports about a massacre in Morazán. "Coming on top of everything else, El Mozote, if true, might have destroyed the entire effort," Thomas O. Enders, the Assistant Secretary of State for Inter-American Affairs, told me. "Who knows? I certainly thought that when I first heard about it."

The Embassy began a counterattack, following a pattern that it held to throughout: undermining the reports not by investigating the facts but by casting doubt on their source. In response to the request from the Reverend Wipfler, of the National Council of Churches, Hinton cabled back, on January 8th, that he did "not know what your sources are but the only sources that I have seen alleging something like this are clandestine Radio Venceremos reports." The Ambassador then quoted in full a heavy-handed Venceremos text from January 2nd, in which El Mozote was compared repeatedly to My Lai; added that he "found it interesting" that a guerrilla communiqué two days earlier had not mentioned El Mozote at all; and concluded that he did not "consider Radio Venceremos to be a reliable source."

Hinton—who declined to be interviewed for this account—must have known that the National Council of Churches could not have got its information from Radio Venceremos. (Among other things, Wipfler's cable was sent before the station had resumed broadcasting.) He himself had probably already received reports from sources of his own that something had happened in Morazán; after all, no fewer than ten American advisers were working with the Atlacatl at the time. According to one of them, members of the Milgroup—the Military Advisory Group at the Embassy—had telephoned the Atlacatl base in La Libertad within a few days of the massacre. "They called up and talked to the Special Forces people and told them they wanted Monterrosa to come in—they wanted to talk to him about something that had happened during the operation," this adviser told me. "But Monterrosa just climbed into his helicopter and said, 'If they want to talk to me, I'll be out with my troops.' He wasn't going to go in and talk to those guys. He said, 'If I go in and let them talk to me about this thing, I'll never be able to get anyone to go out there and fight for me again.' And then he got into his helicopter and took off"—heading back to Morazán.

How had the Milgroup officers heard so quickly that "something had happened" in Morazán? Although the adviser believes it was the guerrillas who got word to the Embassy, a number of highly placed Salvadorans, including one prominent politician of the time who had many friends among senior officers, claim that two American advisers were actually observing the operation from the base camp at Osicala. On its face, the charge is not entirely implausible—American advisers had been known to violate the prohibition against accompanying their charges into the field—but it is impossible to confirm. Colonel Moody Hayes, who was then the Milgroup commander, refused to discuss El Mozote with me, explaining that he didn't know "what might still be classified," while officers from the defense attaché's office and from Milgroup who were willing to talk generally dismissed the charge as unfounded. State Department officials, however, were clearly worried about the possibility. "Certainly, one of the issues I remember raising between us and the Embassy was: Were there any American advisers on this sortie?" Enders said. "The Embassy made a great effort to talk to advisers who were with the Atlacatl to try to find out the truth."

Of course, had the truth been that Americans were at Osicala, it would have been a very hard truth to make public—or, for that matter, to confide to a superior. The officers involved would surely have known, as Enders conceded, that admitting such an unfortunate misjudgment "would have ruined those guys' careers—they would have been cashiered. So no one's going to volunteer, 'Hey, I was up there.' " By the same token, Embassy officials would have been acutely aware of the effect such a revelation would have had on the entire American effort in El Salvador. "It would have been devastating," Enders said. "American advisers with a unit that committed an atrocity? Devastating. Can you imagine anything more corrosive of the entire military effort?" Coming at such a time, it might well have made the Salvadoran war, in Enders' expression, "unfundable." Enders insists, however, that "given the small numbers of advisers involved, if they'd been there we would have known about it." (Radio Venceremos, meantime, managed to cast doubt on the entire issue by insisting that Americans had actually accompanied the Atlacatl in El Mozote—a charge for which no evidence exists. The radio also apparently claimed, among other things, that the soldiers had murdered children in El Mozote by baking them in ovens.)

Sometime in mid-December of 1981, "contacts of great confidence on the left" approached Todd Greentree, the Embassy's junior reporting officer, and told him that a massacre had taken place in Morazán. Greentree knew of Operation Rescue from the defense attaché's reports but knew nothing about a massacre. "I first heard about it from the left," Greentree, who is now the Nicaragua desk officer at the State Department, says. "The most important thing was that they offered me a special safe-conduct to go up there and see it for myself. Obviously, a decision had been taken very high up in the FMLN to do this for propaganda purposes. I knew the guerrillas would never have masqueraded something like this, would never have fabricated it, if they were offering safe-conduct. I was convinced that something had gone on, and that it was bad. I mean, it was pretty clear, if they were going to do this, that something must have happened."

Greentree conveyed this message from the left to Ambassador Hinton. A meeting was held. "His response was 'No, you can't do this under guerrilla escort,'" Greentree says. "'That would be too risky, and you would just be playing into their hands.' I mean, I should emphasize that I never got the feeling that they just wanted this to go away. But there were political and military constraints that we were operating under." As Kenneth Bleakley, who was then the deputy chief of mission, told me, "Todd was a very courageous young officer, but it was just too much of a risk to send somebody out there."

The decision was clearly the Ambassador's to make. Peter Romero, who was an El Salvador specialist at the State Department, says, "However much we might have wanted more information, no one in State was going to make that call. It was clearly the Ambassador's call. And at the time, basically, the Embassy staff down there were targets—they were targeted by the FMLN."

Greentree was unable to accept the guerrillas' offer to visit El Mozote and have a look for himself. But, as he soon learned, two other Americans were about to do just that.

Late on the evening of January 3rd, in the mountains near the Salvadoran border, a dusty car pulled to a stop and disgorged into the barren Honduran landscape two Americans in hiking boots, a man and a woman. They slung their backpacks onto the ground, stretched, peered about into the darkness, wandered down the dirt track, and after a few moments of searching found a boy who had been waiting for them—their FMLN contact. The boy watched as the two slung their packs onto their backs and then led them into the quiet darkness, heading down a rocky trail to the bank of a river. In the moonlight, the three stripped and, holding their clothing and their packs above their heads, picked their way unsteadily through the rushing cold water until they reached the far shore—and the border of the guerrilla-held Department of Morazán.

"I was scared shitless," says Raymond Bonner. "All I could think was, 'The military, what if the military ambushes us?' "

It was not an idle fear (scarcely two months later soldiers ambushed and killed four Dutch journalists as they traveled with the guerrillas); for Bonner of *The New York Times* and the photographer Susan Meiselas—together with Alma Guillermoprieto of the *Washington Post*, who followed them into Morazán a few days later—would be the first members of the American establishment press to report on the Salvadoran war from the guerrilla side. "I'd been wanting to go in for a long time," says Bonner. "Any reporter worth anything wanted to get in. I mean, we were fighting this war and who was it we were fighting?"

He and Guillermoprieto had both been working hard for months to arrange a trip in, lobbying through FMLN contacts in Mexico and New York as well as Salvador. In early December, they had finally seen their trips confirmed, only to have them cancelled with the start of Operation Rescue. "I went home for Christmas," says Bonner, who, because the *Times* did not yet have a bureau in Central America, was technically still attached to the paper's Metro desk, "then I went back down. There was all this cloak and dagger stuff about it, you know. Craig Whitney"—then the *Times'* deputy foreign editor—"and I had a code worked out: 'My trip to Alaska may be postponed . . . ,' stuff like that."

Late in December, Bonner's contacts had informed him that the trip was on again. At the time, he didn't connect the green light to El Mozote. "To the charge the guerrillas took us in to report on the massacre, I'd say now, 'You're damn right they did,' " he says. "But at the time I didn't really know about the massacre."

Bonner telephoned Meiselas, who was in New York, and, in a magnanimous gesture, before flying to Tegucigalpa also put in a call to Guillermoprieto in Mexico City, who immediately resumed her own "desperate, intense, round-the-clock phone lobbying" with her FMLN contacts." A few days later, after rendezvousing with a guerrilla contact in the Tegucigalpa market, she found herself being deposited "under a bush in the middle of the night" near the Honduran border, along with a pile of supplies.

"I sat there, shivering, for what felt like ages," she says. "Finally, pushing through the underbrush came maybe eight or ten *compas*. I started babbling, and they told me to shut up. They had already walked in Susan and Ray and the thought of walking in another of these reporters, who couldn't carry equipment, didn't please them. They bitched and moaned about it.

"They loaded up and just started walking. It was pitch black. My heart was thumping so loudly I couldn't hear. By the time we got to the river, the moon had come up and you could see everything. They forded the river, left me standing there. Finally, one of them came up, real embarrassed, and said, 'You have to take your pants off . . . ' They were peasants, you know, puritans. So there I was, on the river bank, in full moonlight, in this tiny bikini bottom. I forded it by myself, and almost drowned. My camera was ruined, my pack was all wet. Someone came over, threw a few cold tortillas at me, and we started walking again. I was wet, miserable, lonely, terrified."

Bonner and Meiselas, and Guillermoprieto, describe the trip the same way: hiking all night through the moonlit mountains and at dawn coming upon the first guerrilla camp—a scattering of tents, under pine trees, that held twenty-five or thirty people. "The guerrillas there were very short-tempered, irritable," says Guillermoprieto. "They were under great stress." The guides would not say where they were, or where precisely they were going. "The guerrillas were very, very spooked about the whole security situation and they didn't want to tell us much," she said.

"It was a military secret where we were; they didn't want to tell us any specifics."

By dawn of the third day—January 6th—Bonner and Meiselas had reached the area of El Mozote. "There were bodies and parts of bodies," Meiselas said. "We saw about twenty-five houses destroyed around Arambala and Mozote. My strongest memory was this grouping of evangelicals, fourteen of them, who had come together thinking their faith would protect them. They were strewn across the earth next to this cornfield, and you could see on their faces the horror of what had happened to them."

Bonner and Meiselas spent a couple of hours walking around the outskirts of Mozote and the neighboring hamlet of Tierra Colorada. The tour appears to have been somewhat haphazard; they were never shown the center of El Mozote, apparently, or the sacristy. Meiselas shot two rolls of film. "By this time in El Salvador, I'd seen a lot," she says. "I'd had to image a lot of death, bodies upon bodies. If I'd thought I was there to *prove* that a massacre had happened I would have imaged many more bodies."

At a burial near El Zapotal, they were introduced to Rufina Amaya, and Bonner interviewed her at length. A few days later, the guerrillas handed him a list of names. "I was sitting on this low brick wall, watching these guerrilla recruits training," Bonner said. "They were marching back and forth with sticks—they didn't know what the hell they were doing—and these guys came up to me with this list, handwritten, several pages." It contained, they said, the names of those who had died at El Mozote and the surrounding hamlets. "I did the tally," Bonner said, "came up with the number seven hundred, tried to get the number of men, women, and children, got a sample of names."

A few days later, after watching the guerrillas retake Jocoatique from the Army, Bonner and Meiselas began the hike back to

Rufina Amaya in January 1982, about a month after
the massacre.

Honduras. At the middle camp, they met a battered Guillermoprieto, one of whose legs was swollen from an accident in-
volving a rock and a mule. At just about the time Bonner reached
Mexico City and began to file his stories, Guillermoprieto was
nearing El Mozote.

"We started smelling it from Arambala," she said. "These kids
started leading me down paths and pointing to houses and saying
again and again, *'Aquí hay muertos, aquí hay muertos.'* The most
traumatizing thing was looking at these little houses where whole
families had been blown away—these recognizable human beings,
in their little dresses, just lying there mummifying in the sun. We
kept walking, got to El Mozote. We walked down these charming
and beautiful roads, then to the center of town, where there was
this kind of rubbly place"—the sacristy—"and, in it, a stupefying
number of bones. There was a charred wooden beam lying on
top of the bodies, and there were bones sticking up, and pieces
of flesh. You could see vertebrae and femurs sticking out. No
attempt had been made to bury the bodies."

In some shock, she was led to La Guacamaya. "Everyone there
had lost someone in his family—everyone—and everyone was in
a state of controlled hysteria. I mean, at that time survival was
in question. There was a real problem of how to eat, how to find
enough food and stay alive."

The great exodus that had begun with the offensive in mid-
December was still under way. "It was that massacre, the most
horrible, that really caused the glass of water to overflow," Licho
told me. "People flowed out of the zone, either toward Honduras
or south toward Gotera or into the guerrillas. A lot of people
joined us as combatants then. We controlled the zone, but there
were no people left there." If it had been Monterrosa's strategy
to "deprive the fish of its water," it had apparently succeeded.

At the urging of Jonás, the guerrilla commander, Guillermoprieto saw Rufina the next day. Later, she spoke to two young men who had seen their families murdered in La Joya. Then, thinking of Bonner and his head start, she scribbled her story in her notebook, folded up the pages, and hid them in a plastic film canister. She found a guerrilla courier and persuaded him, with some difficulty, to carry the precious cargo to Tegucigalpa and deliver it to a colleague, who could telephone the story in to the *Post*.

On January 26th, the day Guillermoprieto got back to Tegucigalpa, the *Times* ran Bonner's first story from Morazán, headlined "WITH SALVADOR'S REBELS IN COMBAT ZONE." Guillermoprieto—who at the time was a stringer for the *Post*, and for whom scooping the *Times* was a very big deal—had already been on the telephone to the *Post*'s foreign editor, and they managed to get her El Mozote story, along with a Meiselas photograph, onto the front page of the first edition of the next day's paper— eighteen hundred words, headlined "SALVADORAN PEASANTS DE-SCRIBE MASS KILLING; WOMAN TELLS OF CHILDREN'S DEATH." Editors in the *Times*' Washington bureau, seeing the piece in the *Post*'s early edition, telephoned New York, where Bonner's El Mozote story had been awaiting editing at the foreign desk. Craig Whitney, the deputy foreign editor, and the deskmen managed to rush Bonner's slightly shorter article, headlined "MASSACRE OF HUNDREDS REPORTED IN SALVADOR VILLAGE," into the paper's late edition. Six weeks after the massacre, El Mozote had made it onto the front pages of America's two most important newspapers.

The following day, Ronald Reagan sent to Congress the Administration's certification that the government of El Salvador was "making a concerted and significant effort to comply with internationally recognized human rights."

El Mozote in January 1982, about a month after
the massacre.

Two days later, on January 30th, Todd Greentree drove out to
Ilopango Airport, climbed into a Salvadoran Army Alouette helicopter, and in a few minutes was sweeping over green volcanic
landscape toward the mountains of Morazán. At his side was
Major John McKay, of the defense attaché's office. A one-eyed
marine (he had been wounded in Vietnam), McKay was known
to have the best contacts among the Salvadoran officers of any
American in the country. The two men were headed for El Mozote to have a look for themselves.

It was not the most propitious time. The Army was tense; three
days before, guerrilla commandos had stormed Ilopango in a
daring raid and had succeeded in destroying a large part of El
Salvador's Air Force as it sat on the tarmac. The raid—which
the guerrillas named Operation Martyrs of Heroic Morazán, in
honor of those killed in December—would not look good in
Washington. The congressional debate loomed large in the minds
of those in the United States Embassy. "It was in the middle of
a phenomenally packed, intense period down there," Greentree
recently told me by telephone. "We had the investigation of the
murders of the nuns, we had the Constituent Assembly elections
coming up, and, of course, we had the certification"—which only
intensified the pressure from "the political microscope in the
States," as Greentree called it. "The primary policy objective at
the time was to get the certification through," he said, and the
spectacular reports of the massacre threatened the certification.
"From the Embassy's point of view, the guerrillas were trying to
make us look as bad as possible. They wanted to shut the whole
thing down."

The Americans landed at the brigade command in San Miguel
to refuel and to receive their first briefing. "The brigade commander was expecting us," Greentree said. "In San Miguel, that

was Flores"—Colonel Jaime Ernesto Flores Grijalba, the overall commander of Operation Rescue. Also present, Greentree
believes—he is not absolutely certain—was Domingo Monterrosa. The officers gave the Americans "a sort of after-action
report, saying which units were where," Greentree said. "As I
recall, the Atlacatl was the main combat unit, and they talked
about this hammer-and-anvil nonsense. We were dismayed, because the Atlacatl was supposed to have developed new tactics,
but now they were back to the same old shit—you know, insert
a blocking force and then carry out a sweep." The message about
El Mozote—the version that the Salvadoran Army had presumably already provided the defense attaché's office—was, in effect,
that the Army had fought hard to dislodge a large company of
guerrillas from the town, and though perhaps a few civilians had
been killed in the crossfire, soldiers certainly had not carried out
a massacre.

Colonel Flores was not particularly happy to see the Americans, and it was clear that his attitude was shared by the other
officers they encountered that day. As McKay—who is now a
colonel attached to NATO headquarters in Brussels, and was
given permission to speak publicly about the events at El Mozote
by the Defense Department—told me, "In general, we had very
little cooperation when we went to Morazán."

They left San Miguel and flew over the Torola toward El Mozote. "You could see there had been a combat sweep through the
area," Greentree said. "You could tell El Mozote had been pretty
much destroyed. Roofs were collapsed, buildings were destroyed,
and the place was pretty much abandoned."

As they flew over El Mozote, Greentree went on, he could see
signs of battle. "There was an escarpment close to the town, an
obvious line of defense, and you could see trench lines there.
There were definitely fortifications in the vicinity." When I

pressed him for details, he said that the fortifications might have been closer to Arambala, a mile or so away.

They made several passes at a couple of hundred feet, then circled around for a better look. "As we lost altitude and got within range, we got shot at," Greentree said. "That was pretty standard stuff out there. It was definitely not a landing situation."

They headed to Gotera, touched down at the barracks, and received another briefing. "The purpose of the briefing was to impress on us that this was a war zone out there," said Bleakley, the deputy chief of mission, who had come to Gotera on another helicopter and met Greentree and McKay there. The officers' point was that "not only were they not out there killing civilians but they were fighting for their lives in that very dangerous war zone to protect the civilians from guerrilla atrocities."

The Americans said they'd like to have a look, talk to some people in and around the town. "It was extremely tense," McKay told me. "The Army was clearly not happy with our presence there. The colonel was obviously taking orders from someone else, and they gave us very little cooperation."

Accompanied by a squad of soldiers, McKay, Greentree, and Bleakley set off for the refugee camp outside Gotera. "We literally went up and down the streets, saying, 'Hey, do you know anyone from El Mozote?' " Bleakley said. "The impression you got from people was that this was a conflict zone, that the people still up there were camp followers, you know, involved in the conflict."

And yet, as Greentree and McKay acknowledged, the presence of the soldiers made the task of conducting what would, in any case, have been difficult interviews almost impossible. The refugees, in effect, were being asked to describe a "conflict zone" from which many had recently fled—a fact which, in the soldiers' eyes, automatically put the refugees under suspicion of being "guerrilla sympathizers" themselves—and to describe it to what was, as far as they were concerned, nothing more than a group of soldiers. "You had a bunch of very intimidated, scared people, and now the Army presence further intimidated them," McKay said. "I mean, the Atlacatl had supposedly done something horrible, and now these gringos show up under this pretense of investigating it, but in the presence of these soldiers. It was probably the worst thing you could do. I mean, you didn't have to be a rocket scientist to know what the Army people were there for."

The three Americans agree that the information they gathered in the refugee camp was not explicit and this lack of direct confirmation would play a key part in what they later reported, or rather didn't report, back to Washington. As Greentree put it, "I did not get any direct eyewitness accounts of what had taken place, of the type that Ray Bonner and Alma Guillermoprieto reported." Not that they expected people to speak so explicitly. "People sitting in a refugee camp," Greentree said, "who have reassociated themselves in some way with the government, who may well have been guerrilla sympathizers, are not going to sit there and give you an eyewitness, blow-by-blow description of what happened—it's just not possible to get that. It was more sort of the way people were talking and the way the kids around were still looking as if they'd been through hell, and people saying, 'Yes, my wife was killed'—that sort of thing."

Greentree did manage to speak to a number of people— including a mayor from one of the towns near El Mozote and several peasants who had lived near the hamlet—out of the soldiers' hearing. "McKay would work the military and keep them distracted while I went out and around and talked to people," Greentree said.

Sometime during these interviews—Greentree remembers having "conversations with more than a dozen people"—he and

McKay became convinced that something had happened in El Mozote. "You could observe and feel this tremendous fear," said McKay. "I was in Vietnam, and I recognized the ambience. The fear was overriding and we sensed it and we could tell that that fear was not instilled by the guerrillas."

"People were freaked out and pretty scared about talking and stuff," Greentree said. "But there was enough to give a pretty strong impression of the horrors of war that these people had suffered." The interviews in the refugee camp, he told me flatly, "convinced me that there probably had been a massacre, that they had lined people up and shot them."

Bleakley, however (who, as deputy chief of mission, was the senior officer of the three), told me that though "it was clear people had been killed, some of them civilians, what we couldn't answer was the fundamental question—you know, the difference between subduing a town and pulling out the civilians, My Lai style, and massacring them."

Still, Greentree said, "each person I talked to confirmed the impression that something bad had happened, but nobody was willing to go ahead and give the exact story." He drew this conclusion "from things they said, their general manner—and their general unwillingness to talk. And that includes the soldiers as well. I mean, you talk to a soldier who thinks he's taken part in some heroic operation—and a Latin soldier, I mean—you can't get him to shut up. But these soldiers would say nothing. There was something there."

Traveling with the squad of soldiers, McKay and Greentree left the refugee camp (Bleakley, who had business in the camp, stayed at Gotera), climbed into a military jeep, and headed up the black road. "We went to five villages," McKay said, including Jocoaitique, within a few miles of El Mozote. "We talked to a priest who gave us oblique information that something horrible had happened, and that it was committed by the Army."

Now the two men, accompanied by the soldiers, set out for El Mozote to see for themselves. "Between five and seven clicks south of Jocoaitique, we were going to turn off the road toward the hamlet and head there cross-country," McKay said. But the soldiers had begun to grow quiet. "There began to be complaints. They were already sensitive about the civilian with me. Now they were getting more and more sullen. You know, they'd look at the ground, mumble something about being out of radio contact." Finally, the group reached the place where they'd have to leave the black road for El Mozote. At that point, the soldiers just stopped. "The sergeant said, 'We're not going any farther, we're not going to help you.' It was made very clear that we would get no more cooperation."

They had come very close to El Mozote. In less than an hour, they could have seen for themselves the burned buildings, the ruined sacristy, and the bodies. But, with the soldiers' refusal to go on, the Americans faced the choice of heading on across open country—guerrilla-controlled country—without protection or turning back. "You want to know what made me decide?" McKay said. "Well, I'd been on that helicopter over there, and we'd received fire, and, the month before, the guerrillas had wiped out a whole company up there. What made me decide—me, the big tough marine? I was scared shitless."

The choice was clear. The Americans, with their soldier escort, turned around and trooped back to Gotera, and from there the helicopter carried them back to the capital. The investigation was over.

CHAPTER 7

Washington's Version

At the Embassy, Greentree sat down and began to write, and by the following day, after consultations with Bleakley and review by others in the Embassy, including Ambassador Hinton, a lengthy cable, over the Ambassador's name, was dispatched to Washington—a cable that provided the basis for what Assistant Secretary of State Enders told Congress two days later. This cable, which was originally obtained in 1983 by Raymond Bonner under a Freedom of Information Act request, is a remarkable document. Its opening paragraph—the all-important "summary" that heads diplomatic cables—reads (with emphasis added) as follows:

> Embassy investigation of reported massacre at El Mozote including visit to the area by assistant [defense attaché] and [Embassy officer] concludes following: *Although it is not possible to prove or disprove* excesses of violence against the civilian population of El Mozote by Government troops, *it is certain* that the guerrilla forces who established defensive positions in El Mozote did nothing to remove them from the path of battle which they were aware was coming and had

prepared for, *nor is there any evidence* that those who remained attempted to leave. Civilians did die during *Operación Rescate* but *no evidence could be found* to confirm that Government forces systematically massacred civilians in the operation zone, nor that the number of civilians killed *even remotely* approached number being cited in other reports circulating internationally. We are still pursuing question as to which Army units were present in El Mozote. End Summary.

In the entire summary, only one point is considered solid enough to be dubbed "certain"—that "the guerrilla forces who established defensive positions in El Mozote did nothing to remove [civilians] from the path of battle." And yet, as Greentree conceded to me, the descriptions of fighting in El Mozote, and of the "defensive positions" there, came largely, if not exclusively, from the Army briefings. "The information that we had presented to us as concrete was, of course, from the Army side, about the conduct of the combat operation," he said. The slender version of what happened in El Mozote seems to be a mixture of Army briefings and, at best, inferences by Greentree and Bleakley. The only point on which the investigators were ready to confer "certainty"—for the rest of the summary consists of careful assertions of what could *not* be proved—was a scenario they seem to have built up by combining Army briefings and their own speculation about what was "a possibility."

How could the investigators be certain that the guerrillas did nothing to remove civilians "from the path of battle"? The day before the trip to Morazán, another junior reporting officer had sent Bleakley a memorandum passing along the report of a source—the name is effaced in the version released by the government this fall—who, while skeptical of the reported numbers of dead, said that "the military did undertake a sweep ('limpieza') of the area, that residents of the area were given time to leave it, that most did and that among the unknown number of victims of the operation were some (unspecified) evangelicals who unwisely chose to stay behind." (Bleakley does not recall the document, but he did say that it "conforms with my memory of the time that there were people who were part of this new evangelical movement in El Salvador who would live in guerrilla areas and manage to stay above the conflict.") It may be that some of the odd language of the summary ("nor is there any evidence that those who remained attempted to leave") was influenced by this memorandum.

In any event, the assertion that guerrillas "did nothing to remove" civilians is actually contradicted later in the cable, when the authors describe an "aged couple" who said that guerrillas "told them to leave in early December." According to the cable, this "aged couple" returned to El Mozote after "the fighting had ended and soldiers were in control." What did they find? "They claimed they saw dozens of bodies." This "claim" is simply quoted, without comment, as is the remark, in the next paragraph, by a man who "knew of violent fighting in El Mozote and other nearby cantons" but was "unwilling to discuss comportment of government forces saying 'This is something one should talk about in another time, in another country.' "

These quotations, together with the flat statements to me from Greentree and McKay that it was clear to them at the time that "something horrible" had happened at El Mozote, that "there probably had been a massacre," make the cable's summary puzzling, to say the least. Read now, the circumspect locutions that dominate the summary take on the aspect of shields—judicious phrases by which the investigators deflected the burden of explicitly recounting what they strongly suspected had happened.

What is curious is how, instead of building on their observations, inferences, and conclusions to present the best version possible of what *probably* happened, they emphasize the gap between what could be *definitively* proved to have happened—which, of course, wasn't much, given the reticence of the people and the constraints on the investigators' movements—and what the newspapers and the guerrillas were claiming had happened. It is a peculiar way of reasoning, built, as it is, on the assumption that in the absence of definitive proof nothing at all can really be said to be known. In effect, officials made active use of the obstacles to finding out the truth—and formidable obstacles certainly existed in El Salvador in 1982—to avoid saying clearly and honestly what they knew and what they suspected.

McKay, at least, seems to have been troubled by this at the time. "We could not have said, 'My God, there's been a massacre,' " he told me. "But, truth be known, the ambiguity of the cable that went out—in my own conscience I began to question it. And then when I saw *The New York Times* piece, and the picture, that really got me to thinking. Bonner and I had gone to Quantico together, went to Vietnam together." McKay finally sent off another cable—"through my own channels," presumably a military or an intelligence circuit—"and though I can't say categorically that I actually wrote 'something horrible happened,' what I said was to the effect that something *had* occurred, because of the fear we had detected from the people there."

McKay, of course, had reviewed the State Department cable before it was sent, but he was not its author; Greentree was. Though he was only twenty-eight years old, Greentree had already earned the respect of his Foreign Service colleagues and—what was much rarer in El Salvador—was considered a competent, trustworthy official by many in the press corps. Indeed, even a decade later, in his understanding of what had happened in El Salvador he seemed to me the most perceptive of the American officials I interviewed. It was Greentree who embodied the United States government in the closest contact it would make to the massacre at El Mozote, and yet it was Greentree who provided the reporting that would enable the government to deny that the massacre had happened. It is tempting to conclude that he simply suppressed what was inconvenient, but the truth of what happened in the writing of the cable, like most of the United States' dealings with the issue of "human rights" in El Salvador, is rather more interesting than that.

Greentree's recollection, during a series of telephone interviews, of the writing of the cable and of its contents followed a fascinating progression. "As I recall," he told me, "I gave the military account the benefit of the doubt, but I probably put in the summary more ambiguity about what I felt." He went on to say, "There were probably a few lines in there that emphasized that, hey, we infer from some of the information we picked up that something happened, and so on." When he was told no such ambiguity could be found in the summary—that, in effect, the only ambiguity in the cable was the conflict, wholly unacknowledged, between its conclusions and some of the observations in the body—he said he "imagined that in the clearing process that got taken out."

The "clearing process," in which the cable made the rounds of officials in the Embassy for review, centered on Kenneth Bleakley, and his recollection of the trip, alone among the recollections of the three, coincides with the conclusions drawn in the cable. Nonetheless, Greentree insisted to me that he "did not feel that what went out distorted beyond acceptability" what he had written. In a later comment, he stated emphatically, "At no time during my tour in El Salvador was a report that I had anything to do with ever distorted by the Embassy. Because those are the standards that Hinton set." Like many in the Embassy, and throughout the Foreign Service, Greentree had great respect for Ambassador Hinton. He describes Hinton as "a totally credible person" and, in writing what he wrote, he clearly felt the pressure to conform to the older man's standards. Yet it is hard not to suspect that Greentree's strong belief that the cable contained more "ambiguity" than in fact it did reflects a lingering unease with the final product—a conflict that persists, even after twelve years, between what he wrote and what he felt he should have written.

"I had been in the Foreign Service for only a couple of years at that time," Greentree told me, "and we had a very strong Ambassador, and our instructions were to be clear and clean— to not distort. You write it down, and then that becomes the eyes and ears of the United States government. And this was especially important because the journalists reporting in El Salvador were thought to be biased. So if I had said everyone was crying, and everything—well, that wouldn't have had any credibility, either. We reported what we saw, and the main requirement was to distinguish between what you saw and what other people said— you know, what was information and what you thought—and, even more than the standards of journalism, to keep your 'slant' out of what you were reporting. What that leads to, though, is great frustration, and that was my feeling. I mean, I was frustrated because it wasn't a satisfactory account."

Had he not been operating under the constraints of politics in Washington, what would he have written differently?

"Well, I would have put in more strongly the impression that abuses against the civilian population probably took place in El Mozote and the surrounding areas during that operation." But he repeated, "It was just an impression. There was no direct corroborating evidence."

Yet this was his strongest impression, and since the limitations caused it to be omitted, didn't they feel rather artificial, at the least?

"That's right," he said. "But that's where, I guess, political judgment came into it. And it was not the judgment that you would think—that, you know, the Ambassador's got to make sure that the information is politically correct. It was that, for the rest of the report to have credibility among people who were far away and whose priorities were—you know, we're talking about people like Tom Enders—whose priorities were definitely not necessarily about getting at exactly what happened: in order for the report to have credibility, all those things have to be kept to a minimum."

Credibility at the Embassy was a special concern, for, looming over its reporting, was the shadow of the former ambassador, Robert White, whom Reagan had cashiered and who had now become an outspoken critic of the Administration's policy in El Salvador. "The problem," Greentree went on, "was because of Robert White before. The end of Bob White's tour, and the transition period before Hinton arrived, and the first six months of Hinton's tour—those were the absolute worst days, really out of control. And the fact that Bob White and everybody in the Embassy had been so thoroughly traumatized by the murders of the nuns, and the AFL-CIO guys, and just the general sort of out-of-control way the military was—it meant that everything we reported could be taken as suspect. Remember," he went on, "there was a new Administration coming in that had a distinctly different approach to things."

At that point, one begins to understand the pressures on the Embassy, and the effect that the great game of politics being played in Washington had on those who were supposedly acting, within El Salvador, as "the eyes and ears of the United States government." Ambassador Hinton was "the guy who sets the standards," Greentree said. "So, of course, since I was a junior officer, my eyes were not on the policy. They were being very affected by the things I was seeing and encountering out there. From the Ambassador's perspective, he had to keep his eye on where we were supposed to be going in the country, and he had to put where the 'truth' was in the context of that. In other words, the possibility that the guerrillas were making a major propaganda ploy over a massacre that might or might not have occurred in El Mozote, and were doing so for the purpose of derailing U.S. policy—well, what the Embassy had to say about that event had to be very, very carefully phrased and controlled, to get as close as possible to what happened and as far away as possible from propaganda on either side, regardless of what might then happen to it once the report got to Washington and was one way or another translated into testimony before Congress."

In reality, then, the admonition to be "clear and clean," to be "professional" and "not distort," served as an excuse to exclude from the cable the very things that had most impressed the men who actually ventured into the war zone. The emphasis on "clean" reporting permitted the blinding and deafening of the government, and served to remove from its field of perception what might have proved to be, in the Washington of early 1982, a very inconvenient fact.

In place of McKay's clear impression that "something horrible happened," and of Greentree's conviction "that there probably had been a massacre, that they had lined people up and shot them," the cable supplied to officials in the State Department a number of arguments that they might find useful in impeaching the press accounts of El Mozote—deeply misleading arguments that would form the basis of the government's effort to discredit the reports of the massacre. After citing the numbers of dead that had appeared in the *Times* and the *Washington Post*, the cable noted, "It is estimated that no more than 300 people were in the entire canton prior to December 1981"—ignoring the fact that both newspapers had made it quite clear that the massacre took place in El Mozote and in *a number of hamlets around it*. As for the names of the dead "subsequently reported in the U.S. press," the cable suggested that those "may well have been extracts in whole or part from the civil registries . . . stolen from Jocoaitique by subversives," though it offered no evidence whatever for this assertion. "I don't recall thinking it was what happened," Greentree said when he was asked about the Jocoaitique claim, "but I thought it was a possibility." And yet he might have learned from Bonner (with whom Greentree was in frequent contact) that the guerrillas had shown the reporter the list several days *before* they attacked and captured Jocoaitique, so the "possibility" that the names were actually drawn from captured civil registries from Jocoaitique—a charge that an Assistant Secretary of State would soon be repeating to the Congress of the United States—was not a possibility at all.

"El Mozote is in the heart of guerrilla territory," one reads on page 2 of the cable, "and its inhabitants have spent most of the past three years willingly or unwillingly cooperating with insurgents"—an odd locution, particularly since the next sentence notes the fact that "Government forces" were last posted in El Mozote in August of 1981, just four months before Operation Rescue. The observation about "willingly or unwillingly cooperating with the insurgents" echoes the attitude of the Salvadoran Army, in which *anyone* living north of the Torola must be, a priori, a guerrilla follower—and was thus, in the officers' view, fair game. And yet Greentree clearly understood that the reality was more complex.

"Most of these people didn't want anything to do with any of this stuff," he told me. "They just wanted people to leave them alone. . . . They were victims of this whole thing. . . . If they could get away by giving guerrillas some corn and chickens, and still live on their farms, that's what they would do. At the same time, if the people had to get by by giving corn and chickens to the half a dozen Guardia Nacional who were living in their town, then they would do that—whatever it took to enable them to live."

It is an eloquent and concise statement of what the civil war had done to many of the people of Morazán by 1981, but, unfortunately, nothing near such depth of understanding is allowed to come through in the cable.

The cable concludes by noting that the defense attaché's office "is attempting to determine which Army units were present in El Mozote during and after the operation." Of course, if the Embassy wanted to discover what had happened in Morazán this should have been the other path of inquiry: putting the question directly to the American-funded and American-trained Army. And yet six weeks after the events were alleged to have taken place the Embassy reported that it had not managed to discover which units were in El Mozote—this although at least ten American advisers were assigned to the Atlacatl, the unit accused in all the press reports.

As several recently released cables confirm, however, matters were a bit more complicated. On the day Greentree and McKay made their trip to Morazán, Ambassador Hinton had a discussion with Salvadoran Defense Minister García—"on margin of dinner," as he puts it in his cable—about El Mozote. The General (García had been promoted on January 2nd) was about to make a trip to Washington to attend "a Congressional prayer breakfast," and the Ambassador warned him that he should "be ready to respond to Morazán massacre story." General García, Hinton writes, "was his usual cocky self. 'I'll deny it and prove it fabricated.' I wished him well and added he would have to explain away details provided by correspondents. It might be possible—we were investigating and were grateful for his help—but he should bear in mind that something had gone wrong. Who did it, when, and in what circumstances was something else."

Two days later, on the afternoon of February 1st, an American officer from the defense attaché's office—it was, as it happened, Major John McKay—traveled out to the Atlacatl headquarters, where he was received by, among others, Major Cáceres, Major José Armando Azmitia Melara, and Lieutenant Colonel Monterrosa. McKay's mission was, he wrote in a subsequent cable, "to specifically determine if the battalion, or elements thereof, were involved in the fighting around and in El Mozote." After "greetings and pleasantries were exchanged," the American put his question to the Colonel. "Monterrosa remained distantly courteous, but he firmly told RO [Reporting Officer] that he was not in a position to discuss these specific subjects, and that RO had better obtain permission from the General Staff of the Armed Forces before he came with such inquiries to his (LTC Monterrosa's) Battalion." Things had begun badly, McKay reports: "Quite frankly, [I] felt that the interview, albeit short, was thus to be terminated." The American hastened to make "the obligatory apologies for what the Colonel may have interpreted as impertinence. RO also pointed out that candid answers to the questions posed would facilitate countering recent press releases which were less than complimentary to the Armed Forces of El Salvador."

Major Azmitia now spoke in "what can only be described as a parable," explaining that "the unit that had fought at El Mozote had had a tough time of it" and that "because of the intensity and duration of the battle . . . there were undoubtedly casualties among non-combatants." Colonel Monterrosa put in that "the

United States Ambassador Deane Hinton with Domingo Monterrosa
in March 1983.

unit involved had had to fight through fixed enemy positions, then, once in the town, fire was received from the houses in the town." Here, according to the American officer, "Monterrosa now utilized the first person: 'I do not have X-ray vision, and I cannot see inside the house from which someone is shooting at me; nor in those type of circumstances am I very disposed to waste time trying to find out who else might be in the house.' . . . At this point LTC Monterrosa said . . . he was only speaking in general, not specific, terms about what had occurred at El Mozote."

The Salvadorans, it seems clear, are giving the American a conspiratorial wink; but McKay doesn't seem to get it—or pretends he doesn't—instead, he blunders on, venturing to ask Monterrosa if any prisoners had been taken. At this, the Colonel again "assumed an adamant demeanor, and suggested that RO consult with the general staff, or get permission from the general staff to ask him such questions." Major Azmitia, as he escorted the American officer to his vehicle, "acted apologetic about the fact that they could not provide more facts about El Mozote, but he was sure that RO understood what LTC Monterrosa had been talking about."

In his summary McKay notes that "the two hours spent with these officers was interesting, to say the least. The nuances, subtleties and indirect comparisons used by LTC Monterrosa and Maj Azmitia were intriguing. Yet the central questions remain without definitive answers." Here the officer ventures a "personal opinion" that the "Atlacatl battalion or elements thereof participated in the attack on El Mozote," but he adds that "precluding permission from General García . . . definitive answers . . . may never be forthcoming."

Ambassador Hinton, clearly a bit frustrated, now asked his Milgroup commander if "it were possible High Command did not know where and when their field forces operated. No, it was not, he told me." The Ambassador sent this officer to see the Salvadoran chief of staff, who informed the American that the "Defense Minister wanted no one other than himself to deal with that question." Hinton, having been rebuffed on his subordinate's level, now paid a personal visit to General García. "We joshed a bit as is our wont," reports Hinton, describing how the General complimented him "on my *Washington Post* interview which he said put things exactly right." Hinton reminds the General that "Tom [Enders] had today gone to Congress to defend the additional 55 million in military assistance" and that "in this connection . . . reports published in the *Washington Post* and *The New York Times* about alleged Morazán massacre . . . caused great concern."

García replied, according to Hinton, that "the Morazán business was a '*novela*,' pure Marxist propaganda devoid of foundation. I said it was clearly propaganda that its timing had been carefully calculated but there were so many details that it was difficult to deal with the stories." The Ambassador now asks the General about some of those details, including the identity, among others, of Major Cáceres. The General replies that Cáceres is "a straightforward, honorable soldier who would never have killed women and children as described in the story." After some discussion, General García acknowledges that "the Atlacatl Battalion had been at El Mozote during the December sweep," but then he "reiterated that the story was a pack of lies." García does promise the Ambassador that he will look into the matter further. "He asked me to leave with him the stories and I did so adding as a sweetener the *Washington Post* editorial of January 29 supporting our common policies."

One gets a vivid sense from these cables of the frustrating position the Americans had placed themselves in in their dealings with the Salvadoran military. The Salvadorans behave with an arrogance that bespeaks their awareness of their own power. Washington was behind them and they knew it: Why should they comply with these local officials, except in those cases where they absolutely had to?

In the case of El Mozote, it was already clear that they didn't have to. Greentree remembers thinking as he sat in the helicopter on the way back to the capital from Morazán, "If we're really going to get to the bottom of this, there's going to have to be a decision to put a tremendous amount of energy into it, to carry out a more formal investigation, like the ones conducted for the Americans"—the four churchwomen. "I remember feeling frustrated and dissatisfied with what we came back with. But, if we'd wanted to go any further with it, it would have taken a decision to expend a tremendous amount of effort."

No such decision was ever made. Everything, in the end, would depend on Greentree and McKay's one-day mission to Morazán; and the guerrilla presence there, together with the recalcitrance of the Salvadoran soldiers, ensured that that mission would not provide evidence considered sufficient to prove something happened. "In the end, we went up there and we didn't want to find that anything horrible had happened," Colonel McKay told me. "And the fact that we didn't get to the site turned out to be very detrimental to our reporting—the Salvadorans, you know, were never very good about cleaning up their shell casings."

Two days after Greentree's cable arrived at the State Department, Assistant Secretary Thomas O. Enders went up to Capitol Hill. Sitting before the House Subcommittee on Inter-American Affairs, he set out to defend the President's certification that the Salvadoran government was making a "concerted and significant effort to comply with internationally recognized human rights."

Since the law, unfortunately, did not set out in clear terms how such an assertion was to be proved, or judged, Secretary Enders proposed to offer to the Congress "a coherent attempt to answer the question that you have raised . . . are we getting some results." "Results" he would interpret to mean improvement. Thus he would be arguing, in essence, that, however horrendous "the human-rights situation" might now be in El Salvador, the last year had in fact been less horrendous than the year before. The effect of this argument was to shift the ground of the debate. "Previously, it had been 'We think this human-rights thing is important and you don't think it's that important,' " Aryeh Neier, then the director of Americas Watch, told me. "What the Reagan Administration did was embrace the principle of human rights and then conduct warfare over the facts. The fight over El Mozote exemplified this."

The human-rights groups had geared up to fight this new war; Americas Watch, for example, which had been founded only the summer before, issued a book-length study, "Report on Human Rights in El Salvador," on January 26th, two days before the certification was sent up to Congress. For the human-rights groups and for leading Democratic congressmen, as well as for the Administration officials, the fight would center on information and how it was gathered.

"Accurate information," Secretary Enders began. "I think we all have found out that is very hard to establish. The responsibility for the overwhelming number of deaths is never legally determined nor usually accounted for by clear or coherent evidence. Seventy percent of the political murders known to our Embassy were committed by unknown assailants." As in the cable, the fact that the killers' identities could not be definitively known, though in most cases few doubted who the killers were, was used as a shield—an excuse to ignore what *was* known. In the absence of conclusive, undeniable proof, the government would feel free to assert that all was darkness.

The Secretary then attacked, by name, most of the better known human-rights organizations—"there is a lot of special pleading going on," as he put it. Socorro Jurídico "strangely lists no victims of terrorist violence," while the Human Rights Commission "has become itself a propaganda vehicle for the insurgency." The Amnesty International report—a very thorough book-length study—"is without historical reference."

"The most difficult of all to assess," the Secretary went on, "are the repeated allegations of massacres. The ambiguity lies in the fact that there are indeed incidents in which the noncombatants have suffered terribly at the hands of guerrillas, rightist vigilantes, government forces, or some or all of them, but at the same time the insurgency has repeatedly fabricated or inflated alleged mass murders as a means of propaganda.

"We sent two Embassy officers down to investigate the reports . . . of the massacre in Mozote," the Secretary went on. "It is clear from the report that they gave that there has been a confrontation between the guerrillas occupying Mozote and attacking government forces last December. There is no evidence to confirm that government forces systematically massacred civilians in the operations zone, or that the number of civilians remotely approached the seven hundred and thirty-three or nine hundred and twenty-six victims cited in the press." Echoing the strategy suggested in Greentree's cable, Enders went on, "I note they asked how many people there were in that canton and were told probably not more than three hundred in December, and there are many survivors including refugees, now. So we have to be very careful about trying to adduce evidence to the certification. We try, our Embassy tries, to investigate every report we receive."

Six days later, Elliott Abrams, the Assistant Secretary of State for Human Rights and Humanitarian Affairs, remarked to the Senate Foreign Relations Committee that the El Mozote case "is a very interesting one in a sense, because we found, for example, that the numbers, first of all, were not credible, because as Secretary Enders notes, our information was that there were only three hundred people in the canton."

The argument about numbers is, of course, deeply misleading—no one who read the *Times* and the *Post* articles could have missed the fact that the killing had taken place in several hamlets; two of the three survivors Guillermoprieto quoted, for example, were from La Joya, not El Mozote. But the argument exemplifies a pattern. Claiming to have investigated "the facts" and to have found "no evidence" of a massacre, American officials then seized on aspects of the charges that, they said, reveal them to be propaganda. "We find . . . that it is an event that happened in mid-December [but it] is then publicized when the certification comes forward to the committee," Abrams told the Senate. "So, it appears to be an incident which is at least being significantly misused, at the very best, by the guerrillas." In an interview more than a decade later, Abrams made the same argument. He pointed out that the massacre had "supposedly" taken place in December, and asked, "If it had really been a massacre and not a firefight, why didn't we hear right off from the FMLN? I mean, we didn't start hearing about it until a month later."

As has been noted, the guerrillas first "publicized" the massacre about two weeks after the event—as soon as they had got Radio Venceremos back on the air. All the same, it is indisputable that the volume of reporting about El Mozote from Venceremos, from human-rights groups, and from the international press grew steadily throughout January, and reached a crescendo the day before Reagan's certification, with the front-page stories in the *Post* and the *Times*. Certainly a significant part of this publicity— it is impossible to say how much—was owing, directly and in- directly, to the efforts of those, beginning with the guerrillas and their international propaganda apparatus, who had a strong in- terest in derailing the Administration's policy in El Salvador. But Administration officials focused obsessively on this unsurprising reality, as if the very fact that the El Mozote story was being used as propaganda—that it was, as Abrams put it, "significantly mis- used . . . by the guerrillas"—in itself constituted proof that the massacre hadn't taken place.

This is not surprising: to many in the Administration, the im- portance of the massacre *was* that it had such propaganda value, and that the propaganda, coming at a crucial time, posed a threat to American aid. Preserving the Salvadoran government and helping it win the war were paramount; "improving human rights" naturally took a back seat since, as the Administration liked to put it, by far the worst disaster that could befall human rights in El Salvador was a Communist victory. This attitude was no mystery to the Salvadoran leaders; despite the periodic brou- hahas over certain atrocities, they could see the bottom line quite clearly, which was, as Abrams phrased it, that "whatever you think of us from a human-rights point of view, what you think of us from a security point of view is determinative."

To say the least, this attitude did not encourage anyone in the State Department to make any additional effort to find out what had happened at El Mozote. As far as the Department officials were concerned, Greentree's cable was the end of the matter. Even had Abrams been a very different kind of man, even had he been inclined to press an investigation, he had been in office barely a month and his Human Rights Bureau was barely staffed (it had been without a chief for ten months because of a bruising Senate fight over Reagan's first nominee) and, as he told me, he received "only the cable traffic that the Latin American bureau wanted us to get."

In any event, the key cable, the Greentree cable, had come from Hinton's Embassy, and Hinton had a great deal of prestige in the Department. By now, however, Hinton himself had taken a rather different view. "I would be grateful if Department would use extreme care in describing my views on alleged massacre," he cabled on February 1st. Apparently, Washington had sent out cables saying that the Ambassador, in his reply to the National Council of Churches, had denied the massacre had taken place. "My letter did not 'deny' incident: it reported that at that time I had no confirmation and . . . had no reason to believe Venceremos reports. I still don't believe Venceremos version but additional evidence strongly suggests that something happened that should not have happened and that it is quite possible Salvadoran military did commit excesses."

Not only McKay and Greentree but now Hinton himself had come to the conclusion that "something happened" at El Mozote—and Hinton had now told the State Department so. To this, he added his blunt appraisal of the Salvadoran officers' credibility. "I find García's assertion . . . 'we have absolutely no information on military actions in El Mozote' to be stonewalling without credibility. I have tried to warn him re need to face up to problem, but my impression is he thinks categoric denial is way to handle question. Department officers may wish to discuss matter with him . . . before U.S. press gets to him."

As it happened, however, "Department officers" seem to have agreed with General García. They had the Greentree cable, and they would make use of it. After all, the question would come down to—as Abrams put it to me—"Do you believe the Embassy, an agency of the United States government, or Americas Watch?" Americas Watch and other human-rights organizations, Abrams said, "did not have a great deal of credibility with us," for, in his view, they had ranged themselves on the side of those who argued, in effect, for an FMLN victory, and thus they served as willing tools of the hypocrites in Congress who now forced Administration officials to undergo a meaningless certification exercise. "Certification was this political game they were playing," Howard Lane, the Embassy press officer, told me. "I mean, everybody knew, Congress knew, what they"—the Salvadoran government—"were doing down there. By then, they had to know, unless they refused to see it. So they beat their breasts, and tore their hair, and yelled about human rights, and made us jump through this hoop called certification. If any Ambassador wanted to keep his job, he had to jump, which meant essentially saying the half-empty glass was really half full. It was a game. I mean, 'improvement'—what's improvement, anyway? You kill eight hundred and it goes down to two hundred, that's improvement. The whole thing was an exercise in the absurd."

So the officials went up to the Hill and made their case, resenting not only the men interrogating them, but their own superiors. "I remember Enders and I were chatting," Abrams said, "and I said, 'You know, I'm delighted to go up there and support the thing, but why is it just us? I mean, where's the Undersecretary—you know, the upper ranks?' And Enders said to me, 'It's a dirty little war and they don't want to touch it.' " Enders told me that James Baker, then White House Chief of Staff, "consciously steered Reagan away from Central America. I couldn't even get Duarte's picture taken with Reagan the first year. The climate was so dominated by charges of violence that the White House didn't want anything to do with it."

Ever the good soldier, Enders on Capitol Hill attacked the numbers from the human-rights groups, put forward the Administration's numbers, explained how, despite all appearances, the Salvadoran government was "making progress." He testified, "The results are slow in coming. I would agree with you on that. But they are coming. . . . The figures show it. We have September, October, November, December figures for 1980, which show something on the order of eight hundred, seven hundred and seventy-nine, five hundred and seventy-five, and six hundred and sixty-five political murders. That is for 1980. We have the same figures for this year which show September, a hundred and seventy-one, October, a hundred and sixty-one, November, three hundred and two. It shows December, two hundred. Our returns are showing markedly different numbers on the same methodology."

That methodology, as anyone who had looked into it knew, was very obviously flawed. The Administration's numbers, drawn from the Embassy's weekly "grim gram," were based on reports in the Salvadoran newspapers, all of which not only ranged from conservative to unabashedly right-wing but weighted their reporting toward the cities. In 1981, fewer people were being killed in the cities, because fewer activists were there to be killed; most of those who had not been liquidated in late 1979 or 1980 had moved to the mountains. And the killings in the mountains, in the isolated hamlets and villages, rarely reached the pages of newspapers in the capital.

"Let me be clear this is not a complete report," Enders told Congress. "Nobody has a complete report. . . . But, nonetheless, it is a coherent attempt to answer the question that you have raised . . . are we getting some results. This is the indication that I submit to you that we are."

To this statement a number of congressmen responded with

outraged eloquence. Gerry Studds, Democrat of Massachusetts, told Enders, "If there is anything left of the English language in this city . . . it is gone now, because the President has just certified that up is down and in is out and black is white. I anticipate him telling us that war is peace at any moment." It was an irresistible quote, and it made for great television. But it didn't make any difference. Enders had supplied a "coherent attempt to answer the question" that Congress had posed, and though Democratic congressmen would not spare their voices, or their sarcasm, in noting "the Orwellian tones of this certification," as Steven Solarz, Democrat of New York, put it—though congressmen attacked the numbers and the methodology, and the hearings became contentious and angry—it was clear that, come what may, there would not be the votes to cut off aid to El Salvador, for that, as everybody knew, would mean "losing" the country to the Communists. At root, nearly everyone tacitly agreed (the Democrats—whose purported "loss" of China three decades before was still a painful Party memory—no less than the Republican Administration and its allies) that that eventuality was too intolerable even to contemplate, and that in the end the Salvadoran government, by whatever means, *had* to win the war, or the country's security would be unacceptably threatened. And so, because of this underlying agreement, the entire debate, loud and angry as it appeared at first glance, was not a debate. It was an exercise for the cameras.

As for El Mozote, since the Salvadoran newspapers said nothing about it, those who had died there merited no place in the numbers Secretary Enders brought to Congress. Had the massacre somehow been "proved" to the State Department's satisfaction—had it been, somehow, impossible for the Administration to deny—El Mozote would have had an ugly effect on the Administration's numbers: political murders would have shown an increase in December from six hundred and sixty-five to well over a thousand, rather than the sharp decline he claimed. Would this have led Congress to reject the certification and cut off aid? Reading the record now, feeling once again the fear in Washington of an FMLN victory and of the blame such a victory might impose on American politicians, the question seems, sadly, difficult to answer. Aid might have been reduced, true, but, at most, Congress might have managed to cut off aid temporarily, only to restore it again in a panic—as Carter had done—at the first new guerrilla onslaught.

But this is speculation. In the event, the dead of El Mozote did not really come into the discussion at all.

On February 10th, the *Wall Street Journal* published a lengthy editorial headed "The Media's War,"[1] in which it noted that the public's "perceptions are badly confused" on the war in El Salvador, and attributed much of that confusion to "the way the struggle is being covered by the U.S. press." In its broad argument, the editorial followed closely the Administration's line on violence in El Salvador. ("Extremists of the right and left do most of their murder in the dark of the night. Some of both factions are soldiers, but both have also learned long ago the trick of dressing in military uniforms to confuse their victims.") Most notable, though, were several paragraphs that took up the question of El Mozote:

Take the recent controversy over charges of a "massacre" by an elite battalion of the El Salvadoran army. On January 27, Raymond Bonner of *The New York Times* and Alma Guillermoprieto of the *Washington Post* simultaneously reported on a visit to rebel territory, repeating interviews in which they were told that hundreds of civilians were killed in the

Susan Meiselas' photograph appeared in *The New York Times Magazine* in February 1982, as Congress debated aid to El Salvador.

village of Mozote in December. Thomas O. Enders, assistant secretary of state for Inter-American affairs, later cast doubt on the reports. There had been a military operation but no systematic killing of civilians, he said, and anyway the population of the village was only 300 before the attack in which 926 people supposedly died.

When a correspondent is offered a chance to tour rebel territory, he certainly ought to accept, and to report what he sees and hears. But there is such a thing as being overly credulous. Mr. Bonner reported "it is clear" the massacre happened, while Miss Guillermoprieto took pains to say that reporters had been "taken to tour" the site by guerrillas with the purpose of showing their control and providing evidence of the massacre. In other words, whatever the mixture of truth or fabrication, this was a propaganda exercise.

Realistically, neither the press nor the State Department has the power to establish conclusively what happened at Mozote in December, and we're sure the sophisticated editors of the *Times* recognize as much. Yet as an institution, their paper has closed ranks behind a reporter out on a limb, waging a little campaign to bolster his position by impugning his critics. A "news analysis" charged the government of sowing confusion by questioning press reports "without presenting detailed evidence to support its position." The analysis posed the question of "how American diplomats gather information abroad," but not the same question about American reporters.

Oddly missing from these paragraphs, and from the rest of that very long editorial, was any acknowledgment that the two reporters had actually seen corpses—in Guillermoprieto's case, at least, dozens of corpses—and that Meiselas had taken photographs of those corpses. Instead, the editorial said that the two journalists "repeat interviews in which they were told that hundreds of civilians were killed in the village of Mozote," and then said immediately afterward that Enders "later cast doubt on the reports"—as if Enders, or his representatives, had actually made it to the village, as if the kind of evidence he was purveying were no different from what were, after all, two eyewitness accounts, if not of the events themselves, then of their aftermath. The reporting done by the journalists and by the Embassy officials is repeatedly yoked together, as if the two parties had visited the same sites, seen the same evidence, talked to the same people, and merely drawn different conclusions. Neither party, the editorial declared, "has the power to establish conclusively what happened at Mozote"—the implication being, as the Administration itself had argued repeatedly in its defense of its Salvadoran allies, that, since there is no "conclusive" account, nothing can be truly known. The idea that much of a journalist's business consists of a studied sifting of what is said and what is observed, of a careful wrestling with gradations of evidence, and a continual judgment of the credibility of witnesses—this notion is nowhere present in the sixteen paragraphs of the *Journal*'s editorial.

Seven days after the *Journal*'s attack on the *Times*' "overly credulous" reporter, the State Department received a cable over the name of the Ambassador to Honduras, John Negroponte, reporting on a visit by an Embassy official and a House Foreign Affairs Committee staff member to the refugee camp at Colomoncagua, to which many of the refugees from Morazán had fled two months before. According to the cable, the refugees described to the American diplomat "a military sweep in Morazán December 7 to 17 which they claim resulted in large numbers of civilian casualties and physical destruction, leading to their exodus." The cable went on to say that "names of villages cited coincide with *New York Times* article of January 28 same subject." The reporting officer added that the refugees' "decision to flee at this time when in the past they had remained during sweeps . . . lends credibility to reportedly greater magnitude and intensity of . . . military operations in Northern Morazán." This information was not made public.

By now, Bonner and his "credulity" had become a minor cause célèbre in the press and on the television talk shows. George Melloan of the *Journal*, who had co-written the editorial, declared flatly during a televised discussion that "obviously Ray Bonner has a political orientation" in his coverage—extending the parallel, already implied in the editorial, with the *Times'* former correspondent in Cuba, Herbert Matthews, who, the *Journal* said, in his "glorification of Fidel Castro in the 1950s became a permanent embarrassment to *The New York Times*." Accuracy in Media, the right-wing newsletter, made this implication explicit in a number devoted solely to Bonner, accusing the reporter of carrying on "a propaganda war favoring the Marxist guerrillas in El Salvador."

Six months after the *Journal*'s attack on him, Raymond Bonner was gone from Central America. Since the El Mozote story and the controversy surrounding it, Bonner had been under great pressure, enduring a steady fusillade of criticism from the Embassy and the State Department, as well as from various right-wing American publications for whom Bonner had come to symbolize the supposed "leftward tilt" of reporting in Central America. In August 1982, Bonner received a telephone call in his Managua hotel room informing him that he should report to the Metro desk in New York.

The *Times'* decision to remove a correspondent who had been the focus of an aggressive campaign of Administration criticism no doubt had a significant effect on reporting from El Salvador.

The New York Times editors appeared to have "caved" to government pressure, and the Administration seemed to have succeeded in its campaign to have a troublesome reporter—the most dogged and influential in El Salvador—pulled off the beat. The public position of A. M. Rosenthal, then the executive editor of the *Times*, has always been, as he told me by telephone, that "at no time did anybody in the United States government suggest to me, directly or indirectly, that I remove Mr. Bonner," and, further, that "anyone who would approach *The New York Times* and suggest to me that I remove or punish a correspondent would have to be an idiot. To imply that a man who devoted himself to journalism would remove a reporter because of the U.S. government or the CIA, or whatever, is ridiculous, naive, cruel, and slanderous."

According to Rosenthal, Bonner was removed because he had never been fully trained in the *Times*' particular methods. Bonner, he said, "didn't know the techniques of weaving a story together. . . . I brought him back because it seemed terribly unfair to leave him there without training." Bonner had been trained as a lawyer, had been an assistant district attorney and a Nader's Raider, and had joined the *Times* as a stringer in Central America. Seymour Topping, then the managing editor, told me that "because we were considerably pressed at the time in getting people into the field in Salvador, we short-circuited what would be our normal process of training people on Metro to learn the style and methods of the *Times*." Bonner, Topping went on, "had done a first-class job of investigative journalism, and there was never any question that he had come up with the facts—that his stories were true. But, if he had been more experienced, the way he had written his stories—qualified them, etc.—would have left him much less open to criticism."

But training was not the only issue—for that matter, as Bonner pointed out to me, he had spent a good part of 1981 on the Metro desk—and, at least in Rosenthal's case, the question of Bonner's "journalistic technique" seems to have been inextricably bound up with what the executive editor came to perceive as the reporter's left-wing sympathies. "If anybody ever asked me to withdraw him, he'd still be there," Rosenthal told me, and certainly the idea that the government simply pressured the *Times* into withdrawing Bonner is wrong. Rosenthal suggests that others have promoted this version of the story because "I was an agent of change in the *Times*, and a lot of people didn't like my politics"; but conversations with a number of *Times* reporters and editors, former and current, persuaded me that the campaign against Bonner was more effective than it might have been because of Rosenthal's own politics. Several people told me that Rosenthal had made no secret that he was unhappy with Bonner, because the reporter, as one characterized the editor's view, "was too willing to accept the Communist side of the story. He was very vocal that Bonner was sympathetic to the Communist side in Central America." The criticism from the right—led by the *Wall Street Journal* editorial on El Mozote—"resonated with Abe, because it reinforced his own suspicions about Bonner. There seemed to be a growing audience out there that agreed with Abe." Several current and former *Times* employees (none of whom would speak for attribution) pointed to a scene in a Georgetown restaurant—it was the evening of the annual Gridiron dinner—in which Rosenthal criticized Bonner and angrily described the sufferings that Communist regimes inflict on their people. Bonner returned to New York and the Metro desk; after taking a leave of absence to write a book, he finally left the *Times* in 1984.[2]

CHAPTER 8

Monterrosa's Prize

El Mozote represented the climax of the era of the great massacres. It was not the last of them—most notably, in August of 1982 the Atlacatl, in an operation similar to that in El Mozote, killed some two hundred people at El Calabozo, in the Department of San Vicente—but after El Mozote the Army relied less and less on search-and-destroy operations that entailed large-scale killing of civilians. It may be that the guerrillas' use of El Mozote for propaganda and the controversy that followed in the United States led senior officers to begin to realize the potential cost of such slaughter. It may be that the highly visible denunciations in Congress finally lent the Embassy's habitual scoldings a bit more credibility. (Even someone as firmly contemptuous of congressional pressure as Elliott Abrams acknowledges that "the good-cop, bad-cop routine with Congress was very effective" and that "there was some positive impact there in reducing the killing.") It may be that the officers realized that lesser massacres— of forty people or fewer, say—could accomplish as much without attracting so much attention.

More important, the key Salvadoran officers no doubt realized that El Mozote had accomplished its purpose. It was not only that in much of northern Morazán the civilians had fled beyond the border—that in several key areas the water had been taken from the fish. It was what El Mozote had meant—what it had *said*—to those who remained. For El Mozote was, above all, a statement. By doing what it did in El Mozote, the Army had proclaimed loudly and unmistakably to the people of Morazán, and to the peasants in surrounding areas as well, a simple message: In the end, the guerrillas can't protect you, and we, the officers and the soldiers, are willing to do absolutely anything to avoid losing this war—we are willing to do whatever it takes.

By late 1982, the tide had begun to turn in Morazán, which is to say not that the Army had begun to win but that it had become less than certain that it would lose. The preceding March, the elections for the Constituent Assembly, on which the Reagan Administration had set much store, had been a huge political success for Administration policy, with a much higher turnout than had been expected. By exerting enormous pressure, the Administration had succeeded in blocking Roberto d'Aubuisson, the best known of the ultra-rightists, from becoming provisional President. Instead, the officers and party leaders and the Americans had agreed, as a compromise, upon Alvaro Magaña Borja, a wealthy aristocrat and international banker with many old friends in the officer corps.

The successful elections and the consequent emergence of the highly presentable, English-speaking Magaña helped the Administration placate Congress. (By the second certification report, delivered six months later, in July 1982, the Administration had significantly altered its position on El Mozote: where, in February, Enders had said that "there is no evidence to *confirm* that government forces systematically massacred civilians in the operations zone," the Administration now claimed there was "no evidence to *support*" charges of "large-scale massacres allegedly committed by government forces"—a shift of emphasis that put the Department in direct contradiction of what Hinton, and even Greentree, had reported.)[1] Congress more than doubled military aid, from thirty-five million dollars to eighty-two million, and increased economic aid to more than twice that. Not only were the Americans sending new, top-of-the-line equipment and plenty of ammunition but they were expanding the Army— training hundreds of officers and soldiers in the States. Most important, Colonel Jaime Flores, apparently because of rather too blatant irregularities in his payroll in San Miguel, incurred the wrath of Magaña, and was consequently "promoted" from command of the all-important Third Brigade to command of the less important First Brigade, and, finally, to that of San Salvador's Fire Department. To replace Flores in San Miguel, Magaña drew on the obvious—the inevitable—choice: Lieutenant Colonel Domingo Monterrosa.

Monterrosa thus became the military commander of the entire eastern zone of El Salvador and entered upon the period of his greatest renown. Very often, the Army publicity people or the American press people steered reporters straight to the dynamic colonel. Monterrosa would make time for them, welcome them onto his helicopter, let them chase along behind him as he strode through one landing zone after another. "He was a phenomenon," Lucía Annunziata, who traveled frequently with Monterrosa as a correspondent for *La República*, told me. "The Americans were always telling us that here he was, here was the new breed of officer they were always promising. He had embraced completely the anti-Communist ideology of the Americans. By then, he talked not like some kind of butcher but like an American. He was completely full of this idea of conquering hearts and minds."

For by this time, as an Atlacatl adviser put it, "it was a different Monterrosa than the man who had done El Mozote." In 1978, Monterrosa had attended the Political Warfare Cadres Academy, in Peitou, Taiwan,[2] and had been trained there in what he described to an interviewer as "war of the masses" and "Communism of this side." He'd returned to El Salvador "very enthusiastic" about the skills he had learned—"how to project ourselves to the civilian population and win them over"—but found to his dismay that senior officers weren't very interested. Now, as commander of the eastern zone, he began to apply what he'd learned.

"He was always tactically very good," Licho, the rebel commander, told me. "Then he began using much more intelligent methods. You know, whenever he would take a village he would come in personally and do political work himself." His soldiers, usually helicopter-borne, would storm a town, flushing out the armed guerrillas, and then Monterrosa would arrive and gather the people together. "He would make a speech there in the plaza," Annunziata said. "He would ask, 'Who is sick? Who needs help?' Then he would say, 'Do you know these people?'— that is, the guerrillas. And, of course, no one would answer. And he would say, in this soft voice, 'Are you sure? Are you sure you don't have a cousin with them?' "

By this time, people all over the countryside recognized the famous figure of Monterrosa. He was short—stooped, even—with a slight paunch. "He was completely nonmartial," Annunziata said. "He always wore this tattered, sweat-stained camouflage-green bandanna on his head, and he had a real Indian face—big nose, receding chin. With that bandanna, he looked like an old aunt. He was a bit of a fop, a bit dandified. He had this young boy always with him, a beautiful young boy of ten or twelve, who took care of his things. He was always touching his soldiers—

very physical, you know. At night, he would get in his red hammock and put on blue gloves and cover his face with a blue towel. He was a real dandy.

"It was late in the afternoon, and we were outside the town of Carolina, on a hill above it. Monterrosa was sitting on a low stone wall, with his feet dangling over the side. He got on the radiophone and he called, 'Charlie, Charlie'—that was his code name—'to Orange,' and he gave the coordinates, and the planes came and bombed and all the while he was directing the planes with the radio. We looked down, and we could see another Army unit entering the town and then the guerrillas leaving from the other side.

"The next morning, the people came out of the town in a long column. You could see them winding their way up the hill in a long line, moving up to where Monterrosa was sitting on the same wall, leaning back, looking halfway between a king and a hero. And, one by one, the peasants passed in front of him, and each of them had an offering. One of them would give him an egg, another some tortillas, another would push forward a young boy to sign up. And Monterrosa would motion to an aide, as he reclined there like a Roman emperor. I remember a father carrying a little boy who had his head covered with a white handkerchief, and then when he came in front of Monterrosa the father unveiled the kid's head and you could see he had this big growth on his face. And Monterrosa nodded to an aide. The aide grabbed the radio and called in the helicopter to take the kid to the hospital in the city."

By 1983, Monterrosa's new tactics had begun to show some success. "He changed the way he related to the local population, and he was less arrogant in his military stance toward us," Villalobos, the E.R.P. *comandante*, told me. "There was this first stage, I think, in which he executed the massacres not only be-

Domingo Monterrosa was that "rare thing: a pure,
one-hundred-percent soldier, a natural leader,
a born military man."

cause it formed part of his military training and it was tactically approved by the High Command but also because he didn't think it would become a political problem. Then, later, he realized that this sort of tactic didn't work. It did not produce a quick military victory."

Annunziata agreed. "He was not bloodthirsty, but he was so neurotically driven—he wanted at all costs to win the war," she said. "The point was to create a turning point, a watershed, to turn the tide, and to do it by scaring the hell out of the enemy. It was a deliberate demonstration of cruelty to show them that the guerrillas couldn't protect them. And he understood that you do this as cruelly, as brutally as possible; you rape, impale, whatever, to show them the cost."

To most of the reporters who covered him now—few of whom had been in the country in 1981—El Mozote was just a distant rumor, a dark echo from the past. "He was the press-corps officer, you know, very personable," Jon Lee Anderson, who was reporting for *Time* magazine, told me, "but there was always this buzz that he was responsible for El Mozote, and, of course, he always denied it." By this time, Monterrosa had a mistress in the press corps—a beautiful young Salvadoran woman who worked for an American television network. Annunziata recalls, "He would helicopter in to the Camino Real"—the San Salvador hotel favored by the international press—"to visit her, and he would burst through the door of the press offices in his combat fatigues and come over and look over your shoulder at what you were writing and say, 'Have you written about me today?'" Monterrosa's girlfriend let her colleagues know—speaking in all confidence, of course—that there had been "a problem" with the El Mozote operation, and although, for understandable reasons, she wasn't free to go into details, all one had to know was that on that particular day the Colonel had unfortunately

"lost radio contact" with his men—with regrettable conse-
quences.

The guerrillas did not find this story very convincing. "He was
well known to all the guerrillas as the man who had ordered the
massacre," Licho said. "Everybody wanted to kill him in combat." Now, however, their adversary had begun doing what they
themselves knew was the most effective thing to do in order to
win the war: "political work" in the countryside. "He started
learning; he began to play football with the people, help their
families," Licho said. "We realized that for someone as militarily
talented as he was to start to do real political work could be very
dangerous. I think it was at the beginning of 1983 that we started
making plans to kill him."

From the beginning, the Salvadoran civil war had been a personal
affair. El Salvador is small, Salvadoran families are large, and,
especially in the countryside, it was not uncommon for a single
family to include soldiers and guerrillas. Cousins—sometimes
brothers—faced one another across the battlefield. It seemed
almost destined, then, that the duel between the most brilliant
officer in the Army and the guerrillas' reputed military genius,
would become a deeply personal matter. "Villalobos and Monterrosa were obsessed with each other's psychology," Annunziata
said. "For Monterrosa, it was like looking in a mirror. He had
this obsession with the guerrillas—with knowing them, understanding them. He had studied all the different groups, and
claimed he could always tell which one had staged an operation.
He felt he was the alter ego of the guerrillas. Every night, out in
the field, he would listen to the radio, first to the BBC and then
to Radio Venceremos, listening to what *they* said he'd done
that day. Every night, you could hear, coming from his hammock,
the 'Internationale' playing over Radio Venceremos."

Domingo Monterrosa was obsessed with Radio Venceremos,
and capturing the rebel station became one of his principal objectives.

As it happened, Monterrosa's fascination with Radio Vence-remos—his capture of the transmitter, after all, had been the high point of Operation Rescue—had not escaped the notice of his alter ego. "A basic principle of warfare is to study the psychology of the enemy commanders," Villalobos told me. "Monterrosa was obsessed with war trophies. He got personally involved in combat situations when his men captured something—to such an extent that at times he lost the ability to coordinate troop movements. Once, he arrived personally to take charge of video records that they had captured from us. Another time, it was a scale model that we had used to plan an attack. Each time, he came himself. And he was desperate to stop Radio Vence-remos. I mean, any cassette or tape recorder he found was turned into a great victory."

Increasingly, in late 1983 and on into 1984, Monterrosa had victories to celebrate. His "beans and bullets" campaign was making progress in Morazán. The area under FMLN control was gradually shrinking, and so, even more critically, was the guerrillas' manpower base. By the summer of 1984, reports had begun circulating that the guerrillas were reduced to conscripting civilians into their ranks—very good news indeed for the Army.

Around this time, General Blandón, the Army Chief of Staff, flew to Perquín to see Monterrosa. "I offered him command of the Army," Blandón told me. "But he said he wouldn't accept it. If that was to happen, he said, it should happen in the normal course of events. You see, he was not driven by any personal ambition to be Defense Minister, but rather by the need to finish the job at hand."

That September, the Americans gave the Army ten new Huey helicopters. "When I saw that news about the helicopters, I told a friend, 'Monterrosa will be coming after us,' " Villalobos said. " 'He will use those helicopters to attack the command post.' "

The delivery of the helicopters, not coincidentally, came at the time of a major diplomatic initiative by the Salvadoran government. On October 15th, President José Napoleón Duarte—he had won an election earlier that year, and replaced Magaña—joined Minister of Defense Carlos Eugenio Vides Casanova and other government representatives in a meeting with guerrilla leaders (among them Guillermo Ungo, who had been Duarte's Vice-Presidential running mate in the stolen elections of 1972), in La Palma, about eighty miles west of Morazán.

Three days after the meeting, Monterrosa launched a major offensive in Morazán, a six-thousand-man sweep called Torola IV. "The war goes on," he told James LeMoyne, of *The New York Times*, as they stood at the base at Osicala, watching the men of the Atlacatl board the new Huey helicopters and lift off into the northern sky. "There are times when you have to make war to gain peace."

Villalobos would be coordinating the response to Torola IV, a campaign that, in its broad outline, appeared much like Operation Rescue, three years before: soldiers from regular Army units were storming north across the Torola, and the helicopter-borne men of the Atlacatl were moving down from Perquín and other mountain towns. This time, however, the guerrillas' response would be somewhat different.

Villalobos and his staff were hard at work preparing an ambush for the town of Joateca, a few miles east of El Mozote. It was a well-planned ambush—they had devoted many hours to its preparation—but an unusual one: the guerrillas were planning to have the Army ambush *them* and thus capture a prize that they very much wanted Monterrosa to claim.

On October 22nd, Monterrosa helicoptered in to Joateca. With him was, among others, Jon Lee Anderson, of *Time*. "It was real air-mobile ops," Anderson told me in an interview. "Flying around from one place to another, inserting troops, choppering around, moving several times a day." In Joateca, he said, an advance platoon had flushed out the guerrillas the day before. Now the people were gathered there, waiting for Monterrosa. "It was this turfy plaza in this ramshackle old hamlet—you know, cobblestones, shaded front porches—and he gathered the townspeople around and gave them this hearts-and-minds sort of speech. He was sitting at a table with a microphone in his hand, and he had a woman social worker and a civilian psychologist there beside him."

Anderson quotes Monterrosa as telling the peasants, "We are your true brothers. We're not the caretakers of the rich. Do you see any rich among us? We give our blood to the soil, but it's up to you to make it fertile."

Around that time, not far from the plaza where Monterrosa was speaking, his men had pounced on a group of hapless guerrillas. "We sent a column of our fighters to fall into an ambush," Villalobos said, "and then they were supposed to leave the transmitter, as if, you know, they'd had to abandon it"—as they'd had to do three years before. "But it didn't work out that way. We weren't able to get the transmitter up to where the combat took place. We were upset—we thought we had blown the operation. I mean, they should have been suspicious."

The rebels had left the transmitter near a graveyard on the outskirts of Joateca. Not far away, Villalobos and his men were waiting tensely, listening intently to their radios. Suddenly, they heard soldiers begin to talk excitedly to one another. "As soon as they found the transmitter, there was a big celebration," Villalobos said. "We could hear them talking about all the prizes they would get, and so on." The soldiers began to congratulate one another, speculating on how happy the Colonel would be when his men brought him this priceless treasure. There was not a hint of suspicion. "Just as vanity blinded Monterrosa, it blinded his soldiers as well," Villalobos said. "We just had to wait for his personal psychology to play itself out."

Late in the afternoon, Jon Lee Anderson sat down to interview the Colonel. "He disappeared for a while, and then he came back very excited," Anderson said. "He sat down next to me on the stoop of this old peasant house, and he confided to me that he thought he'd found the transmitter. It was in this graveyard, in a cemetery at the edge of this little hamlet. This was somewhat far from where things were happening, it's true, but the town had definitely been *theirs*—I mean, there were graffiti everywhere."

Anderson seized that moment, as darkness fell over Joateca, to ask Monterrosa about the rumors that still clung to him about what had happened at El Mozote. "It was late, and we were sitting there, just the two of us, and I said, 'Colonel, *qué pasó en El Mozote?*' And there was this long pause, and he looked away, and finally he said, *'No es como dicen'*—'It's not like they say.' "

Monterrosa would say no more, but Anderson took his answer as a tacit confirmation that *something* had happened there, that Monterrosa had been involved in the massacre. Shortly before, James LeMoyne had asked Monterrosa the same question, and, according to LeMoyne, the Colonel, in the aftermath of a long and exhausting day of combat, had answered more bluntly. "He shrugged and said, 'Yeah, we did it. We carried out a *limpieza* there. We killed everyone,' " LeMoyne told me. "He said, 'In those days, I thought that was what we had to do to win the war. And I was wrong.' "

Late that evening, Anderson and his photographer left, somewhat regretfully, for the capital. They needed to file their stories, but they intended to rejoin Monterrosa in his chopper the following day. The next day, three senior officers and a three-man

Army television crew arrived in Joateca. Along with a local priest and sacristan, they planned to accompany the victorious Colonel as he carried his prize back to the capital. It was to be a triumphal entrance. The capture of the transmitter was an enormous propaganda victory, and Monterrosa wanted to film it, record it, publicize it—to milk it for all it was worth.

The men climbed aboard the helicopter and took their seats, and as the rotors roared overhead soldiers began loading the equipment aboard. Sitting in the place of honor beside Monterrosa, as it happened, was Todd Greentree, of the United States Embassy. "We were sitting together," Greentree said. "He was buckling in, and people were stowing aboard all these duffel bags that belonged to different soldiers—you know, 'Take this back to my wife in San Salvador.' The transmitter must have been in one of those. Then a soldier came over to Monterrosa to tell him he had a radio call, and he got off to take it."

Greentree was in a great hurry to get back to the capital—he has long since forgotten why. "I saw that another helicopter was getting ready to take off, and I was in such a hurry to get back that I got off and climbed aboard."

On a hill northwest of the town, the guerrillas of the E.R.P. watched excitedly as the Huey slowly rose above the tree line. They waited until it had reached its apogee, pointed a remote-control device in a direct line of sight, and pressed the button. Nothing happened. "We didn't know what had gone wrong," Villalobos said. "We thought we had a malfunction. Then we heard his press conference"—Monterrosa was apparently being interviewed by radio, announcing his destruction of Radio Venceremos—"and we realized that it was the wrong helicopter."

They sat tensely on the hill deep into the afternoon, until at last, after what must have seemed an interminable wait, a second helicopter climbed above the treetops and lofted into space. The big aircraft rose high over Joateca, turned, and began to head west, toward the Sapo River—toward the tiny hamlet of El Mozote. Poised high in the blue sky, it caught the sun. Far below, a man from Perquín gazed upward, squinted, and then saw the machine of war—he had seen them so many times over Morazán—suddenly blossom into a great orange-and-black fireball; and then he was deafened by the explosion.

"I remember thinking to myself," said the man, who had been forced to guide Monterrosa's men on their *limpieza* three years before. "I remember thinking, If only he had gone a few minutes more, his blood would have been mixed with the soil of El Mozote."

CHAPTER 9

Unearthing the Truth of

El Mozote

Monterrosa was five years dead before the exiles returned to Morazán. Crowded into the trucks and buses that came over the mountains from the Honduran refugee camps, they flooded back into the deserted villages and hamlets of the red zone. The Salvadoran government could do nothing to stop them, for it was November, 1989, and across the country the guerrillas had unleashed a general offensive that, in the political shock it provoked, would turn out to be the Salvadoran equivalent of Tet: it would put an end to the long civil war.

The fighting was especially brutal in San Salvador, where guerrillas dug themselves in in the crowded slums, and the military managed to extract them only by bombing and strafing civilian neighborhoods. But the turning point of the offensive, and of the war itself, came during the early hours of November 16th, when commandos scaled the back wall of the shady campus of the University of Central America, roused five Jesuit priests from sleep, ordered them to lie with their faces against the ground, and emptied automatic weapons into their brains. Before they departed, the soldiers killed a sixth priest, the Jesuits' cook, and her fifteen-year-old daughter. The scene they left behind—the obliterated skulls of the priests, the green lawn soaked in blood and brains, the fantastically redundant number of spent cartridges—was one of spectacular carnage. And though the soldiers made a halfhearted attempt to scrawl a few leftist slogans, it would very shortly become clear that those who had done this work were the men of the Atlacatl.[1]

It was an enormous political blunder, for it said to the world, and especially to the Americans in Congress, that after the billions and billions of dollars and all the fine words about "training" and "reform," at bottom the Salvadoran Army remained what it had been at El Mozote. But by now Ronald Reagan had gone, and so had the ideological threat he had so feared. The time had come to bring the war to an end.

In the mountains of Morazán, in what was still the red zone, the refugees rebuilt their community. In the Honduran camps, they had made friends among the international aid workers, and now, with help from the European Community and other agencies, they raised up new buildings of straight brown planks: a shoe factory, a handicraft shop, a nursery to hold the children during the day when the people went to work. And they named their community Segundo Montes, after one of the fallen Jesuits.

On October 26, 1990, Pedro Chicas Romero, of La Joya, who had hidden in a cave above the hamlet as the soldiers killed his relatives and his neighbors, went down to San Francisco Gotera and filed a criminal complaint with the Court of the First Instance, accusing the Atlacatl Battalion of responsibility for the killings in El Mozote and the villages around it, and asking that Judge Federico Ernesto Portillo Campos investigate and punish those responsible. Among the first witnesses to give testimony in the case was Rufina Amaya Márquez.

The investigation proceeded haltingly, and although Tutela Legal, among other human-rights organizations, tried to push the

Pedro Chicas Romero, who had hidden in a cave above La Joya, returned to find "everything burned, everything dead—corpses everywhere in the street." Here, he and another La Joya man mourn the dead.

Judge forward—by publishing, in November, 1991, the first full investigation of the El Mozote massacre, including the names of seven hundred and ninety-four dead—it is hard to know what might have come of it had not the government of President Alfredo Cristiani and the *comandantes* of the FMLN come together, in Mexico City in January, 1992, and signed an agreement to end the twelve-year-old war. Among other things, the agreement provided that the Army be purged of "known human rights violators" and reduced by half; that the guerrillas disarm and some of their number join a new civilian police force; and that the Atlacatl and the other rapid-reaction battalions be disbanded. The agreement also provided for a "Truth Commission" that would take on "the task of investigating serious acts of violence that have occurred since 1980 and whose impact on society urgently demands that the public should know the truth."

The experts from the Argentine Forensic Anthropology Unit entered the country in February, and although the investigation was repeatedly stalled, the people of Morazán helped it along (among other things, by staging a boisterous demonstration in front of the Gotera courthouse in April), and so did the three Truth Commissioners when they arrived in June.

Finally, in October, the experts began to dig. And there, on the third day, in the silence of the ruined hamlet of El Mozote, all the words and claims and counterclaims that had been loudly made for nearly eleven years abruptly gave way before the mute force of material fact. The bones were there, the cartridges were there; the sleeping reality of El Mozote had finally been awoken.

They dug and sifted and charted for thirty-five days, and soon the cartridges and the clothing and the bones and bone fragments, all labeled and packed away in bright manila envelopes and fresh new cartons, would depart El Mozote and travel by car to a laboratory in San Salvador, where the experts worked away into

December. The following March, when the United Nations made public the Truth Commission's report, entitled "From Madness to Hope: The 12-Year War in El Salvador," the analysis of the evidence was there, laid out for the reader in clear, precise language, each successive sentence demolishing one or another of the myths put forward during the previous twelve years. Of the hundred and forty-three skulls found, all "were deposited during the same temporal event," which is "unlikely to have occurred later than 1981." El Mozote could not have been a guerrilla graveyard, as some had claimed, especially since all but twelve of the one hundred and forty-three remains identified turned out to be those of children under twelve years of age, including at least one fetus, found between the pelvic bones of one of the adults.

The cartridges recovered in the sacristy showed that "at least twenty-four people participated in the shooting," and the distribution of the shells indicated that they fired "from within the house, from the doorway, and probably through a window to the right of the door." Finally, of the two hundred and forty-five cartridge cases that were studied—all but one from American M-16 rifles—"184 had discernible headstamps, identifying the ammunition as having been manufactured for the United States Government at Lake City, Missouri."

From this evidence and from a wealth of testimony, the Truth Commission would conclude that "more than 500 identified victims perished at El Mozote and in the other villages. Many other victims have not been identified." To identify them would likely require more exhumations—at other sites in El Mozote, as well as in La Joya and in the other hamlets where the killing took place. But the Truth Commission has finished its report, and, five days after the report was published, the Salvadoran legislature pushed through a blanket amnesty that would bar from prosecution those responsible for El Mozote and other atrocities of the civil war. In view of this, Judge Portillo, after allowing two American anthropologists to work in the hamlet for several weeks with inconclusive results, in effect closed down his investigation. The other victims of El Mozote will continue to lie undisturbed in the soil of Morazán.

In July 1993, the Secretary of State's Panel on El Salvador, created in the wake of the Truth Commission report, concluded that the Department's handling of the massacre investigation "undermined the Department's credibility with its critics—and probably with the Salvadorans—in a serious way that has not healed." The panel concluded its review by noting that "a massacre had indeed occurred and the U.S. statements on the case were wrong. On December 11, 1992, two Embassy officers went to El Mozote to attend a ceremony honoring those who had died in the massacre." Only the *Wall Street Journal* remained more circumspect; in February, in a report from El Mozote on its editorial page, entitled "The War's Over, but El Salvador Still Fights Propaganda Battle," the *Journal* conceded that while "it appears that a massacre of some kind took place, questions remain," including, the *Journal* said, "Who were the true perpetrators of this awful crime?"

If you drive out from San Salvador today, along the highway toward Morazán, passing the barracks of the Domingo Monterrosa Third Brigade, and crossing the narrow bridge on the Torola, its wooden planks clattering beneath your wheels, you will find, amid the sorghum and the corn and the tufts of maguey, the clean, new buildings of Segundo Montes, housing the boot factory and the handicraft shop and the other factories brought back from the refugee camps. In one of the buildings, you will find the woman who fled La Joya in 1981, was forced to bury her wounded child in the mountains, went mad, and became the witch of El Mozote that the villagers came to fear. Andrea Márquez works in the nursery, caring for the children of Segundo Montes. Farther up the black road, if you step through the barbed wire you will find Rufina Amaya living in a small house with her little girl, Marta, who is now four years old. And if you head up the black road to Perquín, with its battered central square and its mural of the slain Archbishop Romero, you will come to Radio Venceremos, which has graduated from its various holes in the ground to an actual building on a nearby hill; concrete, single story, and small, it is a museum now, a gallery to exhibit pictures of the station's former subterranean quarters. Out in front, beside a well-preserved bomb crater with a carefully tended stone-and-flower border, and behind a brass plaque, you will find a dramatically twisted and burned torso of steel. As the people there will tell you, it is what remains of a helicopter that was blown from the sky one fine day, and it happens to be the most cherished monument in all Morazán.

The memorial at El Mozote. The inscription reads:
"They did not die, they are with us, with you,
and with all humanity."

NOTES

Most of the interviews for this book were conducted during a trip to El Salvador in November 1992, and during several trips to Washington over the following three months. Some of the farther-flung players—including Todd Greentree, who was then serving as political officer in the U.S. Embassy in Kathmandu, and Colonel John McKay, who had been assigned to NATO headquarters in Brussels—I interviewed by telephone. The only key participant who steadfastly refused to speak to me was Deane Hinton, the former U.S. ambassador in El Salvador who was then serving as ambassador to Panama. The information office of the Salvadoran Army, through which one must seek to interview particular officers, proved itself to be almost entirely uncooperative—though a number of officers, when contacted privately, did agree to speak to me, some on the record, many more of them off.

These notes are not intended to supply an exhaustive sourcing of the text. Rather, they are meant to supplement the narrative and to point those who are interested toward further reading about El Mozote, El Salvador, and Central America.

CHAPTER 1

1 The Argentine Forensic Anthropology Team was established in Buenos Aires, in 1984, during the exhumation of the mass graves of those who had been "disappeared" during the rule of the military juntas. In February 1992, at the invitation of the Salvadoran human-rights organization Tutela Legal, four members of the team—Mercedes Doretti, Claudia Bernardi, Patricia Bernardi, and Luis Fondebrider—came to El Salvador. In October, they were named "technical consultants" to the United Nations Truth Commission. When they finally began to excavate the site, after a series of frustrating delays, they were assisted by technicians from the Salvadoran Institute of Forensic Medicine and from the Special Investigative Unit. The remains were then taken to a laboratory outside San Salvador, where they were examined by an American forensic team led by Clyde Snow (himself a well-known expert who had much to do with the creation of the Argentine team). The reader will find the full texts of both the archeological and the forensic reports in the Documents section at the back of this book. For more about the anthropologists, see Argentine Forensic Anthropology Team Annual Report 1992 (EAAF, Buenos Aires, 1992), especially pages 11–18.

CHAPTER 2

1 The 'ten-month-old peace accord" refers to the so-called Chapultepec Agreements—named for the castle in Mexico City where they were signed on January 16, 1992—between the Salvadoran Government and the Farabundo Martí Liberation Front (or FMLN), which were the culminating step in a three-year negotiation that put an end to the Salvadoran civil war. The

accords provided for the creation of both a Truth Commission, which consisted of three respected non-Salvadoran statesmen who were assigned the task of "investigating serious acts of violence that have occurred since 1980 and whose impact on society urgently demands that the public should know the truth," and a so-called Ad Hoc Commission, which consisted of three Salvadoran politicians who were asked to examine the human rights records of officers of the Salvadoran Army—in effect, "to put in place . . . a purge of the officer corps." At the time the experts were digging at El Mozote, the Ad Hoc Commission was preparing to deliver its report to the United Nations; anticipation of this report engendered enormous tension within the Salvadoran Army and the Cristiani Government. For a useful, concise account of the process leading to Chapultepec, see Terry Lynn Karl, "El Salvador's Negotiated Revolution," *Foreign Affairs,* Spring 1992, pages 147–64.

2 Specifically, President Cristiani said that his government "could not find any record" of who was responsible. "It must be remembered," he said, "that at this moment there was a 'de facto' government . . . and a restructuring of the Armed Forces. We answered what we could, but we cannot make up information." See *Diario Latino,* October 21, 1992. The *Diario de Hoy* "reconstruction" appeared on October 22, 1992.

3 A short but useful account of the growth of the evangelical movement in El Salvador can be found in Marlise Simons, "Protestant Challenge in El Salvador," collected in Gettleman et al. (eds.), *El Salvador: Central America in the New Cold War* (Grove Press: New York, 1986).

CHAPTER 3

1 Santiago, the Radio Venceremos director, recalled this version of the meeting to me during an interview in San Salvador, Santiago—a Venezuelan journalist and diplomat's son whose real name is Carlos Henríquez Consalvi—includes a similar account in his memoirs, *La Terquedad Del Izote* (Editorial Diana: Mexico, 1992), pages 91–92. The memoirs are subtitled "the story of Radio Venceremos" and provide a useful history of the war from the guerrilla side.

2 A very amusing account of this program can be found in José Ignacio López Vigil's oral history, *Las mil y una historias de Radio Venceremos* (UCA Editores: San Salvador 1992), pages 224–31. Though this book covers much the same ground as Santiago's memoirs, it takes a lighter tone and succeeds in giving a vivid picture of daily life among the guerrillas.

3 The peculiarities of the Salvadoran Army are taken up in, among many others, Joel Millman, "A Force Unto Themselves: The Salvadoran Military," *The New York Times Magazine,* December 10, 1989; in Christopher Dickey, "I Obey but I Do Not Comply," in Leonel Gomez, "The Army (March 1981)" and in Richard Millet, "Praetorians of Pariots," all of which can be found in Leiken and Rubin (eds.), *The Central American Crisis Reader* (Summit: New York, 1987). Also useful is Shirley Christian, "El Salvador's Divided Military," which is included in Gettleman et al. (eds.), *El Salvador: Central America in the New Cold War,* cited above. For an oral history with many contributions from both American and Salvadoran officers, as well as ambassadors and politicans, see Manwaring and Prisk (eds.), *El Salvador At War: An Oral History of Conflict from the 1979*

Insurrection to the Present (National Defense University Press: Washington, 1988). Finally, a unique first-hand account of the growth and destruction of the "military youth" movement in the Salvadoran Army, and of the military operations of the guerrillas, can be found in Captain Francisco Emilio Mena Sandoval, *Del Ejército Nacional Al Ejército Guerrillero* (Ediciones Arcoiris).

4 The literature about the political situation in El Salvador at this time is extensive, but the reader can make a useful start with the two collections already cited, in particular the chapter "Origins of the Conflict in El Salvador" in Leiken and Rubin's *The Central American Crisis Reader;* "Social Forces and Ideologies in the Making of Contemporary El Salvador" in Gettleman et al., *El Salvador: Central America in the New Cold War.* A very good general history is James Dunkerley's *Power in the Isthmus: A Political History of Modern Central America* (Verso: London and New York, 1988), supplemented by the same author's "El Salvador, 1930–1989" in his *Political Suicide in Latin America* (Verso: London and New York, 1992). Walter LaFeber's *Inevitable Revolutions: The United States in Central America* (Norton: New York, 1993) is also useful, as is the more journalistic account in Clifford Krauss's *Inside Central America: Its People, Politics, and History* (Touchstone: New York, 1991). Finally, James Chace's *Endless War: How We Got Involved in Central America— And What Can Be Done* (Vintage: New York, 1984) is an excellent account of United States policy toward El Salvador, Nicaragua, and the other Central American countries.

5 The Salvadoran right and the "dirty war" are well covered in the collections already cited, notably in Craig Pyes, "Roots of the Salvadoran Right: Origins of the Death Squads," and, by the same author, "ARENA's Bid for Power," both of them included

in *El Salvador: Central America in the New Cold War;* and, in the same collection, Major Roberto D'Aubuisson's "ARENA: The Salvadoran Right's Conception of Nationalism and Justice"; the staff of Tutela Legal's "Recording the Terror"; and the Maximiliano Hernández Martínez's "Communiqué from a 'Death Squad.' " Also, Ambassador Robert White, "Murder of the FDR Leaders (November 1980)" in *The Central American Crisis Reader.* Among more general histories, Raymond Bonner's *Weakness and Deceit: U.S. Policy and El Salvador* (Times Books: New York, 1984) is recommended. Joan Didion's *Salvador* (Washington Square Press: New York, 1983; reprinted, Vintage: New York, 1994) provides a vivid picture of the feeling in the country in 1982. The "dirty war" has been extensively documented in human rights reports, notable among them, Americas Watch and the American Civil Liberties Union, *Report on Human Rights in El Salvador* (Vintage: New York, 1982) and its various supplements that appeared under the title *The Civilian Toll;* and America's Watch, *El Salvador's Decade of Terror: Human Rights Since the Assassination of Archbishop Romero* (Yale University Press: New Haven, 1991).

6 The classic account of the events of 1931–32 is Thomas P. Anderson's *Matanza: The 1932 "slaughter" that traumatized a nation, shaping U.S.–Salvadoran policy to this day* (Curbstone: Willimantic, CT, 1992; first published 1971). Dunkerley's *Power in the Isthmus,* cited above, gives a brief but very good account of these events. Hector Perez-Brignoli's *A Brief History of Central America* (University of California Press: Berkeley, 1989) places the episode in the broader history.

7 For an introduction to the rebels, see "The Salvadoran Rebels" in *El Salvador: Central America in the New Cold War;* the various

FMLN documents collected in *The Central American Crisis Reader,* especially those on the Dalton Affair. A brilliant and quite savage account of the Salvadoran guerrillas and the internal struggles that led up to the execution of Dalton is contained in Gabriel Zaid's "Enemy Colleagues," which is excerpted in Leiken and Rubin's collection; the interested reader should refer to the full version in *Dissent,* Winter 1982. Another view of the guerrillas can be found in Manwaring and Prisk's *El Salvador at War: An Oral History,* cited above, particularly pages 123–67.

8 Though the "Report of the El Salvador Military Strategy Assistance Team," known as the "Woerner Report," was extremely influential in the formulation of U.S. policy in El Salvador, it was not available to the public until early 1993, when it was finally released to the National Security Archives, a private research institution in Washington, D.C. The report, as well as the Devine cable and other cables cited here that are not contained in the Documents section at the back of the book—can all be consulted at the National Security Archives, 1755 Massachusetts Avenue, NW, Washington, D.C. 20036.

CHAPTER 4

1 The relationship between the peasants and the National Guard in the countryside is forcefully and evocatively described in Manlio Argueta's short novel, *One Day of Life* (Vintage: New York, 1983).

2 For the background of the Reagan policy, see Jeane Kirkpatrick, "The Hobbes Problem" and "U.S. Security and Latin America"; and the Committee of Santa Fe, "A New Inter-American Policy," all contained in *The Central American Crisis Reader.*

3 Colonel Monterrosa gave a fuller version of this philosophy to Christopher Dickey: "It is natural that in these subversive redoubts the armed men are not there alone. That is to say, they need their 'masses'—people, women, old people, or children, including the children who are messengers, or the wives, and they are all mixed up with the subversives themselves, with the armed ones. So in the clashes . . . it's natural that there were a series of people killed, some without weapons, including some women, and I understand some children." See Christopher Dickey, "U.S. Tactics Fail to Prevent Salvadoran Civilian Deaths," *Washington Post,* June 10, 1982.

4 Philippe Bourgeois testified to the House Subcommittee on Inter-American Affairs on February 23, 1982; he also described his experiences in an article that appeared in the *Washington Post* on February 14, 1982.

5 The text of this CIA cable, like most of those cited in this account, is published in full in the Documents section at the back of the book.

6 Mena Sandoval's account can be found in his *Del Ejército Nacional Al Ejército Guerrillero,* cited above, pages 283–88.

7 Investigators from Tutela Legal, the human rights organization of the Archbishopric of San Salvador, traveled to northern Morazán in the spring of 1990 to begin building a case against the authorities for the massacre at El Mozote. Tutela Legal's lengthy report, *"Investigación de la Masacre de El Mozote y Lugares Aledaños,"* was made public on November 9, 1991. Along with a moment-by-moment account of the operation in El Mozote and the surrounding hamlets, the eighty-one-page document included

a list of the names of 794 of those who had died. (A list based largely on that of Tutela Legal is included here as this book's final chapter.) On March 4, 1992, Americas Watch published "The Massacre at El Mozote: The Need to Remember" (*News From Americas Watch*, Volume No. IV, Issue No. 2), which drew on the Tutela Legal report.

8 The story of the ambush at the black road and of the march to Jucuarán is recounted in detail both in Santiago's memoirs, *La Terquedad del Izote*, and in the oral history, *Las mil y una historias de Radio Venceremos*; both books are cited above.

CHAPTER 6

1 As noted in the text, Ambassador Hinton declined to speak to me. The remarks cited are contained in the transcript of an interview he gave to Manwaring and Prisk for their *El Salvador At War: An Oral History*, cited above. The full transcript of all of the interviews conducted for that book is on file at the National Security Archives in Washington.

For a thorough and well-reasoned account of the certification process—how it was developed and how it worked—see Cynthia J. Arnson, *Crossroads: Congress, the President, and Central America, 1976–1993* (Pennsylvania State University Press: University Park, 1993), pages 69–74 and 84–94.

CHAPTER 7

1 Readers will find the full text of this editorial, headed "The Media's War," as well as several more recent *Journal* pieces, in the Documents section.

2 It should be noted that in 1987, Bonner began writing for the *New Yorker* (where much of this book first appeared)—as did, two years later, Alma Guillermoprieto. Bonner left the magazine in 1992; he is now writing special assignments for the *Times*.

For one account of the Bonner affair, see Michael Massing, "About-face on El Salvador," *Columbia Journalism Review,* November/December 1983. The *Wall Street Journal* took up the matter again in its editorial, "On Credulity," March 19, 1993 (set out in the Documents section, below)—to which A.M. Rosenthal responded in "Let's Set the Record Straight," a lengthy letter to the *Journal* published on April 22, 1993. Massing took up the issue once again with his "annotation" of Rosenthal's letter, "Bringing the Truth Commission Back Home: Raymond Bonner and the News From El Salvador That Didn't Fit," *Harper's Magazine,* July 1993.

CHAPTER 8

1 This point was emphasized by the Department's own investigators. See "Report of the Secretary of State's Panel on El Salvador," July 1993, pages 59–60. Excerpts from this report appear in the Document section.

2 For a fascinating account of this period, see Jon Lee Anderson and Scott Anderson, *Inside the League* (Dodd-Mead: New York, 1986).

CHAPTER 9

1 For a good short account of the investigation of the Jesuits, see Philip Bennett, "Letter from El Salvador," *Vanity Fair,* November 1990.

A C K N O W L E D G M E N T S

This book began its life as an article, "A Reporter At Large: The Truth of El Mozote," which occupied the bulk of the December 6, 1993, issue of the *New Yorker*. Among the people at the *New Yorker* to whom I owe thanks are, first, its editor, Tina Brown, who decided that the magazine must have a piece on El Mozote; that I was the one to write it; and that virtually an entire issue would be given over to it. I am grateful as well to Eleanor Gould Packard and to Elizabeth Pearson-Griffiths, for their devoted and unflagging work editing the text; to Peter Canby, for his fact-checking; to William Vourvoulias, for his fact-checking and his help in translating; and to David Kirkpatrick, for his fact-checking and his invaluable efforts in culling the newly declassified documents. Thanks also to Joseph Cooper, Christine Curry-Burris, Hendrik Hertzberg, Caroline Mailhot, Gerald Marzorati, Chip McGrath, Françoise Mouly, Pamela McCarthy, Maurie Perl, Crary Pullen, Josselyn Simpson, and Lawrence Weschler. And, not for the first time, to John Bennet, who possesses in abundance those qualities vital to a true editor—determination, judgment, and integrity—I owe a special debt of gratitude.

Thanks also to my colleague Thomas Long, who provided tireless assistance during my reporting in El Salvador; to Mercedes Doretti and Claudia Bernardi of the Argentine Forensic Anthropology Team; to María Julia Hernández and David Morales of Tutela Legal; to Stephen Ferry; to James Chace of *The World Policy Journal;* to Tim Golden and James LeMoyne of *The New York Times;* to Susan Kandel and Linda Garrett of El Rescate; to Peter Kornbluh and Kate Doyle of the National Security Archives; to Cynthia Arnson of Americas Watch; to Aryeh Neier, formerly of Human Rights Watch; to Joel Millman of *Fortune* magazine; to Michael Pollan of *Harper's Magazine;* and to Mark A. Uhlig, formerly of *The New York Times.*

To Raymond Bonner, Susan Meiselas, and, especially, my colleague and friend, Alma Guillermoprieto, I offer my warmest thanks and gratitude: I have tried my best to finish the story that they began telling twelve years ago.

I thank my parents for their unfailing support and enthusiasm. Most of all, I want to thank Catherine Lee, who during the writing of this book, as always, gave generously of her faith, her encouragement, and her love.

My sister, Sheila Beth Danner, believed passionately that the truth must be told, no matter how painful. This book is dedicated to her memory.

January 1994

In the debate over what happened at El Mozote, secrecy was never the key obstacle to determining the truth: Some of the most important evidence was available to the public almost from the start—especially the eyewitness testimony presented in Alma Guillermoprieto's article in the *Washington Post* and in Raymond Bonner's in *The New York Times,* and the images in Susan Meiselas' photographs. Most of the documents detailing the United States Government's investigation, however, were kept secret, and largely remained so for almost twelve years.

In November 1993, eight months after the United Nations Truth Commission issued its report on human rights abuses during the Salvadoran civil war, the Clinton Administration (following a number of requests from Congress) released to the public some twelve thousand documents having to do with United States policy in El Salvador. A substantial number of these touched on El Mozote, including a series of cables in which officials at the Embassy in San Salvador reported to their superiors in Washington on their efforts to gather information about what had happened in northern Morazán during December 1981.

I have chosen what seemed to me the most important of these

cables and have arranged them, together with newspaper stories and some Congressional testimony, in chronological order. To these I have added excerpts drawn from the Truth Commission report, *From Madness to Hope,* released in March 1993, and from the *Report of the Secretary of State's Panel on El Salvador,* released in July 1993.

1. THE CIA REPORTS ON OPERATION RESCUE

As Salvadoran soldiers mopped up in Morazán, a CIA officer in San Salvador was cabling a progress report on Operation Rescue to his superiors in Langley, Virginia. The cable is dated December 17, 1981—near the end of the operation—but internal evidence, including the "subject" title and a number of other comments (for example: "AS OF 9 DECEMBER, THE HEAVIEST FIGHTING HAD OCCURRED AT EL MOZOTE"), suggests that the intelligence was gathered no later than December 10, the day the Atlacatl occupied El Mozote. This delay between compiling information and reporting it to Langley is intriguing; but it is impossible to know whether the gap is significant—for example, had the reporting officer gathered his material during a visit to operational headquarters at Osicala and not returned immediately to the capital?—or whether it simply reflects some sort of routine delay.

The cable was released in November 1993, with a number of deletions, including a block of ten to fifteen lines at the end.

TOR: 170256Z DEC 81

COUNTRY: EL SALVADOR/HONDURAS
SUBJECT: 1. STATUS OF THE ARMED FORCES MAJOR SWEEP OPERATION
             IN MORAZAN DEPARTMENT AFTER FOUR DAYS
             2. EVIDENCE THAT INSURGENT RADIO STATION "RADIO VEN-

CEREMOS" WAS LOCATED 18 KILOMETERS SOUTHEAST OF THE CITY OF PERQUIN IN MORAZAN DEPARTMENT (DOI: 6–9 DECEMBER 1981)

1. ON 6 DECEMBER 1981, THE SALVADORAN ARMED FORCES INITIATED A TWO-PHASE, 4,000-MAN SWEEP OPERATION IN NORTHERN MORAZAN DEPARTMENT THAT IS EXPECTED TO BE COMPLETED BY 24 DECEMBER 1981. ([DELETION] COMMENT: APPROXIMATELY ONE-THIRD OF THE SALVADORAN ARMY IS INVOLVED IN THIS OPERATION, LEAVING SECURITY FORCES IN THE REMAINDER OF THE COUNTRY VERY THIN.) THE PRIMARY TARGET OF THE FIRST PHASE IS THE AREA SOUTHEAST OF PERQUIN (13-57-30N 88-09-40W) AND NORTH OF THE TOROLA RIVER. THE PRIMARY TARGET AREA OF THE SECOND PHASE OF THE OPERATION WILL BE THE AREA IMMEDIATELY WEST AND SOUTH OF CORINTO (13-48-30N 87-58-20W). OF PARTICULAR INTEREST IN THIS PHASE WILL BE THE VILLAGE OF VARILLA NEGRA (13-46-15N 88-00-50W) WHERE THE INSURGENTS ARE THOUGHT TO HAVE BEEN REGROUPING SINCE THE START OF THE OPERATION. THE SECOND PHASE OF THE OPERATION WILL COMMENCE IMMEDIATELY UPON COMPLETION OF THE FIRST PHASE WHICH HAD NOT BEEN COMPLETED AS OF 9 DECEMBER 1981.

2. ON 7 AND 8 DECEMBER 1981, A TOTAL OF 1,400 TROOPS WERE AIRLIFTED BY HELICOPTERS INTO SAN FERNANDO (13-57-40N 88-11-50W), PERQUIN, AND JOATECA (13-53-40N 88-02-40W). THESE TROOPS WERE TO MOVE SLOWLY TO THE SOUTH, ACTING AS A BLOCKING FORCE FOR THE REMAINDER OF THE TROOPS MOVING NORTH FROM ALONG THE RIO TOROLA BETWEEN COORDINATES 15-50-20N/88-08-40W AND 15-46-20N/88-04-00W. HONDURAS HAS POSITIONED TWO BATTALIONS ALONG THE BORDER NORTH OF PERQUIN IN AN ATTEMPT TO BLOCK THE PRIMARY GUERRILLA ESCAPE ROUTE TO THE NORTH. ([DELETION] COMMENT: PROVIDING A BLOCKING FORCE AGAINST GUERRILLAS ATTEMPTING TO ESCAPE INTO HONDURAS WOULD BE CONSISTENT WITH PREVIOUS HONDURAN MILITARY ACTIVITIES IN SUPPORT OF THE SALVADORAN ARMY.)

3. BETWEEN 7 AND 9 DECEMBER, EVIDENCE WAS FOUND OF AN INSURGENT "RADIO VENCEREMOS" BROADCASTING STATION IN A HOUSE AT COORDINATES 88-04-30N 88-04-30W [*sic*], 18 KILOMETERS SOUTHEAST OF PERQUIN AND 14 KILOMETERS NORTH/NORTHEAST OF SAN

Francisco Gotera (13-41-40N 88-06-20W). A small box, roughly
0.5 meters square, full of assorted papers, including some that
dealt with Radio Venceremos, was found in the house. Also, at
least one coil of cable was found near the house. ([deletion]
comment: the cable was probably used as guy wire for the
broadcasting station antenna.) ([deletion] comment: radio
Venceremos made its last broadcast on 7 December 1981, one
day after the start of the operation.)

4. As of 9 December 1981, the heaviest fighting had occurred at
El Mozote (13-53-5N 88-06-50W) where 30 to 35 insurgents and
four Salvadoran soldiers were killed. ([deletion] comment:
the Salvadoran soldiers were in high spirits during the
operation because of the large number of men involved in the
sweep. They believe that large numbers will decrease their
casualty rate.)

5. While the primary target of the first phase of the operation
is southeast of Perquin, the soldiers will move north of
Perquin toward the Honduran border. These troops will
launch from Perquin (80 soldiers), San Fernando (80 troops),
and Torola (13-54-50N 88-14-00W) with 30 to 40 troops. The
purpose of the movement is to force the insurgents in this area
into the Honduran blocking force along the border.
[deletions]

2. First Inquiries: Ambassador Hinton Replies

Even as, in Morazan, Operation Rescue was winding down,
human rights organizations in San Salvador began to receive word
of atrocities. An official at one of those groups telephoned the
Reverend William L. Wipfler, director of the human rights office
of the National Council of Churches, in New York, and Wipfler
immediately sent a telegram to Ambassador Deane Hinton in
San Salvador, asking "confirmation or otherwise" of the reports.
(Though the telegram, sent under the name of Eugene Stockwell,

Wipfler's boss, bears no date, the archivist at the National Security Archives in Washington, to whom the cable was originally released, has dated it December 15, 1981—four days after the killing at El Mozote. The Reverend Wipfler is certain only that it was sent "before Christmas.")

In the following cable, sent on January 8, 1982, Ambassador Hinton reports to the State Department on the exchange with the National Council of Churches, including the full texts of both Wipfler's original telegram and his own reply.

R 082122Z JAN 82
FM AMEMBASSY SAN SALVADOR
TO SECSTATE WASHDC 7346

SUBJECT: ALLEGED MORAZAN MASSACRE

I. I HAVE RECEIVED FOLLOWING TELEGRAM FROM EUGENE STOCKWELL
NCC 475 RIVERSIDE DRIVE, NEW YORK, NY 10115:

BEGIN TEXT:

RELIABLE REPORTS RECEIVED HERE INDICATE THAT BETWEEN DECEMBER
10 AND 13 A GOVERNMENT JOINT MILITARY AND SECURITY FORCES
OPERATION TOOK PLACE IN MORAZAN DEPARTMENT WHICH RESULTED IN
OVER 900 CIVILIAN DEATHS PRINCIPALLY IN MOSOTES, CERRO PANDO LA
JOYA MEANGUERA, POSA HONDA, TORRILES AND CAPILLA STOP WOULD
APPRECIATE CONFIRMATION OR OTHERWISE OF THESE REPORTS THANK
YOU.
END TEXT

2. I HAVE REPLIED AS FOLLOWS:

BEGIN TEXT:

IT WAS GOOD OF YOU TO SEEK MY "CONFIRMATION OR OTHERWISE" OF
REPORTS OF OVER 900 CIVILIAN DEATHS IN MORAZAN DEPARTMENT AS A
RESULT OF RECENT GOES MILITARY OPERATIONS. I CERTAINLY CANNOT
CONFIRM SUCH REPORTS NOR DO I HAVE ANY REASON TO BELIEVE THEY

ARE TRUE. NONE OF TESTED SOURCES AVAILABLE TO THIS EMBASSY HAS GIVEN US EVEN HINT OF MASSIVE CIVILIAN CASUALTIES WHICH HAS NOT ALWAYS BEEN THE CASE IN THE PAST. MOREOVER, PERSONALLY, I WOULD THINK THAT GIVEN SAVAGE MEASURES OF CIVIL WAR HERE, THAT HAD ANYTHING LIKE THIS NUMBER OF CIVILIAN CASUALTIES BEEN INFLICTED BY GOVERNMENT MILITARY, THE GUERRILLAS WOULD NOT HAVE TAKEN PRISONERS AS THEY DID DURING THEIR COUNTER-ATTACK IN EL MOSOTES SECTOR.

YOU SAY YOU HAVE RELIABLE REPORTS THAT OVER 900 CIVILIAN DEATHS TOOK PLACE. I DO NOT KNOW WHAT YOUR SOURCES ARE BUT THE ONLY SOURCES THAT I HAVE SEEN ALLEGING SOMETHING LIKE THIS ARE CLANDESTINE RADIO VENCEREMOS REPORTS ATTRIBUTED PRIMARILY TO ONE JOSE LEONCIO PICHINTE IDENTIFIED AS A MEMBER OF THE POLITICAL/MILITARY COMMAND OF THE FRANCISCO SANCHEZ EASTERN FRONT. ON JANUARY 2 HE SAID INTER ALIA:

BEGIN QUOTE: THE DIRECT INTERVENTION OF YANKEE IMPERIALISM THROUGH U.S. ARMY OFFICERS IS BECOMING LARGER AND MORE WIDELY KNOWN EVERY DAY. RECENTLY, FRED IKLE, UNDERSECRETARY OF DE-FENSE FOR U.S. GOVERNMENTAL POLICY, (TITLE AS HEARD) ADMITTED IN A REPORT TO THE U.S. CONGRESSIONAL COMMITTEE FOR HEMISPHERIC AFFAIRS THAT EIGHT HIGH-LEVEL U.S. ARMY ADVISORS HAD BEEN SENT TO EL SALVADOR TO DRAFT, PREPARE AND SUPERVISE A NEW NATIONWIDE MILITARY PLAN WHICH, AMONG OTHER THINGS, INCLUDES THE AIRBORNE TRANSPORTATION OF TROOPS AND A STRING OF MILITARY CAMPAIGNS TO BE CARRIED OUT IN VARIOUS FRONTS WITHIN SHORT INTERVALS. THE PURPOSE OF THESE CAMPAIGNS IS TO SHATTER OUR LOGISTICAL BASES, DESTROY OUR RADIO VENCEREMOS AND TO CARRY OUT LIGHTNING ATTACKS AGAINST THE DEFENSELESS AND UNARMED POPULATION. THIS INCLUDES NOT ONLY THE POPULATION IN AREAS CONTROLLED BY US BUT THE INHABITANTS OF NEARBY AREAS AS HAPPENED DURING THE LAST ENEMY CAMPAIGN IN MORAZAN DEPARTMENT, WHERE APPROXIMATELY 1,000 PEASANTS, MOSTLY CHILDREN AND WOMEN, WERE WANTONLY MURDERED.

THIS GENOCIDAL MILITARY METHOD IS NO HAPPENSTANCE. VIETNAM REPRESENTS ITS HISTORICAL PRECEDENT. THE U.S. CONGRESS AND PEOPLE, AS THE WORLD PUBLIC OPINION PROBABLY REMEMBER THE MASSACRE OF MY LAI, WHICH HAD A PROFOUND IMPACT ON THE U.S. PEOPLE, THE U.S. ARMY ITSELF, AND ALL COUNTRIES OF THE WORLD.

INSOFAR AS MURDER, INHUMANITY AND GENOCIDE ARE CONCERNED,

THERE IS NO DIFFERENCE BETWEEN MY LAI AND EL MOZOTE, CERRO
PANDO, LA JOYA, (LA JITA), (POZA HONDA) AND (LA CAPILIA). THOSE
RESPONSIBLE FOR THESE MASS MURDERS ARE THE SAME. IKLE ADMITTED
THAT THIS MILITARY PLAN, DRAFTED BY THE U.S. ADVISORS AND THE
SALVADORAN ARMY'S HIGH COMMAND TO MURDER THE CIVILIAN
POPULATION OF MORAZAN, WAS DIRECTLY SUPERVISED BY THE U.S.
DEFENSE SECRETARY. IN OTHER WORDS, IMPERIALISM ADMITS HAVING
CARRIED OUT THE DESIGN AND SUPERVISION OF GENOCIDE IN EL SALVA-
DOR. IT ADMITS HAVING CARRIED OUT THE DESIGN AND SUPERVISION
OF THE MASSACRE OF 472 PEOPLE IN EL MOZOTE, 143 IN LA JOYA
OF MEANGUERA, 65 IN (LOS TORILES), 20 IN (LA CAPILLA) HAMLET, 183
IN CERRO PANDO, 5 IN ARAMBALA, 16 IN (LA JITA), 8 IN (SOLEDAD
CANTON), 5 IN YANCOLO, 5 IN (FLOR DEL MUERTO), 5 IN RINCON DE
JOCOAITIQUE AND OVER 100 INHABITANTS OF (POZA HONDA).

THESE CRIMES WERE COMMITTED BETWEEN 7 AND 17 DECEMBER,
1981. IN OTHER WORDS, IMPERIALISM SEEMS TO BE PREPARED TO FACE
THE REPUDIATION OF U.S. YOUTHS THEMSELVES, WHO REPUDIATED AND
CONDEMNED THE MASSACRE OF MY LAI. IT SEEMS TO BE READY TO FACE
THE JUDGMENT AND DISAPPROVAL OF THE U. S. CONGRESS ITSELF AND
THE JUDGMENT AND CONDEMNATION OF THE PEOPLES AND
GOVERNMENTS WHO LOVE PEACE AND RESPECT MAN'S FUNDAMENTAL
RIGHTS IN THE WORLD.

THE IMPERIALISTS SEEM TO BE PREPARED TO FACE THE REPUDIATION
OF INTERNATIONAL BODIES LIKE THE UNITED NATIONS AND THE OAS,
WHICH MUST NOT DELAY IN ISSUING A VERY STRONG PROTEST OVER THE
PREMEDITATED CRIMES AGAINST THE CIVILIAN POPULATION.

IN ADDITION, WE WANT TO DENOUNCE PUBLICLY BEFORE THE
SALVADORAN PEOPLE, THE PEOPLES AND GOVERNMENTS IN THE
AMERICAN CONTINENT AND THE WORLD, THE CONSCIENCE OF PEACE-
LOVING MEN, THE FUTURE PLANS OF THE MILITARY-CHRISTIAN
DEMOCRATIC JUNTA AND THE GENOCIDAL GENERAL ARMY COMMAND, IN
THE PREPARATION OF WHICH IMPERIALISM HAS PUBLICLY ADMITTED
THAT IT HAD A DIRECT HAND.

OUR MILITARY INTELLIGENCE SERVICE HAS INFORMED US OF PLANS TO
CARRY OUT LARGE-SCALE MASSACRES AGAINST THE CIVILIAN
POPULATION OF CHIRILAGUA, JUCUARAN AND TOWNSITES NEAR OUR
POSITIONS IN GUAZAPA. THESE GENOCIDAL ACTIONS ARE PREDICATED ON
THE PREMISE THAT A CLIMATE OF STABILITY IS REQUIRED TO HOLD THE
ELECTIONS WHICH, IN THEIR VIEW, MUST NOT BE HELD IN THE SMALL

TOWNS BUT ONLY IN THE LARGER CITIES. IN VIEW OF THE ACTIONS OF
THE REVOLUTIONARY FORCES IN USULUTAN, SAN MIGUEL, LA UNION,
GUAZAPA AND SAN SALVADOR, THE MILITARY-CHRISTIAN DEMOCRATIC
WHICH PROPOSE IT WILL MASSACRE THE CIVILIAN POPULATION, AS WAS
DONE IN MORAZAN DEPARTMENT. (PASSAGE OMITTED) END QUOTE

3. FRANKLY, I DO NOT CONSIDER RADIO VENCEREMOS TO BE A RELIABLE
SOURCE, I FIND IT INTERESTING THAT A MILITARY COMMUNIQUE FROM
THE FMLN, ISSUED IN THE NAMES OF COMMANDERS JORGE MELANDEZ
AND JUAN RAMON MEDRANO, TWO DAYS BEFORE THE ABOVE ACCOUNT
(DEC 31) WAS CARRIED AND MADE NO MENTION OF ANY MASSACRE OF
CIVILIAN IN ITS TREATMENT OF RECENT OPERATIONS IN MORAZAN. THIS
WAS FOLLOWED ON JAN I BY ANOTHER STATEMENT SIGNED BOTH BY
JOSE LEONCIO PICHINTE AND COMMANDER JUAN RAMON MEDRANO
WHICH INDEED DID MAKE THE CHARGE. ON JAN 2 CAME THE
PREVIOUSLY QUOTED LONG STATEMENT FROM CAMPANERO JOSE LEONCIO
PICHINTE WHO IS IDENTIFIED BY THE FMLN AS "POLITICALLY IN CHARGE
OF RADIO VENCEREMOS". IN PLAIN ENGLISH, HE IS THE PROPAGANDA
CHIEF.

4. ON JANUARY 5, RADIO VENCEREMOS REPORTED THAT ROGELIO
PONCEL (A BELGIAN PRIEST NOW WITH THE FMLN WHO EARLIER WAS
POLITICALLY ACTIVE WITH EXTREMIST FORCES IN EL SALVADOR UNTIL
WITHDRAWN BY HIS ORDER WITH INSTRUCTIONS TO RETURN TO EUROPE
WHICH HE IGNORED CHOOSING TO JOIN THE GUERRILLAS) WAS
SPONSORING A MASS FOR THE "1,000 PEASANTS OF THE MORAZAN
DEPARTMENT WHO HAD BEEN MURDERED BY THE SALVADORAN JUNTA."

5. FINALLY, LET ME EXPRESS MY APPRECIATION FOR YOUR LETTER OF
DECEMBER 10, 1981 REPLYING TO MY LETTER OF NOVEMBER 24. A
SMALL POINT, HOWEVER, PLEASE ADDRESS ME IN THE FUTURE VIA APO
MIAMI, FLORIDA 34023 SINCE YOUR LETTER TOOK ALMOST A MONTH TO
REACH ME THROUGH INTERN MAIL.

6. WITH BEST WISHES FOR THE NEW YEAR.

SINCERELY,
DEANE R. HINTON. END LETTER.

END TEXT.
HINTON

3. THE FRONT PAGE STORIES

In late December, FMLN officials contacted Raymond Bonner of *The New York Times* and informed him that his oft-postponed trip to report from behind guerrilla lines had been approved. On January 6, after an arduous three-day hike from Honduras, Bonner and the photojournalist Susan Meiselas reached El Mozote; Alma Guillermoprieto of the *Washington Post* arrived a few days later. Both articles appeared on the front pages of their respective newspapers on January 27, 1982.

Salvadoran Peasants Describe Mass Killing; Woman Tells of Children's Death
By Alma Guillermoprieto,
Special to *The Washington Post*

MOZOTE, EL SALVADOR, JAN. 14 (DELAYED) Several hundred civilians, including women and children, were taken from their homes in and around this village and killed by Salvadoran Army troops during a December offensive against leftist guerrillas, according to three survivors who say they witnessed the alleged massacres.

Reporters taken to tour the region and speak to the survivors by guerrilla soldiers, who control large areas of Morazan Province, were shown the rubble of scores of adobe houses they and the survivors said were destroyed by the troops in the now deserted village community. Dozens of decomposing bodies still were seen beneath the rubble and lying in nearby fields, despite the month that has passed since the incident.

In Washington, Salvadoran Ambassador Ernesto Rivas Gallont said, "I reject emphatically that the Army of El Salvador" was engaged in "killing women and children. It is not within the armed institution's philosophy to act like that." He acknowledged that the "armed forces have been active in that part of the country," particularly during a December offensive against the guerrillas, but said that their actions had "definitely not been against the civilian populations."

The survivors, including a woman who said her husband and four of her six children were killed, maintained that no battle was under way during the second week in December when the alleged massacre took place.

The woman, Rufina Amaya, a 38-year-old housewife, said that the troops entered the village one morning and, after herding the residents into two separate groups—men divided from women and children—took them off and shot them. Amaya said she had hidden during the shooting and later escaped to the guerrilla-protected camp where she was interviewed.

At the same time, troops allegedly spread into the nearby countryside and smaller surrounding villages. José Marcial Martínez, 14, from nearby La Joya, said he had hidden in a cornfield and watched his parents, brothers and sisters killed. José Santos, 15, said he had witnessed the similar slaying of his parents, three younger brothers and two grandparents.

A dozen other persons from the area interviewed by this correspondent said they had fled their homes during the December offensive and claimed to have lost family members in the military assault.

To reach the heart of Morazán Province from the north, it is necessary to walk for several days, passing through villages and guerrilla camps. After several months of requests, the Farabundo Marti Liberation Front agreed to take this correspondent into the province in early January, two weeks after the guerrillas' clandestine radio station first reported the alleged massacres in Morazán. It was clear that the guerrillas' purpose was not only to demonstrate to journalists their control of the region, but also to provide what they said was evidence of the alleged massacre in December.

As we neared Mozote, the group of young guerrillas who were my guides and I passed on foot through the village of Arambala, whose pretty, whitewashed adobe houses appeared to have been looted of all contents. The village was deserted.

About 45 minutes farther down the road, we entered another small town. Here the houses also were gutted and looted, but the overwhelming initial impression was of the sickly sweet smell of decomposing bodies. This was Mozote.

The muchachos, boys, as the guerrillas are called, walked us toward the central square where the ruins of what had been a small, whitewashed church stood. The smaller sacristy beside it also appeared to have had its adobe walls pushed in. Inside, the stench was overpowering, and countless bits of bones—skulls, rib cages, femurs, a spinal column—poked out of the rubble.

The 15 houses on the main village street had been smashed. In two of them, as in the sacristy, the rubble was filled with bones. All of the buildings, including the three in which body parts could be seen, appeared to have been set on fire, and the remains of the people were as charred as the remaining beams.

Several small rural roads led away from the village to other groups of houses that collectively are known as the Mozote community. We walked down one, an idyllic path where every house had a grove of fruit trees, a small chicken pen and at least one beehive. Only the fruit trees were intact; the hives were overturned, the bees buzzing everywhere. The houses were destroyed and looted.

The road was littered with animal corpses, cows and horses. In the cornfields behind the houses were more bodies, these unburned by fire but baked by the sun. In one grouping in a clearing in a field were 10 bodies: two elderly people, two children, one infant—a bullet hole in the head—in the arms of a woman, and the rest adults. Although local peasants later said they had buried some of the bodies in the area, the guerrilla youths acknowledged they had asked that the corpses be left until someone from the outside could be brought to see them.

It was getting dark, and we traveled to a guerrilla military encampment.

The camp was populated by about 20 young guerrillas, all armed and obviously under military discipline. Farther down the road was a civilian camp, like the other a collection of small adobe houses, with about 80 peasants, refugees and guerrilla sympathizers. It was from this camp the next morning that the guerrillas sent for Amaya, who said she was the only survivor she knew of from Mozote.

The guerrillas left me alone to talk to her. She said that it was on the evening of Dec. 11, although she spoke more of days of the week than dates, that troops of the Atlacatl Brigade had come to Mozote. The brigade is an elite, 1,000-man unit of the Salvadoran Army, well known at least by name to most Salvadorans, that has been trained for rapid deployment and antiguerrilla offensives by U.S. military advisers here.

"The Army people had warned Marcos Díaz, a friend of theirs from our village, that an offensive was coming and that there would be no more traffic allowed from San Francisco Gotera [the provincial capital] in December and that we should all stay in Mozote where no one would harm us. So we did. There were about 500 of us in all living in the village."

The soldiers, she said, took those villagers who were in their homes and made them stand outside "in the road for about 1½ hours. They took our money, searched the houses, ate our food, asked us where the guns were and went away. We were happy then. 'The repression is over,' we said. They didn't kill anybody."

Amaya spoke with what appeared to be controlled hysteria. During our conversation, she broke down only when speaking of what she said were the deaths of her children. She said that while her two surviving sons have joined the guerrillas since the December incident, Mozote was not predominantly pro-guerrilla, although it is in the heart of a rebel zone.

She said the guerrillas had gone around the villages in early December warning the population of an impending government offensive and instructing civilians to head for towns and refugee camps outside the area.

"But because we knew the Army people, we felt safe," she said. Her husband, who Amaya said was on very good terms with the local military, "had a military safe conduct."

At around 5:30 the morning after their initial visit, she

said, the troops, headed by the same officer she called Lt. Ortega, returned to Mozote. She said they herded the people into the tiny village square in front of the church, men in one line and women and children in another.

"Marcos Díaz, who had been told by the Army we would be safe, and my husband were in the men's line. I counted about 80 men and 90 women not including the children."

She said the women were herded with their children into a house on the square. From there they saw the men being blindfolded and bound, kicked and thrown against each other, then taken away in groups of four and shot.

"The soldiers had no fury," she said. "They just observed the lieutenant's orders. They were cold. It wasn't a battle.

"Around noon they began with the women. First they picked out the young girls and took them away to the hills. Then they picked out the old women and took them to Israel Márquez's house on the square. We heard the shots there. Then they started with us in groups. When my turn came and I was being led away to Israel Márquez's house I slipped behind a tree and climbed up. I saw the lieutenant then. He was personally machine-gunning people.

"I heard the soldiers talking," she continued tonelessly. "An order arrived from a Lt. Cáceres to Lt. Ortega to go ahead and kill the children too. A soldier said, 'Lieutenant somebody here says he won't kill children.' 'Who's the son-ofabitch who said that?' the lieutenant answered. 'I am going to kill him.' I could hear them shouting from where I was crouching in the tree.

"I could hear the children crying. I heard my own children. When it was all over late at night the lieutenant ordered the soldiers to put a torch to the corpses. There was a great fire in the night."

Amaya said she escaped while the fire was still burning. "I heard the soldiers say 'Let's go. Witches could come out of the fire.' Then they left to go on what they called a 'combing operation' in the houses on the hills. I started walking and walked for three nights. In the daytime I hid because there were troops everywhere."

Amaya, as well as the two boys who said they witnessed

their families being killed, emphasized that the troops appeared to be in regular radio contact with someone.

I later saw Amaya in the civilian camp down the road, where I also met the two boys. Although they were the only ones who claimed to have witnessed the killing, nearly everyone in the camp said they had come there because of "the repression in December" and claimed to have lost members of their families.

[In Washington, Ambassador Rivas, in denying the accuracy of this account Tuesday, said that "serious efforts" were being made to stem armed forces abuses and that this was the "type of story that leads us to believe there is a plan" to discredit the ongoing electoral process in El Salvador, and to discredit the armed forces "or to take credit away from the certification President Reagan must make to Congress."

This week the Reagan administration must by law certify to Congress that the Salvadoran leadership "is achieving substantial control over all elements of its own armed forces, so as to bring to an end the indiscriminate torture and murder of Salvadoran citizens by these forces," or risk a cutoff of aid to El Salvador under congressional restrictions.]

Massacre of Hundreds Reported in Salvador Village
By Raymond Bonner, Special to *The New York Times*

MOZOTE, EL SALVADOR From interviews with people who live in this small mountain village and surrounding hamlets, it is clear that a massacre of major proportions occurred here last month.

In some 20 mud brick huts here, this reporter saw the charred skulls and bones of dozens of bodies buried under burned-out roofs, beams and shattered tiles. There were more along the trail leading through the hills into the village, and at the edge of a nearby cornfield were the remains of 14 young men, women and children.

In separate interviews during a two-week period in the rebel-controlled northern part of Morazán Province, 13 peasants said that all these, their relatives and friends, had been

killed by Government soldiers of the Atlacatl Battalion in a
sweep in December.

733 VICTIMS LISTED

The villagers have compiled a list of the names, ages and villages of 733 peasants, mostly children, women and old people, who they say were murdered by the Government
soldiers. The Human Rights Commission of El Salvador,
which works with the Roman Catholic Church, puts the
number at 926.

A spokesman for the Salvadoran armed forces, Col. Alfonso Cotto, called the reports about "hundreds of civilians"
being killed by Government soldiers "totally false." Those
reports were fabricated by "subversives," he said.

It is not possible for an observer who was not present at
the time of the massacre to determine independently how
many people died or who killed them. In the interviews, the
peasants said uniformed soldiers, some swooping in by helicopters, did the shooting. The rebels in this zone are not
known to wear uniforms or use helicopters.

'A GREAT MASSACRE'

"It was a great massacre," 38-year-old Rufina Amaya told a
visitor who traveled through the area with those who are
fighting against the junta that now rules El Salvador. "They
left nothing."

Somewhere amid the carnage were Mrs. Amaya's husband,
who was blind, her 9-year-old son and three daughters, ages
5 years, 3 years and 8 months.

Mrs. Amaya said she heard her son scream: "Mama,
they're killing me. They've killed my sister. They're going to
kill me." She said that when the soldiers began gathering the
women into a group, she escaped and hid behind some trees
in back of the houses.

From Dec. 8 to Dec. 21, according to Salvadoran newspapers, soldiers from the Atlacatl Batallion took part in a
sweep through Mozote and the surrounding mountain villages as part of one of the largest search-and-destroy opera-

tions of the war against the leftist guerrillas who are fighting to overthrow the United States-supported junta. According to the villagers, no Americans accompanied the troops on the sweep.

Asked whether the Atlacatl Battalion had been involved in an operation in the northern mountainous region of Morazán in December, Col. Cotto said he could not provide specific details about military operations.

"We have been at war since 1979 against the subversives," he said. As part of that war, he said, air force and army units, including the Atlacatl Battalion, are continually conducting operations throughout the country.

280 CHILDREN REPORTED SLAIN
In Mozote, 280 of the 482 peasants killed, according to the list the villagers have prepared, were children under 14 years old. In Capilla, villagers say the soldiers murdered a father and his nine children, a mother and her five; in Cerro Pando, 87 adults and 62 children.

The Human Rights Commission has at other times also charged the army with killing large numbers of civilians during its operations. According to the commission, more than 100 were killed in the northern part of the province of Cabanas in November; 143, including 99 children under 16 years old, were said to have been killed in San Vicente in October, and about 300 in Usulutan in September.

Under banana trees at the edge of a cornfield near this village were 14 bodies. A child of about 5 or 6 years old was among the heap. Spent M-16 cartridges littered the dirt about 15 to 20 feet from the bodies. The rebels do have some M-16 rifles captured from army units, and they are standard issue for the Atlacatl Battalion.

A few peasants, handkerchiefs or oranges pressed against their noses to help block the stench, poked among the rubble for anything salvageable.

Up the mountain trail a short distance, 12 recently cut wood planks about 10 inches by three-eighths of an inch by 12 feet were propped against the trees. On the patio of the adobe hut, saws and crude homemade machetes and hammers were stained with blood.

Inside, five skulls were strewn among the smashed tiles. The men were carpenters, according to a boy who was working among beehives behind the mud hovel.

Mrs. Amaya said the first column of soldiers arrived in Mozote on foot about 6 P.M. Three times during the next 24 hours, she said, helicopters landed with more soldiers.

She said the soldiers told the villagers they were from the Atlacatl Battalion. "They said they wanted our weapons. But we said we didn't have any. That made them angry, and they started killing us."

Many of the peasants were shot while in their homes, but the soldiers dragged others from their houses and the church and put them in lines, women in one, men in another, Mrs. Amaya said. It was during this confusion that she managed to escape, she said.

She said about 25 young girls were separated from the other women and taken to the edge of the tiny village. She said she heard them screaming.

"We trusted the army," Mrs. Amaya said when asked why the villagers had not fled. She said that from October 1980 to August 1981, there had been a regular contingent of soldiers in Mozote, often from the National Guard. She said that they had not abused the peasants and that the villagers often fed them.

Rebel leaders in this region said Mozote was not considered a pro-rebel village. But the guerrillas did say that 3,000 of their supporters had fled the area when the army came in.

MEN AND BOYS FLED

When the soldiers and helicopters began arriving in the village of La Joya, the older boys and men fled, said 46-year-old César Martínez.

"We didn't think they would kill children, women and old people, so they remained," he explained. But, he said, the soldiers killed his mother, his sister and his sister's two children, ages 5 and 8 years. He said that among the others the soldiers killed were a 70-year-old woman and another woman and her 3-day-old baby.

On the wall of one house, Mr. Martínez said the soldiers scrawled "the Atlacatl Battallion will return to kill the rest." Sitting next to Mr. Martínez as he talked was 15-year-old Julio. Julio said his mother, father, 9-year-old brother and two sisters, ages 7 and 5 years, had been killed by the soldiers in La Joya. He said that when he heard the first shooting, he ran and hid in a gulley.

Julio said that he has returned to his village once since the massacre, to bury his family and two of his friends, ages 7 and 10 years.

WHETHER TO LEARN OR FIGHT

Julio has never been to school, and unlike many boys his age in this area, he had not been involved in the revolutionary movement. Now he is confused: He doesn't know whether to attend the school for children that is operated by the guerrillas or learn to use a rifle so "I can fight against the enemy," he said.

Another La Joya peasant, 39-year-old Gumersindo Lucas, said that before he fled with his wife, children and other relatives, he took his 62-year-old mother, who was too sick to walk, to a neighbor's house and hid her under some blankets. He said the soldiers shot her there and then burned the house.

Holding his half-naked chubby-cheeked 4-month-old daughter, who was wearing a red T-shirt and a tiny red bracelet, Mr. Lucas said that he had not sympathized with the rebels. Now, he said, "I want my wife and children to go to Honduras, but I am going to stay and fight."

4. The Embassy Begins the Search

The *Post* and *Times* stories created a furor in Washington, appearing, as they had, the day before President Reagan sent up to Congress his "certification" that the Salvadoran regime was "making a concerted and significant effort to comply with internationally recognized human rights." Within days, State Department officials would be testifying before Congress, defending the certification; they would need to provide an explanation of the spectacular reports of a massacre in Morazán. At the embassy in San Salvador, American officials began gathering information in earnest.

Two days after the newspaper stories appeared, Carl Gettinger, a reporting officer at the Embassy, sent the following memorandum to Kenneth Bleakley, the Deputy Chief of Mission, summarizing what he had learned from his sources about the reports of a massacre in Morazán. Gettinger's memorandum is particularly interesting for its acknowledgment that among those killed were evangelicals who "unwisely chose to stay behind." The memorandum was released in November 1993, with the deletions indicated.

Morazan Memorandum

DATE: January 29, 1982
REPLY TO ATTN OF: Carl Gettinger
SUBJECT: Mozote and Arambala
TO: DCM: Bleakley
  THRU: POL Driscoll

This morning I spoke with [deleted] about the alleged massacre in Morazán. Their comments are summarized below.

[Deleted] told me what he knows about the issue. [Deleted] is the source of allegations that 1000 people were killed in and around Mozote and Arambala during a military operation there in December.

[Deleted]; she reportedly heard the story from a Protestant evangelical who made it out of the area of the supposed massacre and arrived in [Deleted] story is backed up by a Radio Venceremos broadcast which reported 1009 victims of machine gunning during the December operation.

[Deleted] does not believe that any massacre such as the one described above ever occurred. He has two bases for his rejection of the story. First of all, he dismisses both [Deleted] and the FMLN broadcast as obviously biased sources. Secondly, and more substantially, he has obtained a statement [Deleted]/which includes the two affected cantons which refutes the [Deleted]/FMLN allegations. [Name Deleted] reports that the military did undertake a sweep ("limpieza") of the area, that residents of the area were given time to leave it, that most did and that among the unknown number of victims of the operation were some (unspecified) evangelicals who unwisely chose to stay behind. According to [Name Deleted] has denied that any massacre such as that described by [Deleted] occurred.

[Deleted] believes that the supposed victims of a massacre are now—living—in San Francisco Gotera.

[Deleted] in Cacaopera but who resides in Gotera has recently requested assistance from Caritas in San Miguel for additional assistance for 2000 plus refugees. [Deleted] believes that among that number are many from Mozote and Arambala. He is currently engaged in getting San Miguel Caritas chief Mendoza to determine what percentage of the 2000 are from the area where the massacre supposedly took place.

[Deleted] whose source is [deleted] told me the same story but in less detail.

5. THE GREENTREE CABLE

On January 30th, Todd Greentree and Major John McKay flew to Morazán. After observing El Mozote from the air, they landed in San Francisco Gotera, where they spoke to Army officers and interviewed refugees before traveling by jeep up the black road to within a few kilometers of El Mozote. That evening, Greentree sat down and wrote a lengthy report. That report, after gaining approval from Kenneth Bleakley and Ambassador Hinton, among others, was cabled to the State Department the following day. The conclusions drawn in the Greentree cable would form the heart of the Reagan Administration's public response to the charges that the Salvadoran Army had committed a massacre at El Mozote. The cable, with some deletions, was released to Raymond Bonner following a Freedom of Information request in 1983; the full text was released in November 1993.

O 312020Z JAN 82 ZFF-4
FM AMEMBASSY SAN SALVADOR
TO SECSTATE WASHDC NIACT IMMEDIATE 7665
CONFIDENTIAL

1. C - ENTIRE TEXT.

2. DEPARTMENT MAY WISH TO RELEASE PORTIONS OF THIS REPORT AS APPROPRIATE.

3. SUMMARY: EMBASSY INVESTIGATION OF REPORTED MASSACRE AT EL MOZOTE INCLUDING VISIT TO THE AREA BY ASSISTANT DATT [DEFENSE ATTACHE] AND EMBOFF [EMBASSY OFFICER] CONCLUDES FOLLOWING: ALTHOUGH IT IS NOT POSSIBLE TO PROVE OR DISPROVE EXCESSES OF VIOLENCE AGAINST THE CIVILIAN POPULATION OF EL MOZOTE BY GOVERNMENT TROOPS, IT IS CERTAIN THAT THE GUERRILLA FORCES WHO ESTABLISHED DEFENSIVE POSITIONS IN EL MOZOTE DID NOTHING TO REMOVE THEM FROM THE PATH OF BATTLE WHICH THEY WERE AWARE WAS COMING AND HAD PREPARED FOR, NOR IS THERE ANY EVIDENCE THAT THOSE WHO REMAINED ATTEMPTED TO LEAVE. CIVILIANS DID DIE DURING OPERATION RESCATE BUT NO EVIDENCE COULD BE FOUND TO CONFIRM THAT GOVERNMENT FORCES SYSTEMATICALLY MASSACRED CIVILIANS IN THE OPERATION ZONE, NOR THAT THE NUMBER OF CIVILIANS KILLED EVEN REMOTELY APPROACHED NUMBER BEING CITED IN OTHER REPORTS CIRCULATING INTERNATIONALLY. WE ARE STILL PURSUING QUESTION AS TO WHICH ARMY UNITS WERE PRESENT IN EL MOZOTE. END SUMMARY.

3. THE SETTING: MORAZAN DEPARTMENT

MORAZAN, LOCATED IN NORTHEASTERN EL SALVADOR, IS A SPARSELY POPULATED MOUNTAINOUS DEPARTMENT OF SMALL TOWNS AND WIDELY SCATTERED COMMUNITIES OF SUBSISTENCE FARMERS. TODAY THE DEPARTMENT IS IN A STATE OF WAR. MOST OF THE COUNTRYSIDE IS GUERRILLA DOMINATED. GOVERNMENT FORCES MAINTAIN POSTS IN SAN FRANCISCO GOTERA, THE DEPARTMENTAL CAPITAL, AND ABOUT A DOZEN SMALL TOWNS, MOST OF THEM STRUNG ALONG THE NORTH-SOUTH HIGHWAY THAT RUNS THROUGH THE DEPARTMENT. IN MOST TOWNS, THE CIVILIAN POPULATION CONSISTS LARGELY OF FAMILIES DISPLACED FROM THEIR SMALL PLOTS IN THE COUNTRYSIDE BY THE WAR. THEY OCCUPY HOUSES OF FORMER TOWN DWELLERS, WHO IN TURN HAVE FLED THE VIOLENCE FOR THE RELATIVE SAFETY OF THE LARGER CITIES. MILITARY PRESENCE IN THE DEPARTMENT CONSISTS OF THE 6TH INFANTRY BRIGADE, LOCATED IN THE DEPARTMENTAL CAPITAL, WITH SMALL DETACHMENTS ROUGHLY EQUALLY DIVIDED BETWEEN SECURITY FORCES AND CIVIL DEFENSE POSTED IN THE SMALL TOWNS.

EL MOZOTE IS A TYPICAL RURAL CANTON (COMMUNITY) LOCATED APPROXIMATELY 25 KILOMETERS NORTH OF THE DEPARTMENTAL CAPITAL. ACCESSIBLE BY DIRT ROAD, IT CONSISTS OF A SMALL CLUSTER OF BUILDINGS, INCLUDING A CHAPEL AND A STORE, SURROUNDED BY SCATTERED SINGLE FAMILY ADOBE HOUSES. MANY HAVE FLED THE VIOLENCE IN THE AREA IN RECENT YEARS, AND THE POPULATION OF EL MOZOTE AT THE TIME OF THE DECEMBER OPERATION WAS ESTIMATED AT NO MORE THAN 300, PRIMARILY CAMPESINOS (SUBSISTENCE FARMERS). RELIGIOUS INFLUENCES IN THE AREA HAVE BEEN WEAK FOR SEVERAL YEARS, BUT BOTH CATHOLICS AND EVANGELISTS LIVED IN EL MOZOTE.

EL MOZOTE IS IN THE HEART OF GUERRILLA TERRITORY AND ITS INHABITANTS HAVE SPENT MOST OF THE PAST THREE YEARS WILLINGLY OR UNWILLINGLY COOPERATING WITH INSURGENTS. GOVERNMENT FORCES HAVE NOT BEEN POSTED IN EL MOZOTE SINCE AUGUST 1981. CONSEQUENTLY GUERRILLAS HAVE BEEN FREE TO ESTABLISH THEMSELVES IN THE AREA.

4. OPERATION RESCATE AND EL MOZOTE

REGULAR GOVERNMENT FORCES HAVE MOUNTED PERIODIC OPERATIONS IN MORAZAN TO DECREASE INFLUENCE OF INSURGENT ELEMENTS AND TO ATTEMPT TO ESTABLISH A DEGREE OF GOVERNMENT CONTROL IN CONTESTED AREAS. COMBINED ARMY UNITS, INCLUDING THE ATLACATL

BATTALION, CONDUCTED SUCH AN OPERATION, CALLED OPERATION RESCATE IN CENTRAL MORAZAN FROM DECEMBER 6 THROUGH DECEMBER 17, 1981. THE SPECIFIC DEPLOYMENT OF FORCES IS UNKNOWN AT THIS TIME.

THE DECEMBER MILITARY OPERATION UTILIZED A BLOCK FORCE STRETCHED FROM EAST TO WEST ABOUT 30 KILOMETERS NORTH OF EL MOZOTE. MANEUVERING UNITS WERE SENT NORTH FROM THE DEPART-MENTAL CAPITAL, SWEEPING THE TERRITORY BETWEEN THEM AND THE BLOCKING FORCES. GUERRILLAS HAD KNOWN ABOUT THIS OPERATION SINCE AT LEAST NOVEMBER 15, AND HAD MOBILIZED THEIR FORCES, INCLUDING CIVILIAN SUPPORTERS TO HARASS GOVERNMENT TROOPS WHILE WITHDRAWING LARGE NUMBERS FROM THE OPERATION ZONE.

BOTH GUERRILLAS AND CIVILIANS WERE PRESENT THERE WHEN GOVERNMENT FORCES APPROACHED EL MOZOTE FROM THE SOUTH DURING MID-OPERATION ON ABOUT DECEMBER 11. ATTACKING TROOPS ENCOUNTERED STIFF GUERRILLA RESISTANCE FROM A TRENCH LINE SOUTH OF THE SETTLEMENT. FIGHTING THERE LASTED ABOUT FOUR HOURS UNTIL TROOPS WERE ABLE TO PENETRATE THE LINE WITH 90MM RECOILLESS RIFLE FIRE. SOLDIERS THEN MOVED FORWARD INTO THE SETTLEMENT WHERE THEY AGAIN CAME UNDER FIRE AND TOOK CASUALTIES. FIGHTING CONTINUED AND THE TOWN WAS PARTIALLY DESTROYED. CIVILIANS REMAINING IN ANY PART OF THE CANTON COULD HAVE BEEN SUBJECT TO INJURY AS A RESULT OF THE COMBAT.

AN ARMY COMPANY WHICH DID NOT PARTICIPATE IN THE OPERATION RELIEVED TROOPS IN EL MOZOTE ON DECEMBER 19 AND REMAINED THERE UNTIL GUERRILLAS OVERRAN THEM AND RE-TOOK EL MOZOTE ON DECEMBER 29 KILLING THEM AND TAKING PRISONERS. THE CANTON REMAINS IN INSURGENT HANDS TODAY.

5. DISPLACED PERSONS FROM THE OPERATION ZONE

THOUSANDS OF REFUGEES HAVE CONGREGATED IN THE TOWNS MAKING UP THE MAJORITY OF THE POPULATION EVERYWHERE EXCEPT FOR PERQUIN AND SAN FRANCISCO GOTERA. THOUSANDS OF DISPLACED PERSONS UNABLE TO RETURN TO THEIR HOMES IN THE COUNTRYSIDE HAVE OVERWHELMED THE CAPACITY OF THESE TOWNS TO SUPPORT THEM AND HAVE MOVED EN MASSE ON SEVERAL OCCASIONS SEARCHING FOR SEMI-PERMANENT REFUGE.

AN UNDETERMINED NUMBER OF REFUGEES FROM EL MOZOTE ARE LOCATED IN THE TOWNS OF SAN FRANCISCO GOTERA, PERQUIN AND

JOCOAITIQUE. IN JOCOAITIQUE, AN AGED COUPLE, WHO LEFT EL MOZOTE DURING THE ATTACK, SPOKE FRANKLY OF THEIR EXPERIENCE. ACCORDING TO THEM, GUERRILLAS HAD TOLD THEM TO LEAVE IN EARLY DECEMBER BECAUSE THEY WERE SO OLD, BUT THEY DID NOT WANT TO BECAUSE THEY HAD SPENT THEIR WHOLE LIVES THERE AND HAD NEVER BEEN OUTSIDE THE COMMUNITY. THEIR ADOBE HOUSE LOCATED TO THE SOUTH OF THE MAIN SETTLEMENT WAS DESTROYED BY ARTILLERY BOMBARDMENT, PROBABLY ON THE MORNING OF DECEMBER 11. BY THE TIME THEY REACHED THE MAIN CLUSTER OF HOUSES LATER IN THE DAY, THE FIGHTING HAD ENDED AND SOLDIERS WERE IN CONTROL. THEY CLAIMED THEY SAW DOZENS OF BODIES. SOLDIERS DID NOT MOLEST THEM, AND THE NEXT DAY THEY WALKED EIGHT KILOMETERS TO TAKE REFUGE IN JOCOAITIQUE.

THE MAYOR OF JOCOAITIQUE INTIMATED THAT HE KNEW OF VIOLENT FIGHTING IN EL MOZOTE AND OTHER NEARBY CANTONS. AT THAT TIME AS MANY AS A THOUSAND PEOPLE TOOK REFUGE UNDER MILITARY PROTECTION IN THE TOWN WHERE ALMOST ALL OF THE 3,500 INHABITANTS ARE REFUGEES FROM THE COUNTRYSIDE. HE WAS UNWILLING TO DISCUSS COMPORTMENT OF GOVERNMENT FORCES SAYING, "THIS IS SOMETHING ONE SHOULD TALK ABOUT IN ANOTHER TIME, IN ANOTHER COUNTRY."

ONE OF THE FEW PRIESTS REMAINING IN NORTH MORAZAN TRAVELS FREELY ALONG THE MAIN ROAD BUT STATED HE IS UNWILLING TO GO THROUGH GUERRILLA TERRITORY TO REACH THE SMALL SETTLEMENTS OFF THE ROAD. ACCORDING TO THE PRIEST, EL MOZOTE AND SURROUNDING CANTONS HAVE BEEN POLITICIZED BY THE LEFT FOR SEVERAL YEARS AND PROVIDE A WILLING SUPPORT BASE. HE AGREED WITH THE MAYOR OF JOCOAITIQUE THAT MANY OF THE REFUGEES IN THAT TOWN WERE FROM GUERRILLA FAMILIES.

DISPLACED CAMPESINO FAMILIES FROM THE CANTONS OF ARAMBALA, TIERRA COLORADA, AND GUACAMAYA TO THE NORTH AND SOUTH OF EL MOZOTE ACKNOWLEDGED THAT THEY LEFT THESE AREAS FOR THE TOWNS IN EARLY DECEMBER TO AVOID THE IMPENDING OPERATION, OR IN LATE DECEMBER TO AVOID THE IMPENDING GUERRILLA COUNTEROFFENSIVE.

6. ATTACK ON JOCOAITIQUE

IN LATE DECEMBER, FOLLOWING OPERATION RESCATE, INSURGENTS LAUNCHED A COUNTEROFFENSIVE WHICH SUCCESSFULLY DISPLACED

GOVERNMENT TROOPS EAST OF THE NORTH-SOUTH HIGHWAY FROM THE RIO SAPO NEAR THE TOWN OF OSICALA NORTH TO ARAMBALA.

IN THE EARLY MORNING OF JANUARY 12 GUERRILLAS BEGAN TO FIRE ON THE TOWN OF JOCOAITIQUE FROM THE SURROUNDING HILLSIDES. THEY MOVED IN AND CONTINUED FIRING ON THE SMALL NATIONAL GUARD AND CIVIL DEFENSE POSITIONS IN AND AROUND THE TOWN UNTIL THE DEFENDERS RAN OUT OF AMMUNITION. GUERRILLAS MOVED QUICKLY INTO THE TOWN, KILLING FOUR NATIONAL GUARDSMEN AND TWENTY SEVEN OTHER INHABITANTS, PRIMARILY CIVIL DEFENSE AND THEIR FAMILY MEMBERS. SOME OF THE LATTER DID NOT DIE DURING THE ASSAULT ON THE TOWN, BUT WERE SHOT AFTER BEING CAPTURED. TWO WOMEN AND FOUR CHILDREN WERE WOUNDED DURING THE FIGHTING. THE INSURGENTS TOOK TWENTY FIVE CAPTIVES AND KEPT THEM FOR EIGHT DAYS BEFORE RELEASING THEM. DURING THE OCCUPATION, THREE JOURNALISTS, INCLUDING AN AMERICAN MALE AND FEMALE, ALLEGEDLY ACCOMPANIED GUERRILLAS IN JOCOAITIQUE.

GUERRILLAS HELD THE TOWN FOR SIX DAYS UNTIL GOVERNMENT TROOPS ARRIVED ON THE 18TH, AT WHICH TIME THEY WITHDREW INTO THE HILLS WITHOUT A FIGHT. UPON DEPARTING, THEY TOOK WITH THEM ALL OF THE TYPEWRITERS AND MEDICINES IN THE TOWN, ALSO REMOVING THE TOWN HALL REGISTRIES LISTING THE NAMES OF ALL THE INHABITANTS OF SURROUNDING CANTONS. THEY DID NOT HARM THE TOWNSPEOPLE IN ANY OTHER WAY. SEVERAL REFUGEE FAMILIES WENT WITH THEIR HUSBANDS WHEN THE GROUP DEPARTED ON THE 18TH.

THE TOWN IS CURRENTLY SURROUNDED BY GUERRILLAS. SOLDIERS REMAIN IN THE TOWN OR IN NEARBY FORTIFIED POSITIONS. PEOPLE ARE UNABLE TO LEAVE TO TEND CROPS. THERE IS INADEQUATE FOOD, AND NO MEDICINES. THE MAYOR OF THE TOWN SAID GUERRILLAS SPARED HIS LIFE ONLY BECAUSE HE ASKED THEM TO KILL HIS SEVEN CHILDREN FIRST. HE IS DOING HIS BEST TO MAINTAIN POLITICAL NEUTRALITY. AS SOON AS SOLDIERS DEPART, GUERRILLAS WILL RETURN. HE STATED THAT HIS MAJOR PROBLEM IS WHAT TO DO ABOUT "ALL OF THE WIDOWS AND THEIR CHILDREN."

7. CONCLUSION

MORAZAN IS A WAR-RAVAGED DEPARTMENT. AGRICULTURAL PRODUCTION IS SEVERELY DISRUPTED. LARGE AREAS ARE ENTIRELY ABANDONED, TOWNS CONSIST LARGELY OF REFUGEES AND THOU-SANDS HAVE DIED AT THE HANDS OF BOTH GUERRILLAS AND THE

MILITARY. MOST CIVILIANS ATTEMPT TO MAINTAIN A TENUOUS
NEUTRALITY. WITH THE GOVERNMENT CONTROLLING THE TOWNS AND
THE GUERRILLAS DOMINATING THE COUNTRYSIDE, SMALL CLASHES ARE
DAILY OCCURRENCES AND LARGER CONFRONTATIONS A CONSTANT
POSSIBILITY.

EXCEPT FOR BRIEF PERIOD IN DECEMBER WHEN IT WAS OCCUPIED BY
GOVERNMENT FORCES, EL MOZOTE HAS BEEN IN GUERRILLA HANDS
CONTINUOUSLY SINCE AUGUST 1981. THE INHABITANTS WERE CERTAINLY
PASSIVE AND PROBABLY ACTIVE GUERRILLA SUPPORTERS THROUGHOUT
THE GUERRILLA DOMINATED COUNTRYSIDE. CIVILIANS REMAINING IN EL
MOZOTE DURING THE ATTACK FOUND THEMSELVES SUBJECTED TO
COMBAT. ALTHOUGH IT IS NOT POSSIBLE TO PROVE OR DISPROVE
EXCESSES OF VIOLENCE AGAINST THE CIVILIAN POPULATION OF EL
MOZOTE BY GOVERNMENT TROOPS, IT IS CERTAIN THAT THE GUER-
RILLA FORCES WHO ESTABLISHED DEFENSIVE POSITIONS IN EL
MOZOTE DID NOTHING TO REMOVE THEM FROM THE PATH OF BATTLE
WHICH THEY WERE AWARE WAS COMING AND HAD PREPARED FOR, NOR
IS THERE ANY EVIDENCE THAT THOSE WHO REMAINED ATTEMPTED TO
LEAVE.

CIVILIANS DID DIE DURING THE OPERATION RESCATE, BUT NO
EVIDENCE COULD BE FOUND TO CONFIRM THAT GOVERNMENT FORCES
SYSTEMATICALLY MASSACRED CIVILIANS IN THE OPERATION ZONE. AS
MANY AS ONE THOUSAND VOLUNTARILY DEPARTED FROM THE CANTONS
TO SEEK RELATIVE SAFETY IN THE TOWNS PRIOR TO THE OPERATION.

FILE REVIEW INDICATES RADIO VENCEREMOS FIRST ISSUED REPORT OF
MASSACRES ON DECEMBER 27, CLAIMING 192 HAD DIED IN EL MOZOTE.
ON JANUARY 2 IT REPORTED 472 WERE MASSACRED. ON JANUARY 27
THE WASHINGTON POST REPORTED THAT THE NUMBER "IN AND
AROUND" EL MOZOTE WAS 700. A DAY LATER THE NEW YORK TIMES
REPORTED 482. BOTH US PRESS ACCOUNTS REPORT SEEING UNSPECIFIED
"DOZENS OF BODIES" IN THREE DESTROYED STRUCTURES IN THE
SETTLEMENT AND A PILE OF TEN TO FOURTEEN BODIES NEARBY,
NOTHING NEAR THE TOTAL NUMBERS CLAIMED.

IT IS ESTIMATED THAT NO MORE THAN 300 PEOPE WERE IN THE
ENTIRE CANTON PRIOR TO DECEMBER 1981. NAMES OF "VICTIMS"
SUBSEQUENTLY REPORTED IN THE U.S. PRESS AND CIRCULATED WIDELY
IN EUROPE MAY WELL HAVE BEEN EXTRACTS IN WHOLE OR PART FROM
THE CIVIL REGISTRIES FOR THE AREA STOLEN FROM JOCOAITIQUE BY
SUBVERSIVES.

8. SOURCES

CIVILIAN AUTHORITIES, CHURCH OFFICIALS, RELIEF WORKERS, AND
SOCORRO JURIDICO REPRESENTATIVES WERE UNABLE TO PROVIDE FIRST-
HAND INFORMATION ON EL MOZOTE.
INTERNATIONAL RED CROSS DELEGATES IN CHARGE OF RELIEF TO
DISPLACED PERSONS NORTH OF SAN FRANCISCO GOTERA WERE UNABLE
OR UNWILLING TO DISCUSS THE SUBJECT, DEFERRING INSTEAD TO
SUPERIORS IN GENEVA. THE INTERNATIONAL RED CROSS IS THE ONLY
RELIEF AGENCY PERMITTED TO MOVE FREELY IN MORAZAN DEPARTMENT,
MAKING WEEKLY TRIPS WITH RELIEF SUPPLIES TO THE TOWNS ON THE
NORTH-SOUTH ROAD AND IN OTHER AREAS. DELEGATES MIGHT BE ABLE
TO PROVIDE MORE ACCURATE INFORMATION ON MASSACRES IN EL
MOZOTE AND OTHER CANTONS DURING THE MID-DECEMBER OPERATION.
EMBOFF AND ASSISTANT DEFENSE ATTACHE VISITED LOCATIONS
THROUGHOUT MORAZAN ON JANUARY 30, INTERVIEWING INHABITANTS
AND OBSERVING CONDITIONS IN THE AREA. THEY CONDUCTED
INTERVIEWS WITH REFUGEES FROM EL MOZOTE AND NEARBY CANTONS IN
SAN FRANCISCO GOTERA, JOCOAITIQUE, AND PERQUIN. DAO IS
ATTEMPTING TO DETERMINE WHICH ARMY UNITS WERE PRESENT IN EL
MOZOTE DURING AND AFTER THE OPERATION.
HINTON

6. THE AMBASSADOR AND THE DEFENSE MINISTER, I

On January 30th, even as Greentree and McKay were interviewing refugees in Morazán, Ambassador Hinton was conducting his
own investigation—over dinner, with General José Guillermo
García, the Salvadoran Minister of Defense.

The ambassador cabled his report on February 1st. CESPDES
refers to the Salvadoran Army's propaganda office.

O 011616Z FEB 82
FM AMEMBASSY SAN SALVADOR
TO SECSTATE WASHDC IMMEDIATE 7683
SECRET SAN SALVADOR 0796
EXDIS
E. O. 12065: GDS 2/1/88 (HINTON, DEANE R.) OR-M
SUBJ: (S) CHAT WITH GENERAL GARCIA

I. (S-ENTIRE TEXT.)

2. DEFENSE MINISTER GARCIA IS ON HIS WAY TO STATES TO ATTEND, AMONG OTHER THINGS, A CONGRESSIONAL PRAYER BREAKFAST. IN TALK JANUARY 30 ON MARGIN OF DINNER WE DISCUSSED: (A) MORAZAN MASSACRE ALLEGATIONS, (B) ARMY ATTACK ON HOUSE WHERE AMERICAN LIVED, (C) CESPDES ATTACK ON JESUITS, AND (D) LATEST THINKING ON NUNS MURDER CASE.

3. WARNED GARCIA TO BE READY TO RESPOND TO MORAZAN MASSACRE STORY. HE WAS HIS USUAL COCKY SELF, "I'LL DENY IT AND PROVE IT FABRICATED." I WISHED HIM WELL AND ADDED HE WOULD HAVE TO EXPLAIN AWAY DETAILS PROVIDED BY CORRESPONDENTS. IT MIGHT BE POSSIBLE—WE WERE INVESTIGATING AND WERE GRATEFUL FOR HIS HELP—BUT HE SHOULD BEAR IN MIND THAT SOMETHING HAD GONE WRONG. WHO DID IT, WHEN, AND IN WHAT CIRCUMSTANCES WAS SOMETHING ELSE.

4. I TOLD GARCIA THAT "I DID NOT LIKE THE RAID CONDUCTED THE NIGHT BEFORE ON A HOUSE WHERE AN AMERICAN WAS LIVING." HE REPLIED, "WE ARE LOOKING INTO IT."

5. FOR GOOD MEASURE, I SUGGESTED TO GARCIA THAT IT WAS TIME HE GOT CESPDES UNDER CONTROL, SINCE ITS LATEST ATTACK ON THE JESUITS WAS TOTALLY IRRESPONSIBLE. (SAN SALVADOR 0704) I ADDED THAT THE POPE HAD CHANGED THE ORDER'S COMMANDER, THAT THE JESUITS WERE CLEANING HOUSE, THAT THEY WERE UNDER NEW ORDERS AND COMMANDERS, INCLUDING THE LOCAL BISHOP. THEY SHOULD HAVE BENEFIT OF DOUBT. MOREOVER, IN WORST OF TIMES THERE HAD BEEN INDIVIDUALS WHO HAD STRAYED NOT ENTIRE ORDER. ATTACKERS HAD TO DISCRIMINATE NOT CONDEMN ALL. FINALLY, I REMINDED HIM OF POSITIVE ROLE OF CHURCH IN NICARAGUA AND POLAND, ASKING IF HE DID NOT WANT CHURCH ON HIS SIDE. HE TOOK THIS IN, NOTED ATTACKS WERE "DANGEROUS," AND CHANGED SUBJECT TO NUNS.

6. HERE HE AGAIN ASSURED ME ALL MOVING WELL AND THAT GOVERNMENT HOPED TO MAKE STATEMENT IN DAY OR TWO. HE VOLUNTEERED GOOD NEWS THAT THOUGHT IS BEING GIVEN TO TRYING CASE "AT PLENARY LEVEL." THIS IS NEW IDEA FOR ME BUT WERE IT

FEASIBLE, IT MIGHT ASSUAGE SOMEWHAT CONTINUING GOES CONCERNS
ABOUT POSSIBLE INTIMIDATION OF TRIAL JUDGE. IN ANY CASE, I
WELCOME THESE REMARKS AS EVIDENCE THAT INTERNALLY MILITARY
AND CIVILIAN AUTHORITIES HAVE ENGAGED DIALOGUE TO CONSIDER
STEPS WHICH HAVE TO BE SURMOUNTED WHEN MILITARY TURN ACCUSED
OVER TO CIVIL COURTS.
HINTON
NOTE BY OC/T: CAUTION - THIS MESSAGE APPEARS TO CONTAIN SENSITIVE
INTELLIGENCE INFORMATION

7. "DEBRIEFING" MONTERROSA

On February 1st, an American officer from the Defense Attaché's
office drove to Sitio del Niño—the headquarters of the Atlacatl
Battalion—to put the question about El Mozote directly to Lieutenant Colonel Domingo Monterrosa and his officers. Later that
evening, the American cabled the following report to the Defense
Intelligence Agency at the Pentagon. It was released in November
1993.

FROM: USDAO SAN SALVADOR ES
TO: DIA WASH DC//JSI-4B/OS-1 /DB-3E2//DB-3E
CONFIDENTIAL NOFORN
SUBJ: EL SALVADOR/CONVERSATION WITH ATLACATL BATTALION OFFICERS
CONCERNING ALLEGED MIS-CONDUCT OF THE ARMY IN MORAZAN DEPART-
MENT
THIS IS AN INFO REPORT, NOT FINALLY EVALUATED INTEL

1. CTRY: EL SALVADOR (ES)

2. IR NO: 6 829 0038 82

3. TITLE: CONVERSATION WITH ATLACATL BATTALION OFFICERS
CONCERNING ALLEGED MIS-CONDUCT OF THE ARMY IN MORAZAN
DEPARTMENT.

4. DATE OF INFO: 820201

5. ORIG: USDAO SAN SALVADOR, ES

6. [DELETED]

7. SOURCE: [DELETED]

8. (C/NOFORN) SUMMARY: (ENTIRE TEXT CONFIDENTIAL/NOFORN) THIS IR
PROVIDES A SUMMARY OF REMARKS MADE BY LIEUTENANT COLONEL JOSE
DOMINGO ((MONTERROSA)), COMMANDING OFFICER OF THE ATLACATL
BATTALION; MAJOR JESUS NATIVIDAD ((CASERES)), EXECUTIVE OFFICER
OF THE ATLACATL BATTALION; MAJOR JOSE ARMANDO ((AZMITIA))
MELARA, S-3 OF THE ATLACATL BATTALION ON THE ALLEGATIONS THAT
ATROCITIES WERE COMMITTED BY ELEMENTS OF THE ARMED FORCES OF
EL SALVADOR. THE INCIDENT DISCUSSED IN THESE CONVERSATIONS IS
ALLEGED TO HAVE TAKEN PLACE IN THE VICINITY OF EL MOZOTE
(1355N-8808W), MORAZAN DEPARTMENT, DURING OPERATION
"RESCATE" (6-17 DECEMBER 1981). THE ATLACATL BATTALION
PARTICIPATED IN OPERATION "RESCATE".

(1) THE EXACT PURPOSE OF RO'S [REPORTING OFFICER'S] VISIT TO THE
ATLACATL BATTALION (I.E. TO DETERMINE THE MISSION ASSIGNED, AND
SUCCESSIVE POSITIONS OCCUPIED BY THE BATTALION DURING OPERATION
"RESCATE"; AND TO SPECIFICALLY DETERMINE IF THE BATTALION, OR
ELEMENTS THEREOF, WERE INVOLVED IN THE FIGHTING AROUND AND IN
EL MOZOTE, MORAZAN DEPARTMENT DURING THAT OPERATION) WAS PUT
TO THE COMMANDING OFFICER, LTC MONTERROSA SHORTLY AFTER
GREETINGS AND PLEASANTRIES WERE EXCHANGED. LTC MONTERROSA
REMAINED DISTANTLY COURTEOUS, BUT HE FIRMLY TOLD RO THAT HE
WAS NOT IN A POSITION TO DISCUSS THESE SPECIFIC SUBJECTS, AND
THAT RO HAD BETTER OBTAIN PERMISSION FROM THE GENERAL STAFF OF
THE ARMED FORCES BEFORE HE CAME WITH SUCH INQUIRIES TO HIS (LTC
MONTERROSA'S) BATTALION. (RO NOTE: QUITE FRANKLY, RO FELT THAT
THE INTERVIEW, ALBEIT SHORT, WAS THUS TO BE TERMINATED). RO
MADE THE OBLIGATORY APOLOGIES FOR WHAT THE COLONEL MAY HAVE
INTERPRETED AS IMPERTINENCE. RO ALSO POINTED OUT THAT CANDID
ANSWERS TO THE QUESTIONS POSED WOULD FACILITATE COUNTERING
RECENT PRESS RELEASES WHICH WERE LESS THAN COMPLIMENTARY TO
THE ARMED FORCES OF EL SALVADOR.

(2) AT THIS POINT MAJOR AZMITIA INTERJECTED WITH WHAT CAN
ONLY BE DESCRIBED AS A PARABLE: THE UNIT THAT HAD FOUGHT AT EL
MOZOTE HAD HAD A TOUGH TIME OF IT, AND THAT BECAUSE OF THE
INTENSITY AND DURATION OF THE BATTLE (RO NOTE: MAJOR AZMITIA
SEEMED TO SLIP HERE, AS HE USED THE FIRST PERSON PLURAL "WHEN
WE APPROACHED EL MOZOTE IN THE EARLY AFTERNOON. . . ."----
"CUANDO NOS ACERCAMOS A AQUEL PUEBLO EN LA TARDE. . . . .")
THERE WERE UNDOUBTEDLY CASUALTIES AMONG NON-COMBATANTS. COL
MONTERROSA THEN TOOK UP THE NARRATIVE. HE SAID THAT THE UNIT
INVOLVED HAD HAD TO FIGHT THROUGH FIXED ENEMY POSITIONS, THEN,
ONCE IN THE TOWN, FIRE WAS RECEIVED FROM THE HOUSES IN THE
TOWN (RO NOTE: LTC MONTERROSA NOW UTILIZED THE FIRST PERSON: "I
DO NOT HAVE X-RAY VISION, AND I CAN NOT SEE INSIDE THE HOUSE
FROM WHICH SOMEONE IS SHOOTING AT ME; NOR IN THOSE TYPE OF
CIRCUMSTANCES AM I VERY DISPOSED TO WASTE TIME TRYING TO FIND
OUT WHO ELSE MIGHT BE IN THE HOUSE.") LTC MONTERROSA THEN
STATED (IN THE THIRD PERSON) THAT 90MM RECOILLESS RIFLES WERE
USED AGAINST THE HOUSE FROM WHICH FIRE WAS RECEIVED. AT THIS
POINT LTC MONTERROSA SAID HE WANTED TO REITERATE TO RO THAT HE
DID NOT KNOW WHICH DAY (OF THE OPERATION) RO WAS INTERESTED
IN, AND THAT HE WAS ONLY SPEAKING IN GENERAL, NOT SPECIFIC,
TERMS ABOUT WHAT HAD OCCURRED AT EL MOZOTE.

(3) MAJOR AZMITIA COMMENTED THAT "THEY HAD BEEN THERE (EN
LA ZONA DE MOZOTE) FROM EARLY AFTERNOON UNTIL LATE IN THE
AFTERNOON (DESDE LAS TEMPRANAS HORAS DE LA TARDE HASTA MUY
TARDE) FIGHTING." THEN HE SWITCHED TO THE THIRD PERSON AND
SAID THAT CASUALTIES HAD BEEN HEAVY (NFI) AMONG GOVERNMENT
TROOPS. AS AN ASIDE, HE SAID THE FIGHTING IN ARAMBALA (1356N-
8808W), MORAZAN DEPARTMENT, HAD NOT BEEN SO HEAVY.

(4) RO ASKED LIEUTENANT COLONEL MONTERROSA IF HE KNEW IF
ANY PRISONERS HAD BEEN TAKEN DURING OR AFTER THE BATTLE FOR EL
MOZOTE. AGAIN, THE COLONEL ASSUMED AN ADAMANT DEMEANOR,
AND SUGGESTED THAT RO CONSULT WITH THE GENERAL STAFF, OR GET
PERMISSION FROM THE GENERAL STAFF TO ASK HIM SUCH QUESTIONS. HE
THEN PROCEEDED TO REPEAT THAT HE COULD NOT ANSWER RO'S
QUESTIONS ABOUT HIS BATTALION'S PARTICIPATION IN THE RESCATE
OPERATION UNTIL HE HAD PERMISSION FROM THE GENERAL STAFF TO DO
SO. THEN HE SEEMED TO MELLOW SOMEWHAT, AS HE EXPRESSED WHAT
APPEARED TO BE GENUINE INTEREST IN REVIEWING THE PARTICIPATION

OF THE ATLACATL BATTALION, WITH RO, IN THE ENTIRE OPERATION. IF THE GENERAL STAFF WOULD NOTIFY HIM THAT HE COULD DO SO, HE WOULD SIT DOWN WITH RO AND SHOW HIM HOW HIS BATTALION MOVED, THE ORDERS HE ISSUED (HE CLAIMED HE KEPT THESE), AND HOW THE ENEMY REACTED. LACKING GENERAL STAFF APPROVAL, HE COULD NOT, AND HE STATED HE WAS SORRY HE COULD NOT, PROVIDE RO WITH THE ASSISTANCE HE WAS SEEKING. THE INTERVIEW HAD COME TO AN END.

(5) RO WAS ESCORTED TO HIS VEHICLE BY MAJOR AZMITIA, WHO ACTED APOLOGETIC ABOUT THE FACT THAT THEY COULD NOT PROVIDE MORE FACTS ABOUT EL MOZOTE, BUT HE WAS SURE THAT THE RO UNDERSTOOD WHAT LTC MONTERROSA HAD BEEN TALKING ABOUT.

(1) THE ABOVE INTERVIEW WAS ARRANGED BASED ON AN INQUIRY BY THE AMBASSADOR TO TRY AND DETERMINE WHAT UNIT OR UNITS PARTICIPATED IN THE ATTACK ON EL MOZOTE DURING OPERATION "RESCATE". RO ARRIVED AT ATLACATL BATTALION HEADQUARTERS SHORTLY AFTER 1500 HOURS (L) ON 1 FEBRUARY 1982. HE LEFT SHORTLY AFTER 1700 HOURS (L).

(2) MAJOR AZMITIA WAS PRESENT DURING THE ENTIRE PERIOD RO SPENT WITH LTC MONTERROSA; MAJ CASERES ENTERED ABOUT MID-DISCUSSION.

(3) ALL THREE OFFICERS MENTIONED IN THIS REPORT WERE IN MORAZAN DEPARTMENT DURING OPERATION "RESCATE", ALTHOUGH MAJOR CASERES APPARENTLY SPENT PERIODS AT THE BATTALION HEADQUARTERS AT SITIO DEL NINO (1348N-8922W) DURING THE OPERATION.

(4) THE TWO HOURS SPENT WITH THESE THREE OFFICERS WAS INTERESTING TO SAY THE LEAST. THE NUANCES, SUBTLETIES AND INDIRECT COMPARISONS USED BY LTC MONTERROSA AND MAJ AZMITIA WERE INTRIGUING. YET THE CENTRAL QUESTIONS REMAIN WITHOUT DEFINITIVE ANSWERS.

(5) RO'S PERSONAL OPINION, AND HE EMPHASIZES "PERSONAL", IS THAT ATLACATL BATTALION OR ELEMENTS THEREOF PARTICIPATED IN THE ATTACK ON EL MOZOTE. PRECLUDING PERMISSION FROM GENERAL GARCIA, MINISTER OF DEFENSE, DEFINITIVE ANSWERS AS TO THE MISSION, POSITIONS, AND ACTIONS PARTICIPATED IN, OF THE ATLACATL BATTALION IN OPERATION "RESCATE" MAY NEVER BE FORTHCOMING.

8. THE AMBASSADOR CORRECTS THE STATE DEPARTMENT

On February 1st, Ambassador Hinton cabled the State Department to correct what he apparently saw as a misimpression that had taken root about his response to the National Council of Churches inquiry (see "First Inquiries," above). The tone of the cable—and the unexplained reference to "additional evidence"—suggests that the Ambassador may have already been briefed on that afternoon's attempt to get some straight answers out of Colonel Monterrosa and his officers.

C Q11617Z FEB 82
FM: AMEMBASSY SAN SALVADOR
TO: SECSTATE WASHDC IMMEDIATE 7684

C O N F I D E N T I A L SAN SALVADOR 0797

SUBJ: (C) ALLEGATIONS OF MASSACRE IN MORAZAN

1. (C-ENTIRE TEXT.)

2. I WOULD BE GRATEFUL IF DEPARTMENT WOULD USE EXTREME CARE IN DESCRIBING MY VIEWS ON ALLEGED MASSACRE. CASE IN POINT IS DESCRIPTION IN PARA 3 OF *REFTEL* REFERRING TO MY LETTER TO STOCKWELL AS "DENYING THE INCIDENT". MY LETTER DID NOT "DENY" INCIDENT: IT REPORTED THAT AT THAT TIME I HAD NO CONFIRMATION AND ARGUED FROM AVAILABLE EVIDENCE FROM RADIO VENCEREMOS AND FROM LACK OF OTHER REPORTS THAT I HAD NO REASON TO BELIEVE VENCEREMOS REPORTS. I STILL DON'T BELIEVE VENCEREMOS VERSION BUT ADDITIONAL EVIDENCE STRONGLY SUGGESTS THAT SOMETHING HAPPENED THAT SHOULD NOT HAVE HAPPENED AND THAT IT IS QUITE POSSIBLE SALVADORAN MILITARY DID COMMIT EXCESSES. ALLEGATIONS THAT IT WAS UNIT FROM ATLACATL BATTALION IN EL MOZOTE REMAIN TO BE CONFIRMED OR DISCREDITED.

3. INCIDENTALLY, I FIND GARCIA'S ASSERTION (SAN SALVADOR USINFO 698), "WE HAVE ABSOLUTELY NO INFORMATION ON MILITARY ACTIONS IN EL MOZOTE" TO BE STONEWALLING WITHOUT CREDIBILITY. I HAVE TRIED TO WARN HIM RE NEED TO FACE UP TO PROBLEM, BUT MY IMPRESSION IS HE THINKS CATEGORIC DENIAL IS WAY TO HANDLE QUESTION. DEPARTMENT OFFICERS MAY WISH TO DISCUSS MATTER WITH HIM AND AMBASSADOR RIVAS GALLONG BEFORE U.S. PRESS GETS TO HIM. HINTON

9. SECRETARY ENDERS GOES TO CONGRESS

On February 2, Assistant Secretary of State Thomas O. Enders went up to Capitol Hill to defend the Administration's "certification" that the United States' Salvadoran allies were "making a concerted and significant effort to comply with internationally recognized human rights." Following are excerpts from his testimony before the House Subcommittee on Western Hemisphere Affairs, chaired by Representative Michael Barnes, Democrat of Maryland.

Mr. ENDERS. Thank you very much, Mr. Chairman. It is a pleasure to be back. I do welcome the opportunity to come and discuss with the committee the certification that the President has made under law, and I welcome very much your opening remark that we should attempt to achieve a bipartisan approach to this very difficult problem that we all must face in Central America, a problem we cannot turn our backs on, however much we might wish to do so at times.

And let me say that on behalf of the administration that it is fully committed to the goals which were set out in the Foreign Assistance Act with regard to El Salvador. We understand the act to say yes, there is a challenge to our national security, and that is why economic and security assistance are authorized. But it says at the same time, we must use our assistance to help El Salvador control the violence in that country, make land reform work, develop a democratic process, and bring the murderers of our countrymen and countrywomen to justice. The certification that was made by the President last week shows that there has indeed been substantial progress toward each of the goals laid out in law.

PROGRESS IN THE VIOLATION OF HUMAN RIGHTS

Let me start if I could with the human rights issues. The law requires us to certify that El Salvador is making a concerted and significant effort to comply with internationally recognized human rights and is achieving substantial control over all elements of its armed forces. It does not say that human rights problems must be eliminated. It does demand progress.

There is no question that the human rights situation in El Salvador is deeply troubled, as is detailed in our annual report which has just been submitted to the Congress. The explosion of violence and counterviolence following the extreme left's receipt of outside support for guerrilla warfare has accentuated already high historic levels of violence, strained the system of justice to the breaking point, and eroded normal social constraints against violence. Countless violations of human rights have arisen from partisan animosities of both left and right, personal vendettas, retaliations, provocations, intimidation, and sheer brutality. The breakdown in this society has been profound and will take years to heal.

Accurate information—I think we all have found out that is very hard to establish. The responsibility for the overwhelming number of deaths is never legally determined nor usually accounted for by clear or coherent evidence. Seventy percent of the political murders known to our embassy were committed by unknown assailants. And there is much special pleading going on also in this. For example, many of you have read about something called the Legal Aid Office of the Archbishopric—Socorro Judico [sic] is its Spanish name; it is often cited in the international media. It strangely lists no victims of guerrilla and terrorist violence. Apparently they do not commit violence. In January the Apostolic Delegate Rivera y Damas deprived this legal aid office of any right to speak on behalf of the Archbishopric. That was a statement which was approved by the other bishops of El Salvador.

There is another organization, the Central American University, that collects statistics, too. Its bias may be apparent from the fact that it does include a category of persons killed by what I believe

Congressman Bonker referred to as paramilitary organizations. And they are called in Spanish *ajusticiados,* referring to persons that have received justice at the hands of their executioners.

Finally, I should say that the organization that calls itself the Human Rights Commission, which occasionally issues statistics from outside the country, just did recently on the incident in Mozote, has become itself a propaganda vehicle for the insurgency. It has no independent information-gathering capability.

ALLEGED MASSACRES

The most difficult of all to assess are the repeated allegations of massacres. The ambiguity lies in the fact that there are indeed incidents in which the noncombatants have suffered terribly at the hands of the guerrillas, rightist vigilantes, Government forces, or some or all of them, but at the same time the insurgency has repeatedly fabricated or inflated alleged mass murders as a means of propaganda.

Last year in a widely publicized case, the massacre of 1,000 people in a cave was related by Radio Venceremos. Actually this charge had just been repeated by a Belgian priest broadcasting for the radio. It was picked up in the media in convincing detail until geologists determined that there was no large cave in that region, and the atrocity could not have occurred.

There was another incident in April when 600 people were alleged to have been killed crossing the border from El Salvador into Honduras at the Rio Lempa. We asked the United Nations High Commissioner for Refugees representatives if they could have a look, and they did and found that there was no evidence of the outrage occurring.

On the other hand, as you yourself indicated in your opening statement, there are terrible incidents that occur. In my belief, one did occur 2 nights ago. The 19 people that died in San Salvador, I do not know whether there were weapons found there, whether these people were members of guerrilla organizations, but I find it hard to accept that there was a firefight, that this was a military action as had been alleged. And I deeply deplore as this Government does the excessive violence of the Salvadoran forces in this incident.

We sent two embassy officers down to investigate the reports that you referred to, Mr. Chairman, of the massacre in Mozote in the

Morazán Province. It is clear from the report that they gave that there has been a confrontation between the guerrillas occupying Mozote and attacking Government forces last December. There is no evidence to confirm that Government forces systematically massacred civilians in the operations zone, or that the number of civilians remotely approached the 733 or 926 victims cited in the press. I note they asked how many people there were in that canton, and were told probably not more than 300 in December, and there are many survivors including refugees now.

So we have to be very careful about trying to adduce evidence to the certification. We try, our embassy tries to investigate every report we receive, and we use every opportunity to impress on the El Salvador Government and army that we are serious about practicing human rights and that they must be, too.

The results are slow in coming. I would agree with you on that. But they are coming. Since October 1979, the Salvadoran authorities have done much more than repeatedly emphasize to officers and men the need to protect human rights. They have broken the traditional links between large landowners and the security forces by outlawing the paramilitary organization ORDEN. They have promulgated a military code of conduct that highlights the need to protect human rights. They have transferred, retired, cashiered, or punished 1,000 officers and men for various abuses of authority, and they have gradually reasserted their control over scattered local security force personnel by strengthening the authority of the high command.

LEVEL OF NONCOMBATANT VIOLENCE
In consequence, the level of noncombatant violence, to judge by our best estimates and by the trends that appear in the two other agencies that I cited, the figures that they have, appear to have declined by more than half over the last year.

Mr. Chairman, let me focus on this because I think it is a matter of some importance here. The American Civil Liberties Union report, which I have read with deep interest, was published in or contained information which was up through or up to September 1981. It did not have available to it the figures that our own Embassy has been very carefully compiling since September 1980, and it did not have the advantage of the short-term trends rather than the broad general treatment that that report or those reports which are issued weekly can provide.

I would say that the same is true of the Amnesty International report, which actually is without historical reference. It does not compare the earlier years, so that you cannot tell whether the crucial issue that has been posed by the certification process, the issue of whether there has been progress, can be judged, because I assume what is meant by progress in this instance is progress from the time of American involvement in El Salvador, progress recently, and sustained progress.

The figures show it. We have September, October, November, December figures for 1980 which show something on the order of 800, 779, 575, 665 political murders. That is for 1980. We have the same figures for this year which show September, 171, October, 161, November, 302. It shows December, 200. Our returns are showing markedly different numbers on the same methodology.

Let me be clear this is not a complete report. Nobody has a complete report. The embassy says that maybe it is within 30 percent of the total, but I cannot say for certain that that is the case. But nonetheless, it is a coherent attempt to answer the question that you have raised, are we getting something more than merely exhortations or sweet words, are we getting some results. This is the indication that I submit to you that we are.

Let me make clear, Mr. Chairman, the control of violence is at the center of our relationship with the Salvadoran Government. We mean to see it reduced to the minimum level consistent with existing civil strife. . . .

CERTIFICATION REMOVES INCENTIVE FOR MILITARY

I don't think that there can be any mistake at all in the El Salvadoran Army or Government about how seriously we believe in the need to get on with improving human rights and controlling violence.

Not only have we communicated this to them repeatedly at the very highest level of the American Government and through our Embassy there, but we have demonstrated I think quite straightforwardly and simply that there must be, for the continuation of support for the political reforms process in El Salvador, there must be a broad consensus in the United States that the behavior of the Government is acceptable, within acceptable norms for us.

In this case, there must be progress. I don't think that there is the shadow of a doubt of that down there.

Now, I have been in this business a long time, Mr. Chairman. One of the things that it seems to me is necessary in order to obtain performance from other countries is to be able to set standards that are reachable, to be able to identify steps that can be taken which are within their ability to deliver in a short time.

This law was completed and signed by the President on December 29. It was certified under law, by the way, on January 29, a month later, as required. I think that if we had gone to the El Salvadorans and said to them: "We have noted that you have made some improvement, but we must see an end to all politically motivated murders in which you might have had some hand, regardless of what your enemies do," they would have said to us simply—they would have regarded that the United States was pulling out with a massive blow to the psychology of that society, which would have interpreted it as an American abandonment.

I do not think that that would have been an advisable tactic, but I think the message is there.

Let me say one other thing. The Salvadoran Army and security forces are decentralized and are only gradually being recentralized. They were decentralized in the past because there was an effort to provide checks and balances in a militarily run government between four services and also to prevent the accumulation of too much power in any one hand in the center over the cities.

It takes a long time to pull that back into a disciplined structure that knows how to deal with human rights. I don't think it does any good to ask an organization to transform itself overnight when you know it can't do that. But it can make progress.

Mr. BARNES. You say there cannot be a shadow of a doubt in the military of the importance of this issue to the United States and to continued support to them from the United States.

Yet, 2 or 3 days after the President makes the certification, by your own account and your testimony this afternoon, the military apparently—none of us know all the facts—engaged in what amounted to a rather tragic occurrence.

You said that you didn't think it was a firefight. Your best guess is that that is not what it was. The evidence reported in the newspapers is that some of those who were murdered had their hands tied behind their backs. Other witnesses testified to rapes of children by military personnel. This is a couple of days after the President makes the certification.

If the message has been sent, if it is so fully understood down there, what is the explanation for this?

Mr. ENDERS. Well, as I said just a moment ago I think it will be some time before the leaders of that society are able fully to assert control over all elements of those services what we have attempted to demonstrate and believe we have demonstrated, which is progress toward that goal, not achievement of the absolute standard which, for example, Representative Bonker has stated.

I am not trying to say to you, Mr. Chairman, that there will not be further incidents on both the left and right. I believe there will be. What we are attempting to do is to prevent them in the largest numbers possible, to diminish them.

It would appear that is the standard you have set. If in fact the standard that you have set is that there should be no such incidents in a country of civil strife, then it would be in effect tantamount to saying that we are not going to support this country.

Mr. BARNES. Do you know, or does anyone know, who was responsible for that particular action?

Mr. ENDERS. No, sir, someone may know. I do not know.

CIRCUMSTANCES WHICH WOULD CONSTITUTE
CUTOFF OF MILITARY AID

Mr. BARNES. Are there any circumstances that you can outline for the committee under which you would recommend to the President that assistance to the military government in El Salvador be suspended?

Mr. ENDERS. Well, clearly the President, if he believed that progress were not being made toward the goals that were set, would have to, under these conditions, not certify that. The question arises as to— and I am not able to address that—what would happen then, but we do not believe we are in that situation now. . . .

Mr. BARNES. The gentleman from Massachusetts, Mr. Studds.

Mr. STUDDS. Thank you, Mr. Chairman.

I think someone has done the President a grave disservice. Someone somewhere has obviously prevailed upon him to sign his name to that certification document. If there is anything left of the English language in this city after your long assault by your immediate superior, it is gone now because the President has just certified that up is down and in is out and black is white. I anticipate his telling us that war is peace at any moment.

As the chairman's calmer set of questions has set out clearly here—and I will attempt to remain calm also—there is no evidence of any kind from any source I know of or have heard of, outside this administration and the press of San Salvador—upon which our own Ambassador says we rely for official statistics—to bear out anything of any major substance set out by the President last week.

It is Amnesty International's considered opinion and I quote:

> After reviewing hundreds of detailed accounts reaching our organization, that in the majority of reported cases official security forces have been implicated and these human rights violations have occurred on such a massive scale—this is 1981—that they constitute a gross and consistent pattern of human rights abuses.
>
> Testimony received by Amnesty International implicates all branches of the Salvadoran security forces, whether military, military police or paramilitary, in human rights abuses aimed at the civilian population that had no part in the guerrilla activity.

For the record, I would like to ask you to provide this committee with the sources upon which this statement was based from the President's own certification: "Statistics compiled in El Salvador indicate decreased abuses by security forces."

INCIDENT AT MOZOTE

I would be interested if you could provide for the record the sources of these reassuring statements. I hope some of them are not from the controlled press in El Salvador.

May I say with respect to the incident 2 days ago in the slum section of San Salvador, referred to by several people earlier, without bothering to go back over the killings and rapes, this was not a small rural group of military going wild in the countryside, as you know. It was a planned, orchestrated action of which the military command appears to be quite proud.

It took place in San Salvador and was cold-blooded murder. There were no arrests, no prisoners, no collection of proof, no self-defense—just murder. The bodies, as you know, were found in the streets in the morning.

The only really unusual thing, as far as I can tell about this, is that it involved a reasonably large group rather than a few individuals and a family and was widely reported, as these things have come to be in the past couple weeks, in our own press.

Bodies have turned up every single day of the year, as you know, in El Salvador. What I would like to know is how long you think this administration can continue to shrug away stories of massacre, and torture, and murder of this type and how long you can downplay, as you did in your earlier remarks, killings, such as those which occurred at Mozote and the Rio Lempa before that, the murders of the church-women, the killing of the Archbishop, and an assassination in cold blood in November 1980 of the entire leadership of the opposition.

I don't understand why it is in the best interests of my country to associate itself with acts of terrorism of this sort. Whose guns, whose bullets killed those people in San Salvador this Sunday morning? Chances are they were paid for by our own taxpayers.

Mr. Secretary, the Bingham-Solarz language, which the President has now certified that the Government of El Salvador is in compliance with, was designed by this committee very, very carefully in conference with the Senate, a result of a 26-to-7 bipartisan vote, and designed to give you, the State Department, the executive branch, the leverage to compel the military junta in El Salvador to clean up its act.

I submit to you that you have now pronounced yourself—you, the Government, the President—by signing this certification, satisfied with the current Government's efforts.

Mr. ENDERS. No, sir.

Mr. STUDDS. You take empty rhetoric and call it reform. You accept promises without having demanded action. You look at a 14-month gap between a murder and the application of a lie detector test and call it an investigation.

We have given El Salvador more military aid than we have ever bestowed on any Latin American country, and it hasn't worked. In response, you—and you have had some experience in this area—

have resurrected the State Department approach to Vietnam: If it doesn't work, do more of it.

You have also said to us, in your statement, if, after Nicaragua, El Salvador is captured by a violent minority, who in Central America would not live in fear?

Mr. Secretary, you must know that El Salvador is at the moment captured by a violent minority. It has been run by a violent minority for the duration of this century, and unfortunately a violent minority supported by our own Government.

It seems to me that if you can rationalize—and I will obviously give you a chance to respond—but if one can rationalize signing the certification, as the President of the United States had done, one can rationalize just about anything.

We have said to the military by this certification in El Salvador, no matter what you do, because we think more important things are at stake—namely the decisive battle for Central America—go ahead, we are going to certify that you are in compliance. No matter what massacres, no matter who is killed, no matter whether the land reform program is falling apart, as the report said, whatever. Because we think the security of this country is at stake, we are going to certify your compliance.

There goes your leverage. There goes the full impact of the Bingham-Solarz language, designed to give to the Government of the United States something to hold over the heads of the military of El Salvador. You let them off the hook. If you will tell them their performance in the past couple of months and the past year is OK, you have told them they can do virtually anything they choose to do and the United States will continue to support them.

I suggest to you that this is just one more step, one more poke into that tar baby. How in the world are we going to get out of this one? [Applause.]

Mr. BARNES. The audience will please refrain. I would ask the audience to please not express—

Mr. STUDDS. Let me join the chairman in that. That was not my intention, Mr. Secretary. Those who can deal with tragedies of this dimension without some degree of emotion are those who have other powers to account to.

Mr. BARNES. The guests of the committee will not react to state-

ments of members of the committee or the witnesses. If they do, they
will be asked to leave the committee room.

The time of the gentleman has expired, but certainly the gentleman
and other members of the committee will welcome the response of
Secretary Enders to the questions that were posed.

Mr. ENDERS. I am not aware that any questions were posed in those
remarks by Mr. Studds. I would only say this, that the certification
which was made by the President is not an expression of satisfaction.

Clearly the land reform is not over. The important part of it, the
so-called section 207 part, is a long way from being carried through.
It will take probably another year, maybe another 2 years, before it
is done.

We intend to get it through. It is making progress. Clearly we have
talked a lot about violence. I don't think you and I would perhaps
differ all that much on how much violence remains. There is a substantial amount of violence. We intend to overcome it.

We have been asked to certify that there had been progress and
we think we can show that. We must have more progress. Elections
are only the first step toward a legitimate government. It has to be
followed by the constitution and the larger election for president and
for representatives to a parliament. We intend to see that go on, too.

We are not saying that we are satisfied. We are not saying to anybody
that you are off the hook. We are not saying that the United States
has only one interest here, security, and not its political and humanitarian interests. So, your statement is not accurate, either, as to what
we intend or to what is being heard. . . .

Mr. BARNES. The gentleman from New York.

LEVEL OF VIOLENCE IN EL SALVADOR

Mr. SOLARZ. I am somewhat concerned by the Orwellian tones of
this certification, in the sense that the President seems to be saying
the human rights situation is getting better, when everybody else says
it is getting worse. The President says that the insurgent forces are
unwilling to participate in elections as part of a negotiated settlement,
when the insurgents claim that they are in fact willing to participate
in elections as part of an equitable political resolution.

I would like to ask a number of questions about the certification itself. I gather that if in fact the President came to the conclusion that the realities of the situation there were such that it would not be possible to make a good-faith certification, that he would not have submitted such a certification to us.

Mr. ENDERS. Yes, sir.

Mr. SOLARZ. If that is the case, and I am glad to hear it is, would the President have found that condition No. 2 in the certification had been fulfilled if we had come to the conclusion that the level of Government-related violence had increased in 1981 over 1980?

Mr. ENDERS. Well, condition No. 2 is extending its full control over the armed forces. That obviously is open to a variety of interpretations. We have cited in that regard actions that have taken place and results. I assume that some balance of both would generally be required.

Mr. SOLARZ. My question is, if the U.S. Government had come to the conclusion that the level of violence which could be attributable to the Government and its security forces had increased rather than decreased in 1981 compared to 1980, would you still have certified that condition No. 2—namely, the Government of El Salvador is achieving substantial control over its armed forces—had been met? You claim the level of violence has gone down. If you had come to the opposite conclusion, would you still have submitted the certification on point No. 2?

Mr. ENDERS. Mr. Solarz, we have been given I guess an authoritative interpretation of that in the committee print, and I assume it is authoritative. It says the committee wants to make its intent clear. It expects that the President will certify that this condition has been fulfilled only if the Salvadoran Government has actually made substantial progress in gaining control over all elements of its armed forces. Substantial progress is the criterion which is put here. And the question would be, has substantial progress been made. And that is a question of steps taken, it is a question of results, is it not, or is it a mixture of both?

Mr. SOLARZ. The language in the Senate bill provided for condition No. 2 that the Government of El Salvador is moving to achieve control over the armed forces. That clearly contemplates steps taken. The language in the House bill provided that the Government in El Salvador is achieving substantial control over the armed forces. In the conference we agreed to remove the references contained in the Senate bill, because what we were interested in were not the steps taken but the actual results.

Leaving aside for a moment what steps were or were not taken, in the certification itself, the President pointed to the decline in the level of violence as evidence that the Government of El Salvador was in fact gaining substantial control over its own armed forces.

My question to you, and I would have assumed you would have responded fairly easily to this, is that if you had come to the opposite conclusion, namely that the level of violence had increased in 1981 in comparison to 1980, would you still have said that the Government of El Salvador is achieving substantial control over its armed forces?

Mr. ENDERS. Mr. Solarz, may I read back, because it seems to me that it has been the subject of some dispute here. May I say what the Foreign Affairs Committee said about this? I think it is significant here.

Mr. SOLARZ. Which Foreign Affairs Committee?

Mr. ENDERS. This Foreign Affairs Committee said about this language. In consideration of the second condition of this subsection, the one we are talking about——

Mr. SOLARZ. Are you talking about the conference report, or the bill as it passed the House?

Mr. ENDERS. This committee, sir. It said in consideration of the second condition of this subsection the committee took into account the difficult nature of the task confronting the Government of El Salvador in gaining substantial control over all elements of its armed forces. The committee therefore did not include in the certification requirement a condition that the Government of El Salvador has to achieve total and complete control over all elements of its armed forces. Instead it provided that the President must be able to certify that the Salvadoran Government is achieving a substantial control, a clear distinction made by you.

NUMBER OF NONCOMBATANT DEATHS

Mr. SOLARZ. I submit you have been utterly unresponsive to the question. You claimed in the certification that the level of violence had decreased over the last year. Could you tell us how many people in your judgment were killed over the course of the last year? Can you give us a specific figure provided by the U.S. Embassy?

Mr. ENDERS. The Embassy provided an estimate of roughly 6,000 people, noncombatant deaths in the course of last year.

Mr. SOLARZ. That are attributable to the Government, or overall?

Mr. ENDERS. It was unable to attribute more than 30 percent of that total to one side or the other. Seventy percent is unknown.

Mr. SOLARZ. Do you know what the level of noncombatant deaths was in 1980?

Mr. ENDERS. The figure that was cited I think in our human rights report of 1980 was 9,000.

Mr. SOLARZ. You therefore come to the conclusion that the level of noncombatant deaths went down from 9,000 to 6,000?

Mr. ENDERS. Not on that basis, sir.

Mr. SOLARZ. You just testified that in 1980 in the human rights report you said there were 9,000 noncombatant deaths, and in the certification, while we did not mention a figure, it was based to some extent on the conclusion reached by the Embassy that the number of noncombatant deaths was 6,000.

Mr. ENDERS. The trend during the year.

Mr. SOLARZ. Could you tell us on what basis the Embassy and the administration came to the conclusion that the number of noncombatant deaths had dropped from 9,000 to 6,000? Where is the evidence?

Mr. ENDERS. I would be glad to present the evidence to you. Each week the Embassy does collect evidence which comes from a number of sources. Radio Venceremos is one. Local press reports of deaths are another. Local radio reports, other reports that are available through Government sources. It is an eclectic process.

Mr. SOLARZ. That is the basis rather than some kind of on-the-scene body count, which I gather is not the way in which we collect these figures.

Mr. ENDERS. No.

Mr. SOLARZ. How can you possibly account for the fact that in 1981 our Embassy, based on Radio Venceremos, on death notices in the press, and on other sources, came to the conclusion that there were 6,000 deaths, whereas Archbishop Rivera y Damas estimated that there were 11,700 deaths, the legal aid office estimated there were 12,500 deaths, the Central American University estimated there were over 13,000 deaths? Why has Amnesty International and every other organization that has reported on the human rights situation there said that the level of killings in the country is either at or above the levels that existed in 1980, whereas our Embassy claims it has dropped by 33 percent?

Mr. ENDERS. The totals are different, but the trends are the same. If you look at the trends in the legal aid office, and I pointed out to you earlier something about its own tilt, you will find the same downward trend. That is also true of the statistics collected by the Central American University, but again it has a particular prejudice. They all show this downward trend during the year. That is the basis for the statement, sir.

Mr. SOLARZ. I have a final question. Clearly the critical consideration is not the overall number of deaths, but the number of deaths for which the security forces and the armed forces of the Government of El Salvador are responsible.

Mr. ENDERS. Obviously.

Mr. SOLARZ. On what basis do we decide what percentage of the noncombatant deaths, to attribute to the security forces or the armed forces, and on what basis have we come to the conclusion that the number of noncombatant deaths attributable to the armed forces and the security forces has declined from 1980 to 1981?

Mr. ENDERS. The total number of noncombatant deaths calculated by any one of these three organizations appears to be on a downward trend from month to month. That is the basis, as I said earlier. We are not able to attribute very many of those deaths to one side or the other, and we are not sure even of those that are attributed whether they make sense or not. The point is here that there has been, according to each of these statistics, a downward trend.

The Government has been attempting to get control over it. We find that the insurgents claim that whenever they commit violence it is justified because it is in defense of a new order, and therefore we are not sure that they intend to contribute to lesser violence, and so we assume that there has been some effect, but we do not know in detail how many deaths are caused by people related to security forces.

Mr. SOLARZ. If you say yourself we have no way of knowing how many of the noncombatant deaths are attributable to the security or armed forces, I cannot understand how you then can with a straight face say to the Congress that you believe that the level of Government-supported violence has declined. Even if your statistics are right in suggesting that the overall number of noncombatant deaths has declined, that does not necessarily prove that the number of Government-inflicted noncombatant deaths has declined.

Mr. ENDERS. May I make another comment on this? I do not know whether this can be pressed any further, given the fact that none of us know. For example, in the last 7 months radio Venceremos claimed that it inflicted 2,000 casualties, and it regards the infliction of casualties as a legitimate instrument of revolution and war. I have not heard any statement from anybody representing the insurgents that say that they think that human rights violations must be curbed by them, that this is a problem on their part, so I wonder whether you can attribute what progress has been achieved to the insurgents. The only way that your remark could in logic hold up would be if you said that all the improvements have been done by the insurgents. They do not think any improvement is necessary. . . .

Mr. BARNES. The Chair recognizes the gentlelady from Rhode Island for 5 minutes. . . .

Mrs. SCHNEIDER. Well, I think that testimony here by the members of the committee has very clearly indicated a great deal of displeasure with the absence of any convincing details insofar as satisfying the Members of Congress that the Salvadoran Government is engaged in a "consistent pattern of human rights violations."

And I was wondering if you might be willing to make a commitment to this committee to indicate that the State Department might change their modus operandi in verifying any occurrences of human rights violations.

LEVEL OF U.S. PRESENCE IN EL SALVADOR

Mr. ENDERS. One of the things we have attempted to avoid is the buildup of a very large embassy in the area. I was just asked a question about our military personnel, whether that would go up or not. We have obviously been trying to keep it from being too high. We have five political officers that are responsible for the entire conduct of relations with this Government in the political field, reporting on it, plus all the investigations we do.

I don't know whether we get the best we can on this, but frankly, we do not have people who go out with the units as advisers, you know. These are military trainers. They stay behind. We don't propose to have them and don't think it would be a good idea to have them. We don't know whether we want to send our political officers off into all the areas where there is firing going on to get more statistics or information. We do try to investigate what we can. Now, I can pledge—yes, I realize, Mr. Chairman, that one of the things that this certification process imposes on us is an information requirement. And the requirement to get as credible and detailed information as we can. We are doing everything we can to meet that requirement, and I would be glad to discuss with you how we can do more on this. But we obviously have a certain number of limits.

Mrs. SCHNEIDER. I think that I was not recommending necessarily that the political officers be involved in doing the body counts. But I think it would be appropriate for the State Department to make recommendations as to how they might change their information basis and perhaps use information from other sources or consolidate it, because I would think the members of this committee will continue to be very perplexed by looking at a broad spectrum of different numbers, and being caught up in a situation of not really knowing whom to believe.

So that is my only request and recommendation. I think it would be useful if the State Department would put together a paper or series of alternatives that would say how you might go about changing your modus operandi.

Mr. ENDERS. Let me say in this regard that whenever there is an alleged major incident such as the Mozote incident, we go around and we talk to all of the organizations that claim to have some knowledge.

For example, we went to talk to the Legal Aid Society, because it had put out a figure saying there were almost 1,000 people killed in the massacre. We asked how do you know, did you send somebody there? No, they hadn't sent anybody there, so that eliminated one source of information.

Sometimes they do know. Sometimes they have some information. So we do try to do that. I agree with you that we are going to have to produce more and more detailed information. We will try to do so. . . .

10. THE AMBASSADOR AND THE DEFENSE MINISTER, II

On February 3rd, even as Secretary Enders was testifying before Congress for a second day, Ambassador Hinton, in San Salvador, made another attempt to raise the question of El Mozote with General García. His cable reporting on the meeting was released in November 1993.

R 030559Z FEB 82
FM SECSTATE WASHDC
CONFIDENTIAL STATE 028027
EXDIS - MILITARY ADDEE HANDLE AS SPECAT EXCLUSIVE
E. O. 12065: RDS-1 2/1/02 (HINTON, DEANE R.) OR-M
SUBJ: (C) MORE ON ALLEGED MORAZAN MASSACRE; SAN ANTONIO ABAD:
AND NUNS

1. (C-ENTIRE TEXT.)

2. SINCE DEFENSE ATTACHES HAVE BEEN TRYING FOR DAYS WITHOUT SUCCESS TO IDENTIFY UNITS OF SALVADORAN ARMY IN EL MOZOTE AT TIME MASSACRE ALLEGEDLY OCCURRED, I QUERIED MILGP COMMANDER TODAY IF IT WERE POSSIBLE HIGH COMMAND DID NOT KNOW WHERE AND WHEN THEIR FIELD FORCES OPERATED. NO IT WAS NOT, HE TOLD ME. ACCORDINGLY I ASKED HIM TO GET ANSWER.

3. HE WENT TO CHIEF OF STAFF, WHO SAID DEFENSE MINISTER WANTED NO ONE OTHER THAN HIMSELF TO DEAL WITH THAT QUESTION.

4. THIS AFTERNOON I CALLED ON GENERAL GARCIA. WE JOSHED A BIT AS IS OUR WONT, THEN GARCIA COMPLIMENTED ME ON MY WASHINGTON POST INTERVIEW WHICH HE SAID PUT THINGS EXACTLY RIGHT. I THANKED HIM BUT SAID HE HAD BETTER KEEP THAT OPINION TO HIMSELF SINCE I UNDERSTOOD TOM ENDERS HAD TODAY TOLD THE LONG COMMITTEE THAT HE DID NOT SHARE MY VIEWS ABOUT MILITARY MATTERS.

5. WITH THE MENTION OF ENDERS, I EXPLAINED TO GARCIA THAT TOM HAD TODAY GONE TO CONGRESS TO DEFEND THE ADDITIONAL 55 MILLION IN MILITARY ASSISTANCE TO EL SALVADOR AND THAT FOR A GOOD PART OF THE REST OF THIS WEEK HE WOULD BE BEFORE CONGRESSIONAL COMMITTEES EXPLAINING THE PRESIDENT'S CERTIFICATION WHICH PERMITTED CONTINUED AID TO EL SALVADOR. IN THIS CONNECTION, I SAID, REPORTS PUBLISHED IN THE WASHINTON POST AND THE NEW YORK TIMES ABOUT ALLEGED MORAZAN MASSACRE AND THE INCIDENT OF NIGHT BEFORE LAST CAUSED GREAT CONCERN. I ADDED THERE WAS ONE GOOD SENTENCE IN THE BONNER PIECE AND READ TO HIM THE SENTENCE SAYING THERE WAS NO INDEPENDENT CONFIRMATION WHO DID THE KILLINGS AND HOW MANY HAD BEEN KILLED.

6. HE SAID THE MORAZAN BUSINESS WAS A "NOVELA", PURE MARXIST PROPAGANDA DEVOID OF FOUNDATION.

7. I SAID IT WAS CLEARLY PROPAGANDA THAT ITS TIMING HAD BEEN CAREFULLY CALCULATED BUT THERE WERE SO MANY DETAILS THAT IT WAS DIFFICULT TO DEAL WITH THE STORIES. I WAS PARTICULARLY CONCERNED OVER THE REFERENCES TO THE ATLACATL BATTALION AND LTS. CACERES AND ORTEGA. COULD HE TELL ME IF THE ATLACATL BATTALION HAD ACTUALLY BEEN ENGAGED AT EL MOZOTE. COULD HE TELL ME WHO LTS. CACERES AND ORTEGA WERE. HE SAID IMMEDIATELY THAT THERE WAS A MAJOR CACERES WHO WAS THE DEPUTY COMMANDER OF THE ATLACATL BATTALION AND WHO WAS A STRAIGHTFORWARD, HONORABLE SOLDIER WHO WOULD NEVER HAVE KILLED WOMEN AND CHILDREN AS DESCRIBED IN THE STORY. HE DID NOT KNOW WHO LT. ORTEGA MIGHT BE BUT HE WOULD INQUIRE. AFTER SOME FURTHER DISCUSSION, HE SAID THE ATLACATL BATTALION HAD BEEN AT EL MOZOTE DURING THE DECEMBER SWEEP, BUT HE REITERATED THAT THE STORY WAS A PACK OF LIES. HE WOULD HOWEVER, TALK TO MAJOR CACERES AND GET HIS STORY SO THAT HE WOULD BE PREPARED WHEN HE GOT TO WASHINGTON AND HE WOULD ALSO EXAMINE THE DAILY ACTION REPORTS RECEIVED FROM UNITS IN THE OPERATION REPORTING ON FRIENDLY, ENEMY, AND OTHER CASUALTIES TO SEE WHAT THEY SHOWED. HE ASKED ME TO LEAVE WITH HIM THE STORIES AND I DID SO ADDING AS A SWEETENER THE WASHINGTON POST EDITORIAL OF JANUARY 29 SUPPORTING OUR COMMON POLICIES. AS FOR THE SAN ANTONIO ABAD INCIDENT, THAT TOO WAS BEING DISTORTED BY THE

PRESS AS PART OF A CAMPAIGN. WHAT HAD HAPPENED WAS THAT
NEIGHBORS HAD REPORTED THE EXISTENCE OF SUSPICIOUS MEETINGS IN
A HOUSE. WHEN TROOPS OF THE FIRST BRIGADE WENT TO INVESTIGATE,
THEY HAD BEEN FIRED UPON. BRIGADE TROOPS RESPONDED AND THOSE
KILLED HAD BEEN KILLED IN ACTION. MOREOVER, WEAPONS HAD BEEN
SEIZED. PROOF THAT EVENTS HAD BEEN SUBSEQUENTLY COLORED BY
LEFTIST PROPAGANDISTS WAS THAT THE INVESTIGATING JUDGE HAD
BEEN TOLD NOTHING ABOUT ANY RAPES, WHICH OF COURSE HAD NOT
TAKEN PLACE, NOR HAD MORE THAN TWO WOMEN BEEN KILLED, BOTH
OF WHOM HAD BEEN GUERRILLAS. HE HAD DISCUSSED INCIDENT
DIRECTLY WITH COL. PALACIOS, BRIGADE COMMANDER, AND HE WAS
SURE OF HIS FACTS.

8. I AGREED WITH HIM THAT AGAIN PROPAGANDISTS WERE EXPLOITING
ISSUE BUT I ALLOWED TO HAVING SOME PROBLEMS IN UNDERSTANDING
ALLEGATIONS THAT SOME OF THE DEAD SHOWED SIGNS OF TORTURE
AND MANY OF HAVING BEEN KILLED WITH BULLETS TO THE HEAD.

9. HE DID NOT TRY TO EXPLAIN INCONSISTENCY BUT AVERRED AGAIN
THAT THESE STORIES WERE A PLOT TO DISCREDIT THE ARMED FORCES AT
THIS CRITICAL JUNCTURE. I SAID TIMING WAS INDEED UNFORTUNATE
BUT IT SEEMED TO ME THAT THERE WAS SOME FACTUAL BASIS FOR THE
EXAGGERATED STORIES AND I COULD ONLY URGE HIM ONCE AGAIN TO
EXHORT HIS COMMANDER TO EXERCISE MORE RIGOROUS CONTROL OVER
THEIR FORCES.

10. GARCIA THEN SAID IT WAS INTERESTING THE LEFT WAS NO LONGER
SAYING ANYTHING ABOUT THE NUNS CASE AND WE AGREED THAT THIS
WAS BECAUSE REAL PROGRESS HAS BEEN MADE AND THEY KNOW IT.

11. HE THEN SAID HE WANTED TO TELL ME OF GROWING RESENTMENT
IN THE ARMY OVER PROPOSALS FROM POLITICIANS, THAT THE
ANNOUNCEMENT OF THE TURNOVER OF THE ACCUSED FOR TRIAL MIGHT
BE MADE BY POLITICIANS AND NOT BY THE ARMED FORCES. FROM THIS I
INFERRED THAT HE AND DUARTE ARE BICKERING OVER WHO WILL SAY
WHAT, WHEN. HE ASKED ME FOR MY VIEW.

12. I REPLIED THAT IN MY PERSON OPINION IT WAS NOT TOO IMPORTANT
WHO MADE THE ANNOUNCEMENT BUT THAT IT WAS CRUCIAL THAT THE

PRISONERS NOT BE TURNED OVER TO THE CIVILIAN AUTHORITIES UNTIL THE CIVILIAN AUTHORITIES HAD SORTED OUT HOW TO HANDLE THE PROSECUTION. I SAID I HAD JUST LEARNED THAT AS OF SATURDAY, FISCALIA (ATTORNEY GENERAL'S OFFICE) WAS FAR FROM HAVING DEVELOPED A PROSECUTION STRAGEGY THAT WOULD WORK. NO ONE, IN MY VIEW, NEITHER THE ARMED FORCES NOR THE POLITICIANS, NOR MY GOVERNMENT COULD BENEFIT FROM A LACK OF CARE ON JUDICIAL QUESTIONS WERE THAT TO UNDO THE SPLENDID EFFORTS OF THE MILITARY INVESTIGATION. WHAT WE WANTED WAS FOR THE KILLERS TO BE BROUGHT EFFECTIVELY TO JUSTICE. ONCE THE CASE WAS READY FOR PRESENTATION DETAILED ANNOUNCEMENT SHOULD OF COURSE BE MADE BY WHOM WAS NOT MY PRINCIPAL CONCERN AND, IN THE MEANTIME, GENERAL STATEMENTS SUCH AS HE HAD MADE LAST WEEK COULD BE USEFUL.

13. HE ASKED ME WHEN I THOUGHT THE CIVILIAN AUTHORITIES WOULD BE READY. I SAID I HOPED WITHIN A FEW DAYS. HE SAID HE HOPED SO, TOO, BECAUSE THE GUARD, IN ADDITION TO ITS OTHER PROBLEMS, WANTED TO BE FREED OF GUARDING THE PRISONERS.

14. I TOOK MY LEAVE. HE THANKED ME FOR ALERTING HIM TO THE NEED TO BE WELL PREPARED FOR HIS VISIT TO WASHINGTON, AND I WISHED HIM A GOOD TRIP.

15. COMMENT: GARCIA'S ACCOUNT IN PARAGRAPH 7 OF SAN ANTONIO ABAD INCIDENT IS INCONSISTENT BOTH WITH THE RELEASE ISSUED BY THE HIGH COMMAND LISTING MULTIPLE LOCATIONS THROUGH THE NIGHT AND WITH REPORT BY SE PALACIOS TO [DEFENSE ATTACHE] THAT THERE WAS A FIRE WHICH CAUSED CONFUSION AND LED TO PERHAPS INNOCENT PEOPLE BEING KILLED.
HINTON

11. THE WAR AT HOME

In Washington, meanwhile, where Thomas Enders and other Reagan Administration officials were testifying to both houses of Congress about the certification, the debate over the United

States' policy toward El Salvador was growing in intensity and bitterness. On February 10th, the *Wall Street Journal* devoted its entire editorial column to a lengthy piece entitled "The Media's War," which set off an angry dispute over "bias" in the work of American reporters covering the Salvadoran war. This dispute, carried out in editorial columns and on television discussion shows, went on through the early spring. In August, the editors of the *Times* recalled Raymond Bonner from Central America.

Following is the full text of the *Wall Street Journal* editorial—which the *Journal*'s editors allowed to be reprinted only after imposing rather unusual conditions (see "The War At Home, II" below).

The Media's War

Reprinted with permission of *The Wall Street Journal* © 1982 Dow Jones & Company, Inc. All rights reserved.

A crucial debate on whether the U.S. will step up its aid to the government of El Salvador or leave that government to the tender mercies of Fidel Castro is shaping up in Congress. Central to the debate are public perceptions of what has been going on in El Salvador, and it is quite evident that those perceptions are badly confused. No small part of the problem, it seems to us, is the way the struggle is being covered by the U.S. press.

The El Salvador story is complex. The killing that has been under way there for a decade has reflected a society trying to wrench itself out of Latin-style feudalism. Extremists of the right and left do most of their murder in the dark of the night. Some of both factions are soldiers, but both have also learned long ago the trick of dressing in military uniforms to confuse their victims. Both sides wage propaganda, aimed mainly at the U.S. and Europe. In such a whirlpool the truth is hard to discern. (See the Stanley Karnow article nearby about the difficulties of establishing the "truth" during the Vietnam war.)

*   *   *

Take the recent controversy over charges of a "massacre" by an elite batallion of the El Salvadoran army. On January 27, Raymond Bonner of the *New York Times* and Alma Guillermoprieto of the *Washington Post* simultaneously reported on a visit to rebel territory, repeating interviews in which they were told that hundreds of civilians were killed in the village of Mozote in December. Thomas O. Enders, assistant secretary of state for Inter-American affairs, later cast doubt on the reports. There had been a military operation but no systematic killing of civilians, he said, and anyway the population of the village was only 300 before the attack in which 926 people supposedly died.

When a correspondent is offered a chance to tour rebel territory, he certainly ought to accept, and to report what he sees and hears. But there is such a thing as being overly credulous. Mr. Bonner reported "it is clear" the massacre happened, while Miss Guillermoprieto took pains to say that reporters had been "taken to tour" the site by guerrillas with the purpose of showing their control and providing evidence of the massacre. In other words, whatever the mixture of truth or fabrication, this was a propaganda exercise.

*   *   *

Realistically, neither the press nor the State Department has the power to establish conclusively what happened at Mozote in December, and we're sure the sophisticated editors of the Times recognize as much. Yet as an institution their paper has closed ranks behind a reporter out on a limb, waging a little campaign to bolster his position by impugning his critics. A "news analysis" charged the government of sowing confusion by questioning press reports "without presenting detailed evidence to support its position." The analysis posed the question of "how American diplomats gather information abroad," but not the same question about American reporters.

Further, Times columnist Sydney H. Schanberg launched a personal attack on Mr. Enders. In a column entitled "The Can-Do Bombardier," Mr. Schanberg pointed out that the assistant secretary had been a briefing officer in the Phnom Penh embassy in 1973. Mr. Schanberg suggested Mr. Enders was not to be believed then about American bombing in Cambodia. The unstated implication was that Mr. Enders is lying about El Salvador today.

The issue of government credibility of course came to dominate press coverage of Vietnam, but we wonder whether the press is prudent to start this kind of battle just now. The experience of "Jimmy's World" and the Carter Blair House tapes may account for the greater caution displayed in the *Washington Post*'s version of the Mozote story. But the *Times* has not been without its own experience. Most pointedly, its columnists Anthony Lewis and Flora Lewis were taken in last year by a spurious "dissent paper" purporting to show strong objections within the State Department to U.S. Salvadoran policy.

*   *   *

Mr. Schanberg's own experience in Cambodia is instructive in a broader way. He won a well-deserved Pulitzer Prize for heroically staying behind at the fall of Phnom Penh and writing dramatic dispatches describing the start of Khmer Rouge butchery. But this development came as a surprise to him. The month before the topic he chose for "news analysis" was the "the credibility gap" occasioned by "contradictions and inconsistencies" in U.S. government statements on precisely when the Lon Nol government would run out of money and ammunition.

"If the other side took over, they would kill all the educated people, the teachers, the artists, the intellectuals and that would be a step backward toward barbarism," an American embassy official warned Mr. Schanberg. After reporting this quote he went on to write that an insurgent victory would mean execution or exile "for Marshal Lon Nol and his corrupt entourage at the Presidential palace." But, he added, "unlike Administration officials in Washington and embassy officials here, the Cambodians . . . do not talk much about barbarism or bloodbaths. The average peasant is achingly wearied by the war. . . . He only desires its end. . . . 'When they come' said one businessman of the insurgents 'the war will be over.' "

If Mr. Schanberg had been less preoccupied with Washington's credibility he and the rest of us might have learned earlier of the tragedy that was to ensue. It turned out that U.S. government duplicity was not the big story in Cambodia.

*   *   *

Now, we have no special desire to pick on the *New York Times,* a paper we hold in the highest esteem and whose editors we admire. But while the Bonner-Enders dispute is the most dramatic case, the essential points apply far more broadly. R. Bruce McColm, Central American specialist at Freedom House, has written an excellent monograph titled "El Salvador: Peaceful Revolution or Armed Struggle?" His remarks on the press are worth attention.

"Political bias, ideology, poor sources and deliberate misinformation" are among the sins he charges. Why, he asks, was there almost no reporting of lengthy press conferences with a former guerrilla commander and two captured Nicaraguan pilots that revealed Cuban and Nicaraguan support for the guerrillas? He reports that the Latin press performed far better than the American press.

When it became clear that El Salvador might be another Vietnam, Mr. McColm notes, a host of journalistic adventurers descended on the place. "Noticeably missing, especially among the television press, were people who spoke Spanish, had experience in Central or Latin America, knew anything about El Salvador's history or had battle experience. Much of the American media, it would seem, was dominated by a style of reporting that grew out of Vietnam—in which Communist sources were given greater credence than either the U.S. government or the government it was supporting.

*   *   *

As any viewer of Warren Beatty in "Reds" will appreciate, journalistic romanticizing of revolutionaries is anything but new. But you would think that after being burned enough times serious editors would start to appreciate how such stories tend to end. John Reed's 1917 love affair with the Russian Bolsheviks, currently getting a rerun in "Reds," had no room for any fear that a Stalin might emerge from among his heroes. Theodore H. White has the honesty to admit he never imagined what his

Chinese Communists would become (though without admitting that on this crucial point his home-office editor, Henry Luce, was right all along). An even more penetrating memoir of disillusionment came after the Spanish Civil War by the incomparably honest George Orwell; his "Homage to Catalonia" ought to be required reading for any young correspondent headed for a guerrilla battle.

More recently, Herbert Matthews's glorification of Fidel Castro in the 1950s became a permanent embarrassment to the *New York Times*. David Halberstam and successors played a key role in ridding Vietnam of the supposedly repressive Diem regime, only to help usher in an even bloodier future. Iran is now free of the Shah's secret police and Nicaragua of Somoza; instead we have Khomeini killing the infidel and the Sandinistas closing *La Prensa* and imprisoning business leaders for "antirevolutionary" utterances.

Are we going to have to watch this script replayed again in El Salvador, or can we in the press succeed in bringing some perspective to the story? By now we ought to realize that atrocities, some of them well-documented, have been committed by both sides. We ought to recognize the exceeding improbability of a guerrilla success leading to anything but a Cuban-dominated regime. We ought, especially, to recognize that the incumbent government, for all its problems with right-wing terror, has followed such policies as attempting land reform and nationalizing the banks of the oligarchs, and that it is trying to hold elections. The press will have failed if, in the whirlpool of confusion, these realities are lost.

12. A REPORT FROM HONDURAS

On February 4th—even as the debate over El Mozote was raging on Capitol Hill—an American diplomat and a member of the staff of the House Foreign Affairs Committee visited Colomancagua, a large refugee camp in Honduras that held most of the Salvadorans who had fled over the border from Morazán. What the Americans learned in Colomancagua might have had a direct bearing on the El Mozote debate, but they did not report their findings to Washington until almost two weeks later. In the event, their report was not made public.

P R 172028Z FEB 82
FM AMEMBASSY TEGUCIGALPA
TO SECSTATE WASHDC PRIORITY 6688
INFO AMEMBASSY BOGOTA
C O N F I D E N T I A L TEGUCIGALPA 1250
SUBJ: REPORTS OF ALLEGED MASSACRE BY SALVADORAN ARMY

I. C - ENTIRE TEXT

2. SUMMARY: DURING FEBRUARY 4 VISIT TO SALVADORAN REFUGEE CAMP AT COLOMONCAGUA, POLOFF AND VISITING HOUSE FOREIGN AFFAIRS COMMITTEE STAFFER TOM SMEETON INTERVIEWED SEVERAL NEWLY ARRIVED SALVADORAN FAMILIES FROM MORAZAN DEPARTMENT. LATTER REPORTED A MILITARY SWEEP IN MORAZAN DECEMBER 7 TO 17 WHICH THEY CLAIM RESULTED IN LARGE NUMBERS OF CIVILIAN CASUALTIES AND PHYSICAL DESTRUCTION, LEADING TO THEIR EXODUS. NAMES OF VILLAGES CITED COINCIDE WITH NEW YORK TIMES ARTICLE OF JANUARY 28 SAME SUBJECT. END SUMMARY.

3. POLOFF AND SMEETON WERE INFORMED UPON ARRIVAL AT COLOMONCAGUA THAT 279 NEW SALVADORAN REFUGEES HAD ARRIVED ON JANUARY 15, THE FIRST SIGNIFICANT NUMBER OF NEW ARRIVALS SINCE SEPTEMBER 1981. DURING SUBSEQUENT INTERVIEW, ONE REFUGEE FAMILY SAID THEY WERE FROM CERRO PANDO, NEAR MEANGUERA, WHICH THEY CLAIMED WAS ATTACKED ON DECEMBER 14. THEY SAID THIS WAS THE THIRD MILITARY SWEEP THROUGH THEIR VILLAGE, AND THE MOST INTENSE. IN PAST SWEEPS, A FEW CIVILIAN CASUALTIES HAD BEEN REGISTERED; THIS TIME, THEY CLAIMED, HOUSES WERE BURNED AND MANY RESIDENTS KILLED. AFTER ONE FAMILY FLED THEIR VILLAGE, THEY SPENT A MONTH HIDING OUT IN THE MOUNTAINS AND EVENTUALLY MADE THEIR WAY TO HONDURAS WITH THE HELP OF FAMILIES ON THE WAY WHO GAVE DIRECTIONS AND PROVISIONS.

4. ANOTHER REFUGEE FAMILY SAID THEY WERE FROM NEAR CERRO EL PEDRERO. THIS HAD BEEN THE FOURTH SWEEP OF THEIR DISTRICT. THIS TIME THEY FLED FOR THEIR LIVES. THEY SAID MANY WERE LEFT BEHIND WHO WOULD COME TO HONDURAS IF THEY KNEW THE WAY AND IF THEY COULD GATHER SUFFICIENT SUPPLIES FOR THE JOURNEY.

5. COMMENT: MOST SIGNIFICANT ELEMENT IN REFUGEES REPORTS IS THEIR DECISION TO FLEE AT THIS TIME WHEN IN THE PAST THEY HAD REMAINED DURING SWEEPS. THIS LENDS CREDIBILITY TO REPORTED GREATER MAGNITUDE AND INTENSITY OF THE GOES MILITARY OPERATION IN NORTHERN MORAZAN.

NEGROPONTE

CONFIDENTIAL

13. THE EXHUMATION

In October 1990, a survivor of the massacre, Pedro Chicas Romero of La Joya, went to the Court of the First Instance in San Francisco Gotera and petitioned to open an investigation into the killings. The following May, members of Tutela Legal, the human rights office of the Archbishopric of San Salvador, who were serving as legal advisers to Chicas and others, invited members of the Argentine Forensic Anthropology Team to come to San Salvador to study the possibility of exhuming the site. (The Argentine Forensic Anthropology Team was formed in Buenos Aires, in 1984, during the exhumations of those who had been "disappeared" under the previous military dictatorship.) In April 1992, overcoming a series of obstacles presented by the Salvadoran government, three of the Argentines were appointed "expert witnesses" on the case. The following October, the Truth Commission appointed them "technical consultants" to the Commission.

On October 13, 1992, four Argentine experts—Mercedes Doretti, Patricia Bernardi, Luis Fondebrider and Claudia Bernardi—began work at El Mozote. They were assisted by technicians from El Salvador's Medical–Legal Institute and the Special Investigative Unit. They completed the exhumation of the sacristy on November 17, whereupon the remains were transported to the Medical–Legal Institute, on the outskirts of San Salvador. A team of American experts—including Clyde C. Snow, Robert H. Kirschner, Douglas D. Scott, and John H. Fitzpatrick—performed a forensic investigation.

Following are the reports the Argentine anthropologists and the American forensic experts submitted to the Truth Commission.

Argentine Team of Forensic Anthropologists Archaeological Report

I. INTRODUCTION

The purpose of this report is to describe the results of the archaeological excavation in one of the areas which witnesses say were the burial-places of several dozen victims of the events of 11 December 1981 in the village of El Mozote.

The village of El Mozote is in the canton of Guacamaya (Meanguera jurisdiction) in the department of Morazán. The village has been uninhabited for several years. A dirt road—the only road—leads into the village. On either side of the road, there is a row of dilapidated houses, some built of concrete, others of adobe. Towering over the area are two mountain peaks, El Chingo and Las Cruces. About 40 metres inside the village, there is an open space known as "El Llano de El Mozote," a kind of central square, measuring approximately 30 by 20 metres.

Some 30 metres to the north-east of that geographical centre, are the ruins of the church (also known as "La Ermita") and El Mozote convent. In accordance with the judge's ruling, the excavation began in the area of the convent, an area that will hereinafter be referred to as "Site No. 1."

Archaeological work at Site No. 1 began at 10.30 a.m. on 13 October 1992, and continued until 17 November 1992. During that period, the site was excavated by rotating teams from the Institute of Forensic Medicine of El Salvador and the Commission on Criminal Acts, and on a permanent basis, by three members of the Argentine Team of Forensic Anthropologists. On 23, 26 and 27 October, the Spanish forensic anthropologist, José Reverte Comas, visited the excavation site. Members of the Human Rights Division of the United Nations Observer Mission in El Salvador (ONUSAL) and members of the United Nations Commission on the Truth were frequent visitors to the site. The police contingent of ONUSAL, by maintaining a round-the-clock presence at the site, ensured that evidence was not tampered with. No incidents occurred while excavation was in progress, and the work proceeded normally. Only the weather caused occasional interruptions.

In concluding this introduction, we should note that the hypotheses put forward—which are based directly on the archaeological finds— are attempts to arrive at logical explanations for those finds. When the hypotheses lead to a single possible explanation, that result will be termed a conclusion.

SITE NO. 1

What we have designated Site No. 1 is a rectangular structure measuring about 31.5 square metres (6.94 by 4.63 metres) and surrounded by a stone wall (or foot wall) 50 centimetres high. This stone wall provides a foundation for the building and a support for the walls. The remains of the church are on one side of the stone wall. On the south-western side of the stone wall, there is an opening about 85 centimetres wide, which corresponds to the area where the front door to the building was.

The first task was to clear the area around Site No. 1, which was covered by dense shrubs hiding the ground from view and making it difficult to move freely. That was done with machetes and scythes, so as to avoid disturbing the surface. Once that task was completed, it was possible to observe the building in its entirety and design the archaeological project.

When the shrubs were cleared from the site, it was noted that there were remains of the original adobe walls over the stone wall or foot wall. These walls were made of adobe bricks, similar to those observed at the ruins of other houses in the village. They were at irregular heights, and at no point were they more than 1 metre higher than the stone wall. The roof of the building was missing. About 1.5 metres in a south-westerly direction from the door of the building, there were two wooden posts about 2 metres high, approximately 3 metres apart. The posts, together with the tiles found nearby, formed the porch to the building.

ARCHAEOLOGICAL PLAN

In archaeology, before the excavation of a site begins, a design or work plan is prepared. Essentially this involves determining how best to recover the finds, depending on the specific problems of the archaeological site.

In the case that concerns us, the decision was made to design a grid system using numbers and letters. The result was 20 grid squares, each one measuring 1.5 by 1.5 metres. The four walls of the building were designated "North", "South" "East" and "West", which was simpler than referring to their exact positions on the compass (north-west, south-east, north-east and south-west respectively). Numbers (1, 2, 3, 4 and 5) are used from north to south, and letters (A, B, C and D) from west to east. Each grid square corresponded to an excavation unit, and that allowed us to assign each find to its precise spatial position. Furthermore, in order to have a three-dimensional representation of the positions of the finds, a baseline level of "0" was set as an artificial starting-point for the measurement of all depths. This "0" level was intended to serve as a horizontal fixed plane, established artificially, to compensate for unevenness in the terrain.

Once the archaeological plan had been designed, the next step was to divide up the personnel, assigning them to specific grid squares under the direction of members of EAAF.

The methodology used during the excavation involved seeking to understand the stratigraphy of the site, i.e. the order and relationship of the various strata. The decision was therefore made to excavate in natural layers, following the structure of each layer and trying to have homogeneous levels. As each find appeared, it was represented in three-dimensional form and recorded in a diagram. At the same time, any find that was not part of a skeleton and was not an object pertaining to a skeleton was inventoried in a general log that described what it was, where it was discovered and what it might pertain to.

Once a skeleton that had been found was totally uncovered, it was removed. When the remains were exhumed, data on each skeleton was entered on field forms giving the name of each bone, a description of the condition of the remains, a description of the clothing and personal effects, ballistic evidence and any additional element pertaining to the skeleton.

Lastly, it should be pointed out that all the soil removed since excavation began was sifted with a sieve, so that any evidence not observed *in situ* might be recovered and attributed to its place of origin.

STRATIGRAPHY

The stratigraphy of Site No. 1 reveals three compact and clearly differentiable levels which extend homogeneously throughout the excavated area.

Level 1: This is the level found on the surface of the site, and is the one that extends furthest beneath the surface. It is composed of compact, clayey dirt in small blocks. In appearance, colour, density, morphological characteristics and degree of compaction, these blocks are similar to those observed in the adobe walls resting on the stone wall. Essentially, the adobe is composed of a man-made, sun-dried mixture of clay and water. It is worth noting, therefore, that this stratum is not like a sample of virgin soil, but has been affected by human hand. This layer is, on average, 80 centimetres deep, and shows no signs of disturbance by natural elements (animal burrows, soil displacement, etc.) or deliberate alteration (shovel marks, excavation or other human action).

The main finds at level 1 were nails of varying thicknesses, fragments of burnt wood, probably from the beams of the roof, and possibly from some window frames, cloth remains, some metal fragments and some bullet cartridges (see the inventory of ballistic evidence). These items were all found at a depth close to level 2.

Level 2: This second level is, on average, 15 centimetres deep, and also extends homogeneously throughout the site. It is composed essentially of the remains of reddish tiles, some of them almost whole, others totally fragmented. Many of the tiles have a darkish tinge consistent with the effect of fire. They were found in heterogeneous positions: sideways, concave side up, concave side down. Because of this arrangement, this level intersects with the bottom of the dirt layer. The main finds were tiles, nails of varying sizes and burnt wood. Also at this level, there were no signs of disturbance or alterations whatever.

Level 3: In direct contact with the tiles forming level 2, we find the lowest level, which is composed of human skeletons and related evidence. This level, the last one at the site, is about 30 centimetres deep and in direct contact with the floor.

Floor: The floor of the building is composed of compact bricks, which in some areas have a darkish tinge consistent with the effect of fire. Also discernible on the floor are a number of holes, some of them caused directly by bullets.

II. LEVEL 3: BONE REMAINS

As mentioned under the respective item, this level contains human skeletons and related evidence. From an archaeological standpoint, the type of burial-place that we find at Site No. 1 may be defined as a *primary synchronous common* grave:

• It is a common grave, for it contains more than one body;

• At level 3, there was a total of at least one hundred and seventeen (117) human skeletons, forming complete anatomical units. This means that the persons found at Site No. 1 either died there or had their bodies moved there before rigor mortis set in. The result was that their bones were not out of position, but maintained their anatomical order. Thus, the evidence suggests a primary burial, i.e. bodies buried for the first time;

• The skeletons formed a compact, homogeneous stratum. They were in a confused heap, one on top of the other, without layers of soil or anything else to suggest separation in space or time. In other words, *all* the bodies were buried on the same occasion, not on different occasions separated in time.

All the fragments of jackets and cores and all the bullet cores were found inside the building. A total of 263 bullet fragments (cores and jackets) were recovered, and more than 90 per cent (240 fragments) appertained to the skeletons and clothing of the bodies at Site No. 1.

On the basis of this information, we can affirm that the burial of the bodies and the evidence pertaining thereto are related to a single event that occurred at a specific point in time.

MINIMUM NUMBER OF BODIES RECOVERED—AGE GROUPS REPRE-
SENTED—STATE OF PRESERVATION OF BONE REMAINS

At Site No. 1, at least one hundred and seventeen (117)* intact
human skeletons and twenty-four (24) concentrations of bone remains
were recovered. We used the term "assemblage of bone remains" in
reference to areas at Site No. 1 where the extent of destruction,
carbonization and/or calcination of the bone remains and the density
of such remains made it impossible to recover them as individual
skeletons. Most of those assemblages were in areas—grid squares B3
and B2—where the effect of fire was most intense, causing great
destruction among the bone remains.

Thus *the 117 skeletons recovered represent the minimum number of
bodies, but not the definitive number, recovered at Site No. 1.* It is
possible that the laboratory study may reveal further individual skeletons and raise the initial tally.

It is important to point out that one of the skeletons (No. 33) was
that of a pregnant woman, for the remains of a foetus were wedged
in the pelvic region, with the head between the two coxal bones and
on the sacrum. Laboratory measurements of the long bones of the
foetus will determine how many months pregnant the woman was.
Because parts were missing from many of the skeletons, it can be
said that the bone remains were in an extremely precarious state of
preservation. A number of factors account for this:

• The age characteristics of the group represented: While the laboratory report will give a detailed final estimate of the age of each
skeleton, observations made during the archaeological phase suggest
that nearly 85 per cent of the remains recovered were those of children
under the age of 12. This statement is based on the size of the bones,
the primary and/or secondary centres of ossification not yet fused,
the abundance of primary or deciduous teeth, together with permanent teeth, and the size of the clothes found. The fact that the
bodies had not yet reached maturity contributed to the greater than

---

*During the archaeological work, the tally of skeletons reached 119. After
that phase, another count was taken, and it was found that skeletons 23,
61 and 72 had been misnumbered and that the numbers did not match up.
Also, there were two skeletons numbered "81": that of a child and that of
a new-born baby. Therefore, by subtracting 3 and adding 1, we find that
the total number of bodies recovered at Site No. 1 reaches at least 117.

usual extent of deterioration of the remains, for during the process of skeletal maturation, the bones have a lower mineral content and are less resistant to the effects of exogenous processes, being extremely fragile.

• Exogenous or external factors: when we speak of such factors in this instance, we are referring to four elements that contributed to the deterioration of the remains:

(1) The large quantity of bullet fragments (240) that struck the bodies and clothing of the victims, producing serious lesions immediately prior to their death;

(2) The effect of fire, mainly observed in the large quantity of bone remains, clothing and accompanying objects that were burnt to varying degrees;

(3) The collapse of the roof and walls of the building onto the bodies of the victims, with considerable damage to the bodies from the roof tiles, beams and nails;

(4) The degree of acidity of the earth: the earth found in contact with the skeletons is akin to that of level 1 and of the walls of the building. Although the pH level was not measured during the excavation, it can be speculated that the earth had a corrosive effect on the bones.

SPATIAL DISTRIBUTION OF SKELETONS AND CONCENTRATIONS OF BONE REMAINS

As indicated earlier, the skeletons were all in an intertwined heap. However, they were not lying evenly distributed on the floor of the building; instead, their placement would indicate two areas of concentration:

(1) The first area, denser than the other, comprises grid squares B2, B3, C3 and the south-west corner of C2. In this area alone, approximately 10 metres square, 82 skeletons were concentrated; that is, 70 per cent of the total of 117 bodies exhumed. With regard to the concentrations of bone remains, 80 per cent are to be found in grid squares B3 and B2 alone: concentrations 13, 15, 18, 19, 20, 21, 22, 23 and 24 in B3; and concentrations 2, 3, 5, 6, 7, 8, 9, 12, and 17 in B2.

(2) The second area can be divided into two sub-zones:

(a) One comprises the south-west corner of the site, that is, grid squares B5, B4 and part of C5 and C4. In this zone, there are 17 skeletons, that is, almost 15 per cent of the total;

(b) The other comprises the north-east corner of the site, that is, grid squares C1, part of C2, D1 and D2. Here, there are 18 skeletons, about 15 per cent of the total.

As to the distribution of the concentrations of bone remains, it is important to note that they contain the greatest concentration of burnt bones and associated objects, and that, especially in grid square B3, they form actual compact masses of bones, clothing, metal fragments and other objects. Because of the degree of compaction and melting of some of the objects—like coins, shoes, clothing, glass and eyeglasses—the wave of heat produced in the area must have reached very high temperatures. The presence of a fragment of an explosive device discovered in grid square B3, between levels 2 and 3, may have a bearing on this.

III. EVIDENCE ASSOCIATED WITH THE BONE REMAINS

CLOTHING

Of the bodies exhumed at Site No. 1, 89.7 per cent (105 of the skeletons recovered) were clothed; that is, the individuals were wearing articles of clothing at the time that they were killed. In addition, there were articles of clothing belonging to at least 9 individuals that did not pertain to any bone remains, and these were found in concentrations 1, 6, 11, 17, 18, 20, 21 and 22.

In 23 of the 105 cases of individuals who were dressed at the time of death, fragments of bullet jackets or cores were found embedded in their clothing; in 14 cases, bullet cartridges were found stuck to the clothing. Thus, in 37 instances (35 per cent of the 105 cases), ballistic evidence was found stuck to the clothing.

Furthermore, holes were detected in many of the garments, which were compatible with the passage of a bullet and which in some cases were in direct contact with a bullet fragment. In other cases, the bullet was not found, but beneath the hole in the garment a perimortem lesion could be seen in the bone.

Most of the articles of clothing showed signs of the effect of fire, and it could be seen in many cases that extensive areas with scorched edges were missing.

As to the type of garments represented, the majority of them support the findings in the present report regarding the ages of the victims: dresses, trousers, undershirts, bloomers, underskirts, socks and shoes in very small sizes, belonging to children of both sexes.

PERSONAL EFFECTS

Together with the bone remains and the clothing, various personal effects were found, like coins and bills of different denominations; toys such as marbles, little plastic horses, the head of a doll, and the like; eyeglasses, combs, barrettes, ornamental combs, medals, crucifixes, scapulars, fragments of mirrors, etc. A good part of this material as well was damaged by fire.

HOUSEHOLD GOODS

The household goods found were dishes, cups, nails, spoons, a bottle of Coca-Cola, bottles containing coffee beans, glass bottles of various sizes, hinges, bolts, gourds, two grindstones with their respective pestles, three machetes, iron girders of the kind used in construction, etc.

BALLISTIC EVIDENCE

The ballistic evidence gathered consists of bullets and bullet cartridges. Each one of the ballistic finds was indicated tridimensionally on a map of the site so as to show their exact distribution. Once the archaeological work was done, 257 bullet (jacket and/or core) fragments and 244 spent cartridges were counted. In the process of washing and analysing the bone remains in the laboratory, one cartridge fragment was found in association with skeleton 69; and six bullet jacket and/or core fragments in association with skeletons 6, 74, 44, 42 and 119 and with concentration 16. This raises the figure to *245 spent cartridges and 263 bullet (core and/or casing) fragments.*

Throughout the process of excavation, any material relating to ballistics was gone over by staff of the Commission on Criminal Acts (Comisíon de hechos delictivos), who determined if what was being uncovered was a bullet or a cartridge. The few doubtful cases were listed as "metal fragments" in the listing of ballistic evidence, and they were not counted as bullets.

The bullet fragments were found very shattered, and what was turned up in most cases was part of the jacket of the bullet or of its core. In very few instances, the fragments were more complete, though still misshapen. The spent cartridges, on the other hand, were recovered whole in almost all cases.

With respect to the spatial distribution of the bullets and spent cartridges, various points can be made:

• Virtually all the ballistic evidence was found at level 3, in direct contact with or embedded in the bone remains, clothing, household goods and floor of the building;

• Some bullets (six in all) were found embedded in the foot wall and in the junction between that wall and the floor;

• In at least nine cases, bullets were found which, after passing through the clothing and the body, had become embedded in the floor, leaving a distinct hole in it;

• The spatial distribution of most of the bullet fragments coincides with the area of greatest concentration of skeletons and with piles of bone remains. We are referring to grid squares B2, B3, C3 and the south-west corner of C2, where 82 bodies—almost 70 per cent of the skeletons—and 18 of the 24 concentrations of bone remains—almost 80 per cent—were found. In these grid squares, 159 bullet fragments were found: 102 fragments in B3; 13 fragments in B2; 30 fragments in C3; and 14 fragments in C2. In these grid squares, all these bullet fragments were in direct contact with bone remains. In other words, 159 bullet fragments had struck a large proportion of the 82 skeletons and 18 concentrations discovered in this zone.

The second area of concentration of bullet fragments coincides with the second area of concentration of skeletons. We are referring to the north-east corner of the inside of the building, corresponding to grid squares D1 and D2. In these two grid squares, three bullet fragments were found in D1 and 37 fragments in D2. Thus 40 bullet fragments (approximately 15 per cent of the total) had mainly struck 18 skeletons.

Lastly, the third area of concentration of skeletons coincides with the third area of concentration of bullet fragments. We are referring to grid squares B5, B4 and part of C5 and C4. Fourteen fragments were recovered in B4, five fragments in B5, seven fragments in C4, and four fragments in C5. In other words, 28 bullet fragments (close to 10 per cent) had for the most part struck 17 skeletons.

The remaining 5 per cent were scattered about in other grid squares.

• Most of the skulls and post-cranial skeletons exhibited multiple fractures that could be due to various factors: bullets, fire, the collapse of the roof, etc. This point will be examined more closely in the laboratory. However, on the basis of the ballistic evidence discovered, some facts can already be adduced to explain how some of the fractures occurred.

Of the 117 bodies recovered at Site No. 1, bullet fragments were found in conjunction with 67. The bullet fragments were recovered from the following areas of the body:

Cranium:	14 individuals
Thorax:	14 individuals
Cranium and thorax:	3 individuals
Cranium and upper and/or lower limbs and/or pelvis:	5 individuals
Thorax and upper and/or lower limbs and/or pelvis:	7 individuals
Total:	43 individuals
Upper and/or lower limbs and/or pelvis and/or clothing:	24 individuals
Total:	67 individuals

This means that at least 43 individuals received gunshot wounds in areas of the body where the injury may have caused their death.

It is important to specify that it is possible that more individuals than those indicated here may have been struck by bullets even though the bullet fragments have not been recovered in the field. These preliminary data must be supplemented by the results of the radiographic studies of the bone remains, indicating whether the X-ray plates reveal metal densities that could correspond to bullet fragments.

• In the "A" grid line, corresponding to the west wall and the entrance to the building, only two bullet fragments were found, one in A1 and the other in A5—both on the interior side of the stone wall.

No bullet fragments were found on the exterior side of the west wall.

• The pattern of dispersal of the spent cartridges differs from that of the bullets. The areas where the spent cartridges were found can be divided into two basic zones: (1) grid squares A3, A4 and A5, outside the building and at the front door; (2) grid squares B3 and B4.

• The fact that there were large numbers of spent cartridges in some areas—at the front door of the building in A3, in grid squares A4 and A5 outside the building, and in grid square B4 inside the building—indicates that some of the positions of those shooting may have been close to those. Diagram 8 suggests that there were shooters at the front door and to the south-west inside the building, shooting from inside or into the building, mostly towards central grid squares, such as B3, and towards the north-east. Eighty-five per cent of the skeletons and 75 per cent of the bullet fragments were found in these two areas.

EXPLOSIVE DEVICES

During the excavation, three metal fragments were found with morphological characteristics classified by the staff of the Commission on Criminal Acts as fragments of explosive and/or incendiary devices.

The devices were found in grid squares B3 and D3, the first between levels 2 and 3, and the second over the roof tiles, that is to say, over level 2. The splinter is not shown in diagram 8; it was found in grid square B2, at level 3, accompanying bone remains.

The explosive devices contributed to the destruction of the remains. In particular, the explosive fragment found in grid square B3 corresponds to the area in which there was the greatest density of skeletons, concentrations of bone remains and the greatest damage thereto.

IV. EFFECTS OF FIRE

With respect to the pattern of dispersal of burnt bone remains—and of the accompanying evidence, which was also affected by the heat—it must be stressed that not all the objects found show effects of fire to the same extent. As in the preceding cases, two zones can be delimited:

(1) The first zone corresponds to the area in which most of the concentrations of bone remains were found and consequently where the remains showed the greatest deterioration resulting from fire: grid squares B3, B2, A2 and A1. In the case of the concentrations located in those grid squares—Nos. 1, 2, 3, 4, 5, 6, 7, 9, 13, 14, 15, 18, 19, 20, 21, 22, 23 and 24—the bone remains actually formed compact masses with remnants of clothing, partly melted coins and melted plastic shoes. The floor in some of the zones in question also had a darkish tinge;

(2) The second zone appears to be located on the periphery of zone 1, particularly in grid squares C2 and C3, containing assemblages of bone remains, 12, 16, 10, 11 and 8. There were signs of fire in zone 2 but to a much lesser extent than in zone 1, in which the heat was much more intense.

V. FLOOR OF SITE NO. I

Once all the bone remains and accompanying evidence had been removed, the cleaning of the brick floor was begun. When that operation had been completed, it could be seen that in the floor there were a number of irregularly shaped holes—a total of thirty-eight (38) were found—in some cases approximately 10 millimetres deep. It must be stressed that some of the holes were discovered during the excavation, when skeletons were found, and that when a broken bone was removed, it was found to have been resting on top of a bullet, which itself was resting in a hole in the floor. The details are as follows:

(1) Skeleton 2: the bullet fragment matching the hole in the floor was recovered from beneath the skull;

(2) Skeleton 5: the bullet fragment matching the hole in the floor was found beneath the right shoulder-blade;

(3) Skeleton 9: the bullet fragment matching the hole in the floor was found beneath the right femur;

(4) Skeleton 10: two bullet fragments matching two holes in the floor were found beneath the skull;

(5) Skeleton 26: the bullet fragment matching the hole in the floor was found in a cervical vertebra;

(6) Skeleton 57: the bullet fragment matching the hole in the floor was found beneath the skull;

(7) Skeleton 92: the bullet fragment matching the hole in the floor was found in the skull when it was cleaned in the laboratory;

(8) Skeleton 110: the bullet fragment matching the hole in the floor was found on the skull area;

(9) Skeleton 113: the bullet fragment matching the hole in the floor was found close to the right ribs.

With regard to the pattern of dispersal of the holes, they follow an axis passing diagonally through the building, from the south-west corner to the north-east corner, increasing in terms of density or number of holes. It is precisely in grid squares C3 and C2 that twenty (20) of the thirty-eight (38) holes are concentrated.

VI. DATING OF THE OCCURRENCE

Two types of article recovered from Site No. 1 facilitate determination of the approximate date on which the events occurred: coins and the base of the spent cartridges. With respect to the coins, 33 coins corresponding to 12 skeletons (4, 6, 25, 26, 37, 39, 62, 66, 67, 92 and 101) and two piles of bone remains (9 and 21). In the case of skeletons, the coins were in garment pockets. The skeletons and concentrations of bone remains came from virtually all the grid squares in which there were remains: A3, B1, B2, B3, B4, C1, C2, C3, C4 and D2.

Five of the 33 coins had undergone oxidation, and it was thus impossible to read the date on them. The remaining 28 coins corresponded to the following years: 1952 (1); 1956 (1); 1962 (1); 1966 (2); 1967 (2); 1972 (4); 1974 (2); 1975 (3); 1976 (5); 1977 (5); on one coin only "197 . . ." was legible; and, lastly, there was one quarter-real coin from 1883.

That is to say, there were no coins from years later than 1981, the year in which the events are assumed to have occurred.

The same applies in the case of the dates on the base of the spent cartridges fround at Site No. 1. When a ballistic analysis was carried out by Dr. Douglas Scott, it was found that the date of manufacture could be read in the case of 184 out of a total of 245 spent cartridges, that is to say, in the case of 75.1 per cent of the cartridges. None of the dates of the cartridges is later than 1981.

These findings confirm the assumed date on which the events under consideration in this investigation occurred.

VII. CONCLUSIONS

On the basis of the data obtained during the archaeological excavation of Site No. 1 at El Mozote and the comprehensive analysis carried out solely on the basis of that data, we have reached a set of logical and scientifically tenable conclusions as to what occurred there.

• All the skeletons recovered from the site and the accompanying evidence were deposited during the same temporal event, in a kind of primary synchronous common burial or interment.

Three factors lead to this conclusion:

(1) The great degree of intermingling and great density of the bone remains themselves and with the associated evidence (clothing, bullets, personal effects, etc.);

(2) The total absence of intervening layers of earth or other elements between the skeletons that might be an indication of different inhumation times;

(3) The skeletons formed complete anatomical units; the people concerned therefore died at Site No. 1 or their bodies were deposited there before the flesh decomposed.

The evidence recovered thus excludes the possibility that Site No. 1 was used as a "cemetery" in which the bodies were placed during various temporal events over a period of time.

• It cannot be determined with certainty that all the victims were alive when they were brought to the convent. However, it can be concluded that at least some of the victims were struck by bullets, with an effect that may well have been lethal, inside the building. This conclusion is based on:

(1) The large quantity of bullet fragments found inside the building, both corresponding and not corresponding to the surrounding bone remains;

(2) The bullet fragments embedded in the interior surfaces of the stone wall;

(3) The holes found in the floor of the building directly linked to bullet fragments and bone remains;

(4) The presence and the location of a great quantity of spent cartridges inside the building;

(5) Of the 245 cartridges retrieved, 244 correspond to the same type of ammunition; only one relates to a different type of ammunition;

(6) Such bullet fragments as were found belong to the same type of ammunition as do the spent cartridges.

• In at least nine cases, the victims were shot inside the building while lying in a horizontal position on the floor. The shots were fired downwards. In at least six of the nine cases mentioned, these shots could have caused the victims' deaths.

These assertions are supported by the following:

1) Observation of *peri-mortem* lesions, together with bullet fragments and holes in the floor underneath such fragments. This observation applies to skeletons 2, 5, 9, 10, 26, 57, 92, 110 and 113, located in grid squares C1, C2, C1, D2, B4, C3, B2, B3-C3 and B3 respectively;

(2) The only way such shots could have produced holes in the floor is by shooting downwards, either straight down or diagonally;

(3) In the case of skeletons 2, 10, 92, 110 and 57, the bullets which made the holes in the floor were found in the area of the skull; in the case of skeleton 26, in the cervical vertebrae (very close to the skull).

• Of 117 skeletons identified in the field, 67 were associated with bullet fragments. In 43 out of this subtotal of 67, the fragments were found in the areas of the skull and/or the thorax, i.e. parts of the body where they could have been the cause of death.

• Some of those who fired were probably positioned in the entrance doorway and the south-west part of the building, firing inwards from both outside and inside, mostly in the direction of the central grid squares—B3 and C3—and towards the north-east.

The basis for these assertions is as follows:

(1) The area where most spent cartridges were found is other than that in which most bullet fragments were found:

(a) More than 40 per cent of all the spent cartridges were found in the west wall of the building: in the area of the entrance doorway (64 cartridges in A3, i.e. 25 per cent); in the grid squares to the right of the door, outside the building (24 cartridges in A4 and 18 in A5). Thirty-eight cartridges were found in grid square B4, accounting for some 15 per cent of all the cartridges retrieved;

(b) One hundred and eighty-nine bullet fragments were found in grid squares B3, B2, C3, part of C2 and in the north-east corner of the building (grid squares D2 and D1), these being the same grid squares where most bone remains were found;

(2) Holes in the floor of the building corresponding to bullet fragments and bone remains were located principally in the centre and the north-east corner of the building (31 of the 38 holes found);

(3) No bullet fragments were found in the outside west facade of the foot wall.

• There was substantial burn damage to the victims' bones, clothing and personal effects.

There were many signs of burning at all levels of the building: on the floor, the bone remains and clothing of the victims; at level 2, in fragments of tile and wood from the roof, and in the lower part of level 1, where pieces of burnt wood were also retrieved.

• Approximately 85 per cent of the 117 victims were children under 12 years of age.

The basis of this assertion is as follows:

(1) The simultaneous presence of both deciduous and permanent teeth, as observed in most of the skeletons exhumed from Site No. 1;

(2) The fact that their primary and/or secondary centres of ossification had not fused. A more precise estimate of the victims' ages will be made in the laboratory.

• The remains were exhumed of a woman who had been pregnant at the time of death (skeleton 33). Much of the foetus' bones were found in the area of her pelvis.

• The events under investigation are unlikely to have occurred later than 1981.

The basis for this assertion is as follows:

(1) The date was legible on 28 of the 35 coins retrieved from the pockets of different skeletons. On none was the date later than 1977;

(2) The date of production was legible on 184 of the 245 spent cartridges retrieved. In no case was the date later than 1981.

• After the shots, one or more explosive and/or incendiary devices were thrown into the building.

• All these facts tend to indicate the perpetration of a massive crime, there being no evidence to support the theory of a confrontation between two groups.

Argentine Team of Forensic Anthropologists

(*Signed*) Luis Fondebrider
          Anthropologist

(*Signed*) Patricia Bernardi
Anthropologist
(*Signed*) Mercedes Doretti
Anthropologist

Report of Forensic Investigation El Mozote, El Salvador
10 December 1992

To the Members of the United Nations Truth Commission:
The followng report is based upon an investigation conducted by Clyde C. Snow, Ph.D., forensic anthropologist, Robert H. Kirschner, M.D., forensic pathologist, Dougas D. Scott, Ph.D., archeologist and ballistics analyst, and John J. Fitzpatrick, M.D., trauma radiologist, as consultants to the United Nations Truth Commission in El Salvador. This report reflects the laboratory analysis of skeletal remains and artifacts recovered at El Mozote. The Equipo Argentino de Antropología Forense will issue a separate report regarding the exhumation itself.

During our work in El Salvador, we analyzed the skeletal remains and associated artifacts exhumed at El Mozote, including ballistic evidence, clothing and coins. We visited the exhumation site, and examined photographs, a videotape and diagrams of the exhumation prepared by the Equipo Argentino. We performed our analyses at a special laboratory that had been established at the Institute of Legal Medicine at Santa Tecla, working closely with the Equipo to assure our complete understanding of all aspects of the exhumation. Dr. Gerardo A. Hidalgo Lavin worked with us as dental consultant, and personnel of the Institute provided technical support. Dr. Scott utilized the facilities of the Comisión de Investigación de Hechos Delictivos for his comparative ballistic analysis. The anthropologic data and ballistic analysis are discussed in greater detail in appendices to this report prepared by Dr. Snow and Dr. Scott.

The physical evidence from the exhumation of the convent house at El Mozote confirms the allegations of a mass murder. The evidence is as follows:

1. We have identified the presence of 143 skeletal remains, including

136 children and adolescents and 7 adults. The average age of the children was approximately 6 years; there were 6 women, ages 21–40, one of whom was in the third trimester of pregnancy, and one man of approximately 50 years of age. There may, in fact, have been a greater number of deaths. This uncertainty regarding the number of skeletons is a reflection of the extensive perimortem skeletal injuries, postmortem skeletal damage and associated commingling. Many young infants may have been entirely cremated; other children may not have been counted because of extensive fragmentation of body parts.

2. The skeletons showed evidence of severe trauma, reflecting high velocity gun shot wound injury and postmortem crushing and fire/heat damage.

a. Gun shot injury: Direct skeletal examination showed intact gun shot wounds of entrance in only a few skulls because of the extensive fracturing that is characteristically associated with such high velocity injuries. Skull reconstruction identified many more entrance wounds, but relatively few exit wounds. This is consistent with the ballistic evidence that the ammunition involved in the shootings was a type likely to fragment upon impact, becoming essentially frangible bullets. Radiologic examination of skull bones, including the mandible, demonstrated small metallic densities consistent with bullet fragments in 45.2% (51/115).

In long bones, vertebrae, pelvis and ribs there were defects characteristic of high velocity gun shot wounds. In long bones, these defects typically showed shattering of the bone at the point of impact with longitudinal fractures extending along the shaft. In vertebrae and pelvic bones, concave defects and shattering at the impact site were common. In many cases, evidence of gunshot injury was undoubtedly obscured by postmortem skeletal damage. Small bullet fragments were identified radiologically in 23.3% (12/52) of the post-cranial material examined. Many clearly identified gun shot wounds showed no residual bullet fragments radiologically.

b. Crushing and fire/heat damage: Few skulls were intact, and only 5.5% of the long bones were sufficiently intact to determine diaphyseal length. As described above, there were extensive skull fractures related to the gun shot injuries, with further fracturing due to the combined effects of the fire in the building, the collapse of the roof and the destruction of the walls. The fire was not uniform, being intensely hot in some areas of the room, but showing relative sparing of other portions. This was reflected both by the burn pattern at the crime scene and by the distribution of burning seen on the skeletal remains. Charring of clothing was common, and typical charring and fire fractures of skulls and long bones were noted. There was total destruction of the distal portions of the extremities in many of the victims due to severe postmortem burns. Subsequent to the fire injuries, the weight of the roof tiles and walls of the building produced further postmortem damage to the bodies. It is probable that some young infants (less than 1 year) may have been completely cremated (based on the lower than expected number of such children recovered), but we can not determine the number.

3. Based on the minimal evidence of postmortem insect activity and lack of evidence of other animal scavenging, the deaths were relatively contemporaneous with one another, and the subsequent fire and burial occurred following a relatively short postmortem interval.

4. The specific cause of death could not be determined in all cases because of the absence of soft tissues, the extent of postmortem skeletal damage and the long postmortem interval. Some of the victims might have been strangled, stabbed or suffocated. However, we found no evidence of cutting or stabbing wounds in the skeletal remains, nor of the type of comminuted, depressed skull fractures common with inflicted blunt trauma injury to the head. We have no way of determining if any of the victims were alive at the time of the fire.

5. Two hundred forty five cartridge cases recovered from the El Mozote site were studied. Of these, 184 had discernible headstamps, identifying the ammunition as having been manufactured for the United States Government at Lake City, Missouri. Thirty four cartridges were sufficiently well preserved to analyze for individual as well as class characteristics. All of the projectiles except one appear to have been fired from United States manufactured M–16 rifles; 24 separate weapons were identified, consistent with at least 24 individual shooters. The distribution of the cartridges and projectiles, the pattern of projectile damage to the floor of the convent house, and the specific association of projectiles with the skeletal remains clearly demonstrates that the shooters were firing from within the house, from the doorway, and probably through a window to the right of

the door. Some of the children may have been shot outside the house and subsequently dumped inside, but sufficient rounds of ammunition were fired into the house to account for all of the deaths.

6. There is no evidence to support the contention that these victims, almost all young children, were involved in combat or were caught in the crossfire of combat forces. Rather the evidence strongly supports the conclusion that they were the intentional victims of a mass extra-judicial execution.

All of the above opinions are stated with a reasonable degree of medical and scientific certainty. The authors of this report are willing to testify in an appropriate court of law regarding their conclusions in this matter.

14. THE WAR AT HOME, II

The exhumation at El Mozote was widely reported in the United States—on the front page of *The New York Times,* among other places—and the uncovering of the remains provoked a great many commentaries, many of which pointed out that the discovery had, among other things, "exonerated" the work of those who had first reported the massacre, Alma Guillermoprieto and Raymond Bonner. Some writers took the *Wall Street Journal* to task for its editorial, "The Media's War" (see "The War At Home," above).

In the two pieces that follow, the *Wall Street Journal* answers its critics. I feel obliged to inform the reader, however, that these articles are reprinted here not by the choice of the author but at the insistence of the *Journal*'s editors, who refused to allow their original editorial to be reprinted unless these two recent articles, published on February 26, 1993 and March 19, 1993, were reprinted as well.

The War's Over, but El Salvador Still Fights Propaganda Battle

By David Asman, The Americas

EL MOZOTE, EL SALVADOR—This country is in the midst of an economic and cultural rebirth. While some of El Salvador's Central American neighbors (most notably Nicaragua) continue to experience a depressing Diaspora due to lingering war, corruption and statist economic policies, thousands of Salvadorans who had left for the U.S. are returning home now with capital and newfound expertise. Sworn enemies from the Marxist guerrillas and the legitimate political establishment are beginning to talk—albeit haltingly—about rebuilding the country. The capital city of San Salvador is bursting with traffic jams, office construction and neat, middle-class residential communities that are sold out before construction can be completed.

But if San Salvador has become a living symbol of the country's comeback spirit, the tiny hamlet of El Mozote, in the barely accessible highlands of eastern El Salvador, has become a symbol of the horrors of a divisive war, the deep wounds of which will have to heal before the rule of law is accepted by all. Hindering that healing process is the fact that El Mozote has become the battleground of an international propaganda war in which truth and justice are secondary considerations.

El Mozote first entered international consciousness through newspaper accounts of a massacre that allegedly took place there in December 1981. One month later, reporters from *The New York Times* and the *Washington Post* were introduced to survivors of the massacre by Marxist guerrilla guides. The reporters also saw scores of putrefied bodies scattered around El Mozote and surrounding villages. Many of the dead were women and children.

The guerrillas and their supporters claimed that more than 700 defenseless civilians were massacred by government troops in a noncombat zone. Later this figure was increased to about 1,000 by virulently antigovernment human rights organizations in San Salvador. Salvadoran and U.S. government officials questioned both the number of civilians killed (which they say exceeded the number of people who lived in the area) and the assumption that all were massacred by the army.

Clearly the time to have investigated the veracity of claims on both sides was in 1982. However, due to guerrilla control of the area, thorough investigations were impossible and the truth of El Mozote became obscured by propaganda.

Almost 10 years later, Rufina Amaya, the leading witness interviewed by reporters in 1982, filed charges with the district judge responsible for El Mozote and demanded a full investigation of the massacre. Mrs. Amaya's charges were filed just before the 10-year statute of limitations would have taken effect.

But investigating the scene after 10 years posed extraordinary challenges. Even a four-wheel-drive vehicle has great difficulty negotiating the mountain roads that lead into the area. And in the rainy season, El Mozote is virtually inaccessible by car. Nevertheless, the long-deserted killing fields were soon filled with investigators. In addition to an investigation conducted by local representatives of the Salvadoran Supreme Court, teams of forensic doctors, anthropologists and criminologists arrived from around the world. Even Scotland Yard was called in to help.

On the road to El Mozote, signs of the rebel control of the area still predominate: FMLN guerrilla propaganda is carefully painted on buildings; children are seen wearing FMLN caps; two blond, "internationalist" women with tie-dyed shirts try unsuccessfully to blend in with the Salvadoran peasants. And at the entrance to El Mozote, a new, professionally lithographed sign announces the massacre of "more than 1,000 peasants."

El Mozote itself resembles more an archaeological dig than the scene of a crime. Freshly dug sites are fenced off with twine strung on twigs that designate neat, geometric plots. It's clear that fierce fighting of some kind took place here. Bullet holes indicating gunshots from all angles riddle the few standing walls of the hamlet's nine burned-out structures. Gaping holes are found in some walls, in addition to smaller holes that appear to have been chipped out as gun ports. And bullet holes are clearly visible on the floors of at least two buildings, as if someone had been firing directly into bodies piled on the floor. Of the dozen sites in El Mozote where Mrs. Amaya claimed bodies would be found, four sites have been excavated. Of these, just two have yielded remains. In "site two," one skeleton was found. But the findings at "site one" were horrific. In a small, 10-by-20 convent adjacent to a chuch, 143 skeletal remains were found buried under the collapsed roof and walls of the partially burned-out structure. Of the remains found, it was determined that 136 were children. Most appeared to have been killed by high-velocity weapons. About 150 M-16 and a few AK-47 shell casings were found nearby.

While it appears that a massacre of some kind took place, questions remain: Had El Mozote been a war zone before the killing of innocents began? Were there as many killed as the guerrillas and others claim? Who were the true perpetrators of this awful crime?

Clyde Collins Snow is a world-renowned forensic anthropologist who was called in by the United Nations Peace Commission to help the government with its investigation. "I try to keep an open mind till all the evidence is in," says Mr. Snow. "You have a single living witness, and you have accounts on both sides. The human rights groups tend to have their own agendas, so they tend to give you figures on the high side. On the other extreme you have the government people who say nobody was killed. However, I can't see how you wind up with 136 kids killed without somebody being way out of line. . . . I think a war crime was committed up there."

President Alfredo Cristiani is somewhat hesitant about focusing too much on the El Mozote investigations. "I think it's better for the country if we don't always look back," he said in a recent interview in the presidential palace. But the fact that El Salvador has evolved enough so that apparent war crimes like El Mozote can be investigated without passion is a great sign of hope. Only by taking highly charged cases such as El Mozote out of the realm of propaganda and subjecting them to the bare scrutiny of independent investigators will there be hope that El Salvador's current social and economic boom is rooted not in speculation, but in a lasting respect for the rule of the law.

On Credulity

For more than a year now we've been following the campaign asserting that we victimized former *New York Times* correspondent Raymond Bonner. We held our peace as this charge moved from Aryeh Neier in the *Nation* to Sydney Schanberg in *Newsday* to Anthony Lewis in the *Times* to National Public Radio to the *Columbia Journalism Review* to CBS's "60 Minutes." Our patience broke when the *Times* itself joined in editorially.

The issue concerns Mr. Bonner's reporting on El Salvador in 1981 and 1982, and came to a head over his report of the tragedy in the rebel-held village of El Mozote. It was clear enough at the time that something awful had happened there. It may very well have been a My Lai by government forces, as a U.N.-sponsored Truth Commission has asserted. The excavation of children's bones in Mozote is supposed to vindicate Mr. Bonner and discredit what we said. Or as the *Times* put it, "Some American editorialists who attacked the reporters as credulous were themselves duped."

About this, we would like to make several things clear. In the first place, our editorial ("The Media's War," February 19, 1982) never denied that there was a massacre at El Mozote. Rather, we said, "realistically, neither the press nor the State Department has the power to establish conclusively what happened at Mozote in December." We also took no position on the official human rights "certifications" required by laws Congress passed to duck responsibility for either ending or continuing U.S. support of the anti-guerrilla effort.

In the second place, we did not criticize "reporters," plural. We offered not one word of criticism of Alma Guillermoprieto of the *Washington Post.* Indeed, we held her reports of the same story as a model of proper reporting: "Miss Guillermoprieto took pains to say that reporters had been 'taken to tour' the site by guerrillas with the purpose of showing their control and providing evidence of the massacre. In other words, whatever the mixture of truth and fabrication, this was a propaganda exercise."

In the third place, we did not fire Mr. Bonner in the first place. *The New York Times* did. Or more precisely, after then–Managing Editor A.M. Rosenthal undertook his own reporting visit to Salvador, it pulled Mr. Bonner off the beat and back to New York, where he left the paper. If the *Times* thinks Mr. Bonner has been vindicated, it should stop carping at us and rehire him forthwith.

Before second-guessing Mr. Rosenthal, though, current *Times* editors might want to take a look at Mr. Bonner's interview with Scott Simon on National Public Radio last November 14. We offer the following excerpt for those who may want to make their own judgments about credulity:

> Simon: Do you—do you feel any kind of sense of—of justification? Do—does the terrible loss of the time come back to you?
>
> Bonner: You know, something else has happened in the last couple of weeks. I've gotten all these calls and letters about 'you must feel vindicated.' Yes, I do feel partially vindicated, but do you know what vindication is really important—it is now with Alger Hiss. Now that's a vindication that really means something.
>
> Simon: Mm-hmm.
>
> Bonner: Sure, I took my lumps, but look, we're in this business. We give lumps and we take our lumps. If there's lessons out of this, it's there's got to be limits to which we go when we're fighting a perceived enemy. Now with the Cold War over, communism isn't the enemy anymore. What's the enemy—next enemy going to be? Is it Islamic fundamentalism? Is that the next 'ism' that we're going to worry about? And are reporters who write favorably that or try to put it in some kind of context—are they going to be smeared? Are Peter Arnetts, who tried to do their jobs by staying in Baghdad—I mean, the reporters out there who are sending back the message that we don't want

to hear. We have to be careful before we let our ideological crusades—and that's what it was against communism, what they did to Alger Hiss—and the war was still being fought, of course, in the 1980s.

Simon: Ray, thank you very much for speaking with us.

15. THE COMMISSION ON THE TRUTH

When in January 1992 President Alfredo Cristiani of El Salvador and representatives of the FMLN signed the peace agreement ending the Salvadoran civil war—known as the Chapultepec accords after the castle in Mexico City where they were signed—they agreed to establish a *Comisión de Verdad,* or Truth Commission, which, in the words of article 2, "shall have the task of investigating serious acts of violence that have occurred since 1980 and whose impact on society urgently demands that the public should know the truth." Three commissioners were agreed on by the parties: Belisario Betancur, the former president of Colombia; Reinaldo Figueredo Planchart, former Foreign Minister of Venezuela; and Thomas Buergenthal, Professor of Comparative Law and Jurisprudence at the National Law Center of George Washington University and President of the Inter-American Institute for Human Rights in Costa Rica.

In the summer of 1992, the Commission set up its offices not far from the Sheraton Hotel in San Salvador. Outside the offices were a number of small rooms where, throughout the summer and the early fall, testimony was taken. Advertisements were placed in newspapers, announcements on radio and television, notices were posted—all urging Salvadorans to come and speak to a member of the Truth Commission's young international staff (a number of whom had lost relatives to political violence). During those few months, hundreds and hundreds of Salvadorans came, and many of them spoke about what had happened at El Mozote.

In March 1993, the Truth Commission delivered its report, entitled *From Madness to Hope: The 12-year war in El Salvador,* to the Secretary General of the United Nations. Under Chapter IV, "Cases and Patterns of Violence," and Part C., "Massacres of peasants by the armed forces," El Mozote was listed as an "illustrative case." The Commission ruled out any possibility that El Mozote, along with the massacres at the Sampul River in 1980 and El Calabozo in 1982, could have been "isolated incidents where soldiers or their immediate superiors went to extremes." Instead, they wrote, "everything points to the fact that these deaths formed part of a pattern of conduct, a deliberate strategy of eliminating or terrifying the peasant population in areas where the guerrillas were active, the purpose being to deprive the guerrilla forces of this source of supplies and information and of the possibility of hiding or concealing themselves among that population." Of the bones of El Mozote, the Commissioners wrote, "Those small skeletons are proof not only of the existence of the cold-blooded massacre at El Mozote but also of the collusion of senior commanders of the armed forces, for they show that the evidence of the unburied bodies was there for a long time for anyone who wanted to investigate the facts. In this case, we cannot accept the excuse that senior commanders knew nothing of what had happened.

"No action was taken to avoid incidents such as this. On the contrary, the deliberate, systematic and indiscriminate violence against the peasant population in areas of military operations went on for years."

What follows is the full text of the Truth Commission's chapter on El Mozote.

SUMMARY OF THE CASE

On 10 December 1981, in the village of El Mozote in the Department of Morazán, units of the Atlacatl Battalion detained, without resistance, all the men, women and children who were in the place. The following day, 11 December, after spending the night locked in their homes, they were deliberately and systematically executed in groups.

First, the men were tortured and executed, then the women were executed and, lastly, the children, in the place where they had been locked up. The number of victims identified was *over 200*. The figure is higher if other unidentified victims are taken into account.

These events occurred in the course of an anti-guerrilla action known as "Operación Rescate" in which, in addition to the Atlacatl Battalion, units from the Third Infantry Brigade and the San Francisco Gotera Commando Training Centre took part.

In the course of "Operación Rescate," massacres of civilians also occurred in the following places: 11 December, more than 20 people in La Joya canton; 12 December, some 30 people in the village of La Ranchería; the same day, by units of the Atlacatl Battalion, the inhabitants of the village of Los Toriles; and 13 December, the inhabitants of the village of Jocote Amarillo and Cerro Pando canton. More than 500 identified victims perished at El Mozote and in the other villages. Many other victims have not been identified.

We have accounts of these massacres provided by eyewitnesses and by other witnesses who later saw the bodies, which were left unburied. In the case of El Mozote, the accounts were fully corroborated by the results of the 1992 exhumation of the remains.

Despite the public complaints of a massacre and the ease with which they could have been verified, the Salvadoran authorities did not order an investigation and consistently denied that the massacre had taken place.

The Minister of Defense and the Chief of the Armed Forces Joint Staff have denied to the Commission on the Truth that they have any information that would make it possible to identify the units and officers who participated in "Operación Rescate." They say that there are no records for the period.

The President of the Supreme Court has interfered in a biased and political way in the judicial proceedings on the massacre instituted in 1990.

DESCRIPTION OF THE FACTS

VILLAGE OF EL MOZOTE

On the afternoon of 10 December 1981, units of the Atlacatl Rapid Deployment Infantry Battalion (BIRI) arrived in the village of El Mozote, Department of Morazán, after a clash with guerrillas in the vicinity. The village consisted of about 20 houses situated on open ground around a square. Facing onto the square was a church and behind it a small building known as "the convent," used by the priest to change into his vestments when he came to the village to celebrate mass. Not far from the village was a school, the Grupo Escolar.

When the soldiers arrived in the village they found, in addition to the residents, other peasants who were refugees from the surrounding areas. They ordered everyone out of the houses and into the square; they made them lie face down, searched them and asked them about the guerrillas. They then ordered them to lock themselves in their houses until the next day, warning that anyone coming out would be shot. The soldiers remained in the village during the night.

Early next morning, 11 December, the soldiers reassembled the entire population in the square. They separated the men from the women and children and locked everyone up in different groups in the church, the convent and various houses.

During the morning, they proceeded to interrogate, torture and execute the men in various locations. Around noon, they began taking out the women in groups, separating them from their children and machine-gunning them. Finally, they killed the children. A group of children who had been locked in the convent were machine-gunned through the windows. After exterminating the entire population, the soldiers set fire to the buildings.

The soldiers remained in El Mozote that night. The next day, they went through the village of Los Toriles, situated 2 kilometres away. Some of the inhabitants managed to escape. The others, men, women, and children, were taken from their homes, lined up and machine-gunned.

The victims at El Mozote were left unburied. During the weeks that followed the bodies were seen by many people who passed by there. In Los Toriles, the survivors subsequently buried the bodies.

BACKGROUND

The Atlacatl Battalion arrived at El Mozote in the course of a military action known as *"Operación Rescate,"* which had begun two days earlier on 6 December and also involved units from the Third Brigade and the San Francisco Gotera Commando Training Centre. The Atlacatl Battalion was a "Rapid Deployment Infantry Battalion" or "BIRI," that is, a unit specially trained for "counterinsurgency" warfare. It was the first unit of its kind in the armed forces and had completed its training, under the supervision of United States military advisers, at the beginning of that year, 1981.

Nine months before *"Operación Rescate"* took place, a company of the Atlacatl Battalion, under the command of Captain Juan Ernesto Méndez, had taken part in an anti-guerrilla operation in the same northern zone of Morazán. On that occasion, it had come under heavy attack from guerrillas and had had to withdraw with heavy casualties without achieving its military objective. This setback for the brand new "Rapid Deployment Infantry Battalion" made it the butt of criticism and jokes by officers of other units, who nicknamed it the "Rapid Retreat Infantry Battalion."

The goal of *"Operación Rescate"* was to eliminate the guerrilla presence in a small sector in northern Morazán, where the guerrillas had a camp and a training center at a place called La Guacamaya.

Colonel Jaime Flórez Grijalva, Commander of the Third Brigade, was responsible for overseeing the operation. Lieutenant Colonel Domingo Monterrosa Barrios, Commander of the Atlacatl BIRI, was in command of the units taking part.

On 9 December, clashes took place between Government troops and the guerrillas. That same day, a company of the Atlacatl BIRI entered the town of Arambala. They rounded up the population in the town square and separated the men from the women and children. They locked the women and children in the church and ordered the men to lie face down in the square. A number of men were accused of being guerrilla collaborators. They were tied up, blindfolded and tortured. Residents later found the bodies of three of them, stabbed to death.

In Cumaro canton as well, residents were rounded up in the main square by Atlacatl units on the morning of 10 December. There, however, no one was killed.

There is sufficient evidence that units of the Atlacatl BIRI participated in all these actions. In the course of "Operación Rescate," however, other mass executions were carried out by units which it has not been possible to identify with certainty.

In all instances, troops acted in the same way: they killed anyone they came across, men, women and children, and then set fire to the houses. This is what happened in La Joya canton on 11 December, in the village of La Ranchería on 12 December, and in the village of Jocote Amarillo and Cerro Pando canton on 13 December.

SUBSEQUENT EVENTS

The El Mozote massacre became public knowledge on 27 January 1982, when *The New York Times* and the *Washington Post* published articles by Raymond Bonner and Alma Guillermoprieto, respectively, reporting the massacre. In January, they had visited the scene of the massacre and had seen the bodies and the ruined houses.

In the course of the year, a number of human rights organizations denounced the massacre. The Salvadoran authorities categorically denied that a massacre had taken place. No judicial investigation was launched and there was no word of any investigation by the Government or the armed forces.

On 26 October 1990, on a criminal complaint brought by Pedro Chicas Romero, criminal proceedings were instituted in the San Francisco Gotera Court of the First Instance. During the trial, which is still going on, statements were taken from witnesses for the prosecution; eventually, the remains were ordered exhumed, and this provided irrefutable evidence of the El Mozote massacre. The judge asked the Government repeatedly for a list of the officers who took part in the military operation. He received the reply that the Government did not have such information.

THE RESULTS OF THE EXHUMATION

The exhumation of the remains in the ruins of the little building known as the convent, adjacent to the El Mozote church, took place between 13 and 17 November 1992.

The material found in the convent was analysed by expert anthropologists and then studied in minute detail in the laboratories of the Santa Tecla Institute of Forensic Medicine and of the Commission for the Investigation of Criminal Acts by Dr. Clyde Snow (forensic anthropologist), Dr. Robert H. Kirschner (forensic pathologist), Dr. Douglas Scott (archaeologist and ballistics analyst), and Dr. John Fitzpatrick (radiologist), in collaboration with the Argentine Team of Forensic Anthropologists made up of Patricia Bernardi, Mercedes Doretti and Luis Fondebrider.

The study made by the experts led to the following conclusions:

1. "All the skeletons recovered from the site and the associated evidence were deposited during the same temporal event . . . ." The physical evidence recovered in the site excludes the possibility that the site could have been used as a clandestine cemetery in which the dead were placed at different times.

2. "The events under investigation are unlikely to have occurred later than 1981." Coins and bullet cartridges bearing their date of manufacture were found in the convent. In no case was this date later than 1981.

3. In the convent, bone remains of at least 143 people were found. However, the laboratory analysis indicates that "there may, in fact, have been a greater number of deaths. This uncertainty regarding the number of skeletons is a reflection of the extensive perimortem skeletal injuries, postmortem skeletal damage and associated commingling. Many young infants may have been entirely cremated; other children may not have been counted because of extensive fragmentation of body parts."

4. The bone remains and other evidence found in the convent show numerous signs of damage caused by crushing and by fire.

5. Most of the victims were minors.

The experts determined, initially, after the exhumation, that "approximately 85 per cent of the 117 victims were children under 12 years of age," and indicated that a more precise estimate of the victims' ages would be made in the laboratory.

In the laboratory, the skeletal remains of 143 bodies were identified, including 131 children under the age of 12, 5 adolescents and 7 adults. The experts noted, in addition, that "the average age of the children was approximately 6 years."

6. One of the victims was a pregnant woman.

7. Although it could not be determined with certainty that all the victims were alive when they were brought into the convent, "it can be concluded that at least some of the victims were struck by bullets, with an effect that may well have been lethal, inside the building."

This conclusion is based on various factors:

(1) A "large quantity of bullet fragments [were] found inside the building . . . ." "Virtually all the ballistic evidence was found at level 3, in direct contact with or imbedded in the bone remains, clothing, household goods and floor of the building." Moreover, "the spatial distribution of most of the bullet fragments coincides with the area of greatest concentration of skeletons and with concentrations of bone remains." Also, the second and third areas of concentration of bullet fragments coincide with the second and third areas of concentration of skeletons, respectively.

(2) "Of 117 skeletons identified in the field, 67 were associated with bullet fragments. In 43 out of this subtotal of 67, the fragments were found in the areas of the skull and/or the thorax, i.e., parts of the body where they could have been the cause of death."

(3) "In at least nine cases, the victims were shot inside the building while lying in a horizontal position on the floor. The shots were fired downwards. In at least six of the nine cases mentioned, these shots could have caused the victims' deaths."

(4) "Direct skeletal examination showed intact gunshot wounds of entrance in only a few skulls because of the extensive fracturing that is characteristically associated with such high-velocity injuries. Skull reconstruction identified many more entrance wounds, but relatively few exit wounds. This is consistent with the ballistic evidence that the ammunition involved in the shootings was a type likely to fragment upon impact, becoming essentially frangible bullets. Radiologic examination of skull bones demonstrated small metallic densities consistent with bullet fragments in 45.2 percent (51/115).

In long bones, vertebrae, pelvis and ribs there were defects characteristic of high velocity gunshot wounds."

(5) The weapons used to fire at the victims were M–16 rifles.

As the ballistics analyst described, "two hundred forty-five cartridge cases recovered from the El Mozote site were studied. Of these, 184 had discernible headstamps, identifying the ammunition as having been manufactured for the United States Government at Lake City, Missouri. Thirty-four cartridges were sufficiently well preserved to analyze for individual as well as class characteristics. All of the projectiles except one appear to have been fired from United States-manufactured M-16 rifles."

(6) At least 24 people participated in the shooting. They fired "from

within the house, from the doorway, and probably through a window to the right of the door."

An important point that emerges from the results of the observations is that "no bullet fragments were found in the outside west facade of the stone wall."

The evidence presented above is full proof that the victims were summarily executed, as the witnesses have testified.

The experts who carried out the exhumation reached the following conclusion: "All these facts tend to indicate the perpetration of a massive crime, there being no evidence to support the theory of a confrontation between two groups."

For their part, the experts who conducted the laboratory analysis said that "the physical evidence from the exhumation of the convent house at El Mozote confirms the allegations of a mass murder." They went on to say, on the same point: "There is no evidence to support the contention that these victims, almost all young children, were involved in combat or were caught in the crossfire of combat forces. Rather the evidence strongly supports the conclusion that they were the intentional victims of a mass extra-judicial execution."

ACTION BY THE COMMISSION

Before the Commission on the Truth began its work, the Director of the Human Rights Division of the United Nations Observer Mission in El Salvador (ONUSAL) brought a motion before the judge hearing the case to have qualified foreign experts appointed.

The Commission on the Truth, from the moment it was set up, took a special interest in having the exhumation conducted under conditions that guaranteed the necessary scientific rigour and impartiality.

The Commission also reviewed the available publications, documentation and court records. It took testimony directly from eyewitnesses and was present at the exhumation site.

The Commission wrote three times to the Minister of Defence and once to the Chief of the Armed Forces Joint Staff requesting information about the units and officers who took part in *"Operación Rescate,"* and about any orders, reports or other documents relating to that operation that might be in the archives. The only response it received was that there were no records for that period.

Special mention must be made of the interference in the case by the President of the Supreme Court of El Salvador, Mr. Mauricio Gutiérrez Castro. When on 17 July 1991 representatives of the Legal Protection Office asked the trial judge to appoint qualified foreign experts to conduct the exhumations, he told them that this would require the approval of Mr. Gutiérrez Castro. It was not until nine months later, on 29 April 1992, after ONUSAL stepped in, that he proceeded to appoint them.

On 16 July 1992, when the members of the Commission on the Truth went to see him, Mr. Gutiérrez Castro said that the exhumation ordered by the trial judge would prove that "only dead guerrillas are buried" at El Mozote.

A few days later, the court hearing the case ruled that its appointment of foreign experts was not valid without a complicated procedure of consultation with foreign Governments through the Supreme Court of Justice, with the result that the exhumation was on the point of going ahead without the presence of such experts.

On 21 October, Mr. Mauricio Gutiérrez Castro came to the exhumation site and, in giving his opinion on how future excavations in the zone should be carried out, said that care should be taken not to "favour one of the parties" (presumably the Government and FMLN) "because of the political implications of this process, which override legal considerations."

FINDINGS

There is full proof that on 11 December *1981, in the* village of El Mozote, units of the Atlacatl Battalion deliberately and systematically killed a group of more than 200 men, women and children, constituting the entire civilian population that they had found there the previous day and had since been holding prisoner.

The officers in command of the Atlacatl Battalion at the time of the operation whom the Commission has managed to identify are the following: Battalion Commander: Lieutenant Colonel Domingo Monterrosa Barrios (deceased); Commanding Officer: Major Natividad de Jesús Cáceres Cabrera (now Colonel); Chief of Operations: Major José Armando Azmitia Melara (deceased); Company Commanders: Juan Ernesto Méndez Rodríguez (now Colonel); Roberto Alfonso Mendoza Portillo (deceased); José Antonio Rodríguez Molina (now Lieutenant Colonel), Captain Walter Oswaldo Salazar (now Lieutenant Colonel) and José Alfredo Jiménez (currently a fugitive from justice).

There is sufficient evidence that in the days preceding and following the El Mozote massacre, troops participating in "Operación Rescate" massacred the non-combatant civilian population in La Joya canton, in the villages of La Ranchería, Jocote Amarillo y Los Toriles, and in Cerro Pando canton.

Participating in this operation, in addition to the Atlacatl Battalion, were units of the Third Infantry Brigade, commanded by Colonel Jaime Flórez Grijalba (now retired) who was also responsible for supervising the operation, and units from the San Francisco Gotera Commando Training Centre commanded by Colonel Alejandro Cisneros (now retired).

Although it received news of the massacre, which would have been easy to corroborate because of the profusion of unburied bodies, the Armed Forces High Command did not conduct or did not give any word of an investigation and repeatedly denied that the massacre had occurred. There is full evidence that General José Guillermo García, then Minister of Defence, initiated no investigations that might have enabled the facts to be established. There is sufficient evidence that General Rafael Flórez Lima, Chief of the Armed Force Joint Staff at the time, was aware that the massacre had occurred and also failed to undertake any investigation.

The High Command also took no steps whatsoever to prevent the repetition of such acts, with the result that the same units were used in other operations and followed the same procedures.

The El Mozote massacre was a serious violation of international humanitarian law and international human rights law.

The President of the Supreme Court of Justice of El Salvador, Mr. Mauricio Gutiérrez Castro, has interfered unduly and prejudicially, for biased political reasons, in the ongoing judicial proceedings on the case.

16. THE STATE DEPARTMENT LOOKS AT ITSELF

After the Truth Commission made its report public in March 1993, Warren Christopher, the Secretary of State in the newly-installed Clinton Administration, declared himself "deeply shocked" by what he read. A few days later, the Secretary appointed a three-member panel to "examine the activities and conduct of the [State] Department" during the period covered by the Truth Commission report. The panel included George S. Vest and Richard W. Murphy, both retired Foreign Service Officers, and I. M. Destler, a professor at the University of Maryland.

A little more than three months later, in July 1993, the panel published its report. Its "basic conclusion," as stated in the Executive Summary, was that, "within the parameters of overall U.S. policy, the Department and Foreign Service personnel performed creditably—and on occasion with personal bravery—in advancing human rights in El Salvador." It did, however, list several caveats: "Mistakes were certainly made: in dealing with specific cases, in the handling of reporting during one period of the decade, and particularly in the failure to get the truth about the December 1981 massacre at El Mozote."

Following is the full text of the panel's report on the Department's handling of the El Mozote massacre.

The El Mozote Massacre

The Truth Commission stated that more than 500 men, women, and children were massacred in El Mozote and nearby hamlets on over a three-day period beginning December 11. The massacre was carried out by units of the Atlacatl Battalion, an "Immediate Reaction Infantry Battalion" (the first of its kind in El Salvador), which had completed its U.S. counter-insurgency training earlier that year. The FMLN Radio Venceremos first broke the story of the massacre on December 27. It reached the international press with the publication of front-page articles in *The New York Times* and *Washington Post* on January 27, 1982, following visits by American reporters to the site. The incident was confirmed by autopsy reports on remains in the area ten years later.

Ambassador Hinton informed the Department on January 8 that he had been asked about a massacre in Morazán Department by a representative of the National Council of Churches and had responded: "I certainly cannot confirm such reports nor do I have any reason to believe they are true." He noted that Embassy sources had provided no hint that such a thing had occurred and quoted a Radio Venceremos report of January 2 as the only source he had seen. He then stated that he did not consider Radio Venceremos to be reliable. A discussion a few days later with a freelance American journalist who had apparently accompanied the Salvadoran troops on their sweep in the area and witnessed nothing untoward added to the Embassy's skepticism. Further skepticism, and a belief that the El Mozote story was part of an FMLN pre-certification propaganda campaign, was engendered by a false story filed a few days earlier by one of the same journalists who wrote on January 27 to the effect that U.S. military trainers had observed Salvadorans carrying out torture.

Asked about a massacre when the stories in *The New York Times* and the *Washington Post* appeared on January 27, the Department's spokesman said "if the reports were proven accurate, we would obviously deplore such an incident." He quoted the Ambassador's January 8 response at some length and added that "the Embassy has, and will continue actively, to seek corroboration of such reports." He reiterated the Department's position that "we abhor violence of this type, whether from the right or the left, whether by government troops or guerrilla insurgents."

The January 27 stories prompted the Embassy to carry out its own investigation. It sent the assistant defense attaché and a human rights officer to the area. They were unable to get to the site—which had returned to rebel control—but they flew over it by helicopter and talked to people in the vicinity.

The Embassy reported its conclusions in a cable dated January 31. The summary stated: "Although it is not possible to prove or disprove excesses of violence against the civilian population of El Mozote by government troops, it is certain that the guerrilla forces who established defensive positions in El Mozote did nothing to remove them from the path of battle which they were aware was coming and had prepared for, nor is there any evidence that those who remained attempted to leave. Civilians did die during Operation Rescate but no evidence could be found to confirm that government forces systematically massacred civilians in the operation zone, nor that the number of civilians killed even remotely approached number being cited in other reports circulating internationally." It noted they were still pursuing the question of what army units were present in El Mozote.

The body of the cable described Morazán Department (where El Mozote is located), El Mozote itself (noting its population at the time was estimated at no more than 300), and the military's Operation Rescate. It said there was stiff guerrilla resistance and four hours of fighting. It further noted that "civilians remaining in any part of the canton could have been subject to injury as a result of the combat" and added that El Mozote returned to guerrilla hands December 29. The reporting officers quoted an aged couple who fled the town during the attack as saying they saw dozens of bodies. The mayor of a nearby town was unwilling to discuss the comportment of government forces saying "this is something one should talk about in another time, in another country." He and a priest both agreed that many of the refugees in this nearby town were from guerrilla families.

The conclusion of the cable noted that the area was war-ravaged with the government controlling the towns, the guerrillas the countryside, and "most civilians attempt [ing] to maintain a tenuous neutrality." With El Mozote in guerrilla hands since August 1981, the reporting officers felt "the inhabitants were certainly passive and probably active guerrilla supporters." The cable noted inconsistency in the reported numbers of deaths, adding its estimate that no more than 300 people were in the entire canton. It noted that various contacts in the area had been unable to provide first-hand information on El Mozote, that the officials had visited "locations throughout Morazán" on January 30 and interviewed inhabitants and refugees from El Mozote and nearby cantons.

Ambassador Hinton was clearly uncomfortable about jumping to conclusions on El Mozote. He complained to the Department on February 1 about a cable that referred to his "denying" the incident. "I would be grateful if Department would use extreme care in describing my views on alleged massacre," he wrote, noting that he had said he had no confirmation of it and no reason to believe Radio Venceremos. He added, however, that "additional evidence strongly suggests that something happened that should not have happened and that it is quite possible Salvadoran military did commit excesses." He also dismissed the Salvadoran Defense Minister's denial as "stone-walling without credibility" and told the Minister that something had "gone wrong" with the operation. The next day he pressed him to name the leaders of the battalion involved. The Defense Minister responded by calling the stories a *"novela"* and a "pack of lies."

The Department released the Embassy summary of its investigation to the press on February 1. Assistant Secretary Enders testified at several House and Senate committees over the next few days. His approach before the Subcommittee on Inter-American Affairs of the House Foreign Affairs Committee on February 2 was typical. He commented that there was "no question that the human rights situation in El Salvador is deeply troubled" and discussed the difficulties of gathering accurate information. He said the "most difficult of all to assess are the repeated allegations of massacres. The ambiguity lies in the fact that there are indeed incidents in which the noncombatants have suffered terribly at the hands of the guerrillas, rightist vigilantes, government forces, or some or all of them, but at the same time the insurgency has repeatedly fabricated or inflated alleged mass murders as a means of propaganda." He noted two instances that had not stood up under investigation in 1981 and sharply criticized the killing of 19 persons in San Salvador (San Antonio Abad) two days previously, adding that he "deeply deplored" the "excessive violence of the Salvadoran forces in this incident."

He continued that "we sent two Embassy officers down to investigate the report . . . of the massacre in Mozote in the Morazán Province. It is clear from the report that they gave that there has been a confrontation between the guerrillas occupying Mozote and attacking government forces last December. There is no evidence to confirm that government forces systematically massacred civilians in the operations zone, or that the number of civilians remotely approached the 733 or 926 victims cited in the press. I note they asked how many people there were in that canton, and were told probably not more than 300 in December, and there are many survivors including refugees now." He added that "our Embassy tries to investigate every report we receive, and we use every opportunity to impress on the El Salvador government and army that we are serious about practicing human rights and they must be too."

In the testimony cited above, Enders did not note that the Embassy officers, unlike the reporters, did not actually visit the site. That omission became highly controversial, despite the fact he had told another subcommittee the day before the officers had not reached El Mozote.* So did the phrase "no evidence to confirm."

The controversy on El Mozote was also heightened by the political context. Not only did the President make his first certification of El Salvador on January 28, but critics in Congress and the press were questioning Administration statements of Nicaraguan support to the Salvadoran insurgents (this, of course, was the basis for U.S. covert funding of the contras which had begun two months before). The Administration planned to send new aid to El Salvador, and the Administration had complained repeatedly that press reporting from El Salvador was biased in the favor of the FMLN. The thrust of Enders' testimony was to dispute the press reports on El Mozote. The standard response the Department then used for Congressional and other correspondence went further. It was, in fact, designed essentially to discredit the story by repeating that there had been a battle for the town, that civilians were not removed from the line of fire, and that "the guerrillas have grossly inflated the number of civilian deaths for propaganda purposes."

Embassy San Salvador did not attempt again to go to El Mozote. Embassy Tegucigalpa reported on February 17 that some recently arrived Salvadoran refugees from Morazán Province said there had been intense military sweeps through the province in December and that houses were burned and many residents killed. With the run-up to the March 1982 election and movement on some U.S.-interest cases, Embassy San Salvador found itself with little time to follow up on the El Mozote case. There was apparently also no effort in Washington to obtain and analyze the numerous photographs that had been taken at the site by the American journalists. In May the Embassy reported it had attempted to establish a data base for further investigation of the events in El Mozote, but said it was "unable to reach

---

*Enders had, in fact, noted to the House Foreign Operations (Appropriations) Subcommittee on February 1 that the town of "El Mozote was again in insurgents' hands and we could not go there" and repeated that point a few days later to the Senate Foreign Relations Committee. He provided a classified copy of the original reporting cable to the Senate.

a definite conclusion regarding civilian deaths" there. Reviewing all available sources, it felt that none of them "concretely indicate that anywhere near 1,000 civilians were massacred there."

The El Mozote issue then appears to have been lost in the flood of ongoing embassy business. The election and its aftermath dominated the Salvadoran political scene. People the Panel interviewed underlined that it had dropped off the scope of the Embassy's and the Department's concerns. However, given the enormity and prominence of the charges, this was clearly a case where an extraordinary effort—possibly including pressing for a Salvadoran military operation to escort neutral observers to the site—was needed. The Embassy does not seem to have been inclined to press, and Washington preferred to avoid the issue and protect its policy then under siege. By July, Enders' careful "no evidence to confirm" had become in the certification report "no evidence to support allegations of large-scale massacres allegedly committed by government forces." This conclusion is obviously inconsistent with the January 31 cable and Hinton's subsequent cautionary messages as well as the press reports. It undermined the Department's credibility with its critics—and probably with the Salvadorans—in a serious way that has not healed.

The exhumations in 1992 showed clearly that a massacre had indeed occurred and the U.S. statements on the case were wrong. On December 11, 1991, two Embassy officers went to El Mozote to attend a ceremony honoring those who had died in the massacre.

THE DEAD

Within a few weeks after the killings at El Mozote and the surrounding hamlets, the first attempts were made to compile lists of the dead. Scarcely a month after the massacre, when Raymond Bonner of *The New York Times* visited northern Morazán, the guerrillas there handed him a few scraps of notepaper covered with handwriting: hundreds and hundreds of names. After counting the names himself, Bonner published his total of 733.

During the next weeks and months, the number of dead claimed for the massacre varied widely. The war prevented any independent forensic investigation and encouraged the manipulation of the numbers for use as propaganda. What's more, the great movements of population that the fighting had brought to Morazán presented practical difficulties that made an accurate accounting almost impossible. (In El Mozote itself, for example, where virtually everyone had died, a substantial number of those killed had come to the hamlet from outside, seeking protection.)

In the spring of 1990, investigators from Tutela Legal, the human rights office of the Archbishopric of San Salvador, traveled to Morazán to begin gathering information for the legal case that Pedro Chicas Romero and others would bring the following November. During the course of their investigation, the Tutela workers interviewed scores of survivors, compiled family trees, examined surviving birth records. When Tutela Legal published its report in November 1991, appended to it was a list of those who had died. Tutela's list was certainly the most accurate such effort up to that time; failing further exhumations, it will likely remain the most thorough accounting of those who died during the massacre of El Mozote. It contains just short of eight hundred names. (After its own thorough investigation, the Truth Commission concluded that "more than 500 identified victims perished at El Mozote and in the other villages. Many other victims have not been identified.")

What follows is drawn from the Tutela Legal list, with some changes to take account of more recent information. In general, ages are approximate—particularly in the case of children, many of whom, because of the lack of official records and the limited memories of those who survived, must remain without names.

The Dead

EL MOZOTE

1. DOMINGO CLAROS, 29, wood cutter
2. CRISTINO AMAYA CLAROS, 9, son of Domingo Claros
3. MARÍA DOLORES AMAYA CLAROS, 5, daughter of Domingo Claros
4. MARTA LILIÁN CLAROS, 3, daughter of Domingo Claros
5. MARÍA ISABEL AMAYA CLAROS, 8 months, daughter of Domingo Claros
6. ISIDRA CLAROS, 60, aunt of Domingo Claros
7. BONIFACIA RODRÍGUEZ OR ANASTACIA ARGUETA, 65
8. LEONISIA RODRÍGUEZ OR DIONISIA RODRÍGUEZ, 27, seamstress, daughter of Bonifacia Rodríguez
9. VILMA RODRÍGUEZ, 2, daughter of Dionisia Rodríguez and Manuel Alvarenda
10. MARTINA RODRÍGUEZ, 35, daughter of Bonifacia Rodríguez and sister of Dionisia and Vilma Rodríguez

11. Ruperto Chicas, 40, farmer, husband of Martina Rodríguez
12. Mirna Chicas, 10, daughter of Martina Rodríguez and Ruperto Chicas
13. Child, 6, son of Martina Rodríguez and Ruperto Chicas
14. Child, 4, daughter of Martina Rodríguez and Ruperto Chicas
15. Child, 3, son of Martina Rodríguez and Ruperto Chicas
16. Child, 1, son of Martina Rodríguez and Ruperto Chicas
17. Concepción Márquez, 75
18. Julia Claros, 30, daughter of Concepción Márquez
19. Alberta Claros, 18, daughter of Julia Claros
20. Child, 1, daughter of Alberta Claros
21. Francisca Claros, 11, daughter of Julia Claros
22. Child, 7, daughter of Julia Claros
23. Antolina Claros, 28
24. Francisca Claros, 16, daughter of Antolina Claros
25. Claudio Del Cid, 20, carpenter, companion of Francisca Claros
26. Child, 6 months old, daughter of Francisca Claros and Claudio Del Cid
27. María Del Cid, 60, mother of Claudio Del Cid
28. Girl, 15, daughter of Antolina Claros
29. Child, 11, daughter of Antolina Claros
30. Oscar Claros, 7, son of Antolina Claros
31. Jesús Claros, 5, daughter of Antolina Claros
32. Leonisia Claros, 25, daughter of Concepción Márquez and sister of Antolina Claros
33. Fabián Luna, 20, day laborer, companion of Leonisia Claros
34. Child, 5, daughter of Leonisia Claros and Fabián Luna
35. Lucio Claros, 2½, son of Leonisia Claros and Fabián Luna
36. Child, 7 months old, daughter of Leonisia Claros and Fabián Luna
37. Emilia Claros, 35, daughter of Concepción Márquez and sister of Antolina and Francisca Claros
38. Melesio Argueta Alvarenga, 40, day laborer, husband of Emilia Claros
39. Priscilio Claros, 7, son of Emilia Claros and Melesio Argueta
40. Girl, 18, daughter of Emilia Claros and Melesio Argueta
41. Child, 10 months old, daughter of victim #40 and granddaughter of Emilia Claros and Melesio Argueta
42. Isabel Argueta, 6, daughter of Emilia Claros and Melesio Argueta
43. Child, 4, son of Emilia Claros and Melesio Argueta
44. Child, 2, son of Emilia Claros and Melesio Argueta
45. Cosme Argueta, 45, sister of Melesio Argueta

46. ISRAEL MÁRQUEZ, 80, merchant
47. PAULA MÁRQUEZ, 60, wife of Israel Márquez
48. ELVIRA MÁRQUEZ CHICAS, 34, pregnant at time of death, niece of Israel Márquez
49. SONIA MÁRQUEZ OR SONIA CHICAS, 5, daughter of Elvira Márquez and Leonardo Márquez Del Cid (victim #51)
50. GIRL, 19, daughter of Israel Márquez
51. LEONARDO MÁRQUEZ DEL CID, 40, farmer, father of Sonia Márquez (victim #49)
52. BALBINO MÁRQUEZ DEL CID, 60, farmer, father of Leonardo Márquez
53. FRANCISCA DEL CID, 55, wife of Balbino Márquez
54. ORBELINA MÁRQUEZ, 45, seamstress, companion of Leonardo Márquez Del Cid
55. BRUNO CLAROS, 50, farmer
56. HORTENSIA ROMERO MÁRQUEZ, 39, wife of Bruno Claros
57. MATILDE PEREIRA, 70, farmer, father of Bruno Claros
58. RODOLFO CLAROS, 15, brother of Bruno Claros
59. CHILD, 5, ward of Bruno Claros
60. BOY, 18, son of Bruno Claros and Hortensia Romero
61. GIRL, 16, daughter of Bruno Claros and Hortensia Romero
62. EVA ROMERO, 11, daughter of Bruno Claros and Hortensia Romero
63. IRMA ROMERO, 9, daughter of Bruno Claros and Hortensia Romero
64. BRUNO CLAROS, 7, son of Bruno Claros and Hortensia Romero
65. HIPÓLITA CLAROS, 13, daughter of Domingo Claros (victim #1)
66. MARÍA CONCEPCIÓN ROMERO, 44, mother of Hipólita Claros
67. MELESIO DÍAZ, 65, butcher
68. NORBERTA MÁRQUEZ, 40, companion of Melesio Díaz
69. MÁRTIR DÍAZ, 14, daughter of Melesio Díaz
70. MOISÉS CLAROS, 75, day laborer
71. MAN, 90, father of Moisés Claros
72. EUGENIA CLAROS, 27, maguey spinner, daughter of Moisés Claros
73. DAVID CLAROS, 10, son of Eugenia Claros and grandson of Moisés Claros
74. CHILD, 6, daughter of Eugenia Claros and granddaughter of Moisés Claros
75. CHILD, 8, daughter of Eugenia Claros and granddaughter of Moisés Claros
76. CHILD, 3, daughter of Eugenia Claros and granddaughter of Moisés Claros
77. CHILD, 2, daughter of Eugenia Claros and granddaughter of Moisés Claros

78. CHILD, 9 months old, daughter of Eugenia Claros and granddaughter of Moisés Claros
79. BENJAMÍN ANTONIO CLAROS, 45, son of Moisés Claros
80. ANASTACIA MÁRQUEZ, 40, pregnant at time of death, companion of Benjamín Antonio Claros
81. MATÍAS MÁRQUEZ, 75, carpenter, father of Anastacia Márquez
82. MARÍA ARGUETA, 30, companion of Matías Márquez
83. DOLORES MÁRQUEZ, 25, pregnant at time of death, daughter of Matías Márquez
84. LUCÍO MÁRQUEZ, 45, day laborer, companion of Dolores Márquez
85. CHILD, 7, son of Dolores Márquez and Lucío Márquez
86. CHILD, 5, son of Dolores Márquez and Lucío Márquez
87. DOMINGA MÁRQUEZ, 70, mother of Lucío Márquez
88. CHILD, 5, daughter of Benjamín Claros (victim #79) and Anastacia Márquez (victim #80)
89. CHILD, 6, son of Benjamín Claros (victim #79) and Anastacia Márquez (victim #80)
90. CHILD, 9, son of Benjamín Claros (victim #79) and Anastacia Márquez (victim #80)
91. CHILD, 11, son of Benjamín Claros (victim #79) and Anastacia Márquez (victim #80)
92. FRANCISCO CLAROS, 80, day laborer, cousin of Moisés Claros (victim #70)
93. ROGELIA DÍAZ, 76, wife of Francisco Claros
94. BOY, 16, paralyzed, grandson of Francisco Claros
95. PAULINA MÁRQUEZ CLAROS OR PAULINA CLAROS OR PAULINA DÍAZ, 60
96. TELÉSFORO MÁRQUEZ, 35, deaf and mute, son of Paulina Márquez
97. LORENZO CLAROS OR LORENZO DÍAZ, 25, son of Paulina Márquez and brother of Telésforo Márquez
98. EUGENIO VIGIL, 60, farmer
99. AGUSTINA VIGIL, 25, pregnant at time of death, daughter of Eugenio Vigil
100. CHILD, 7, daughter of Agustina Vigil
101. MARCELINA VIGIL, 22, daughter of Eugenio Vigil
102. DIONISIO MÁRQUEZ, 20, day laborer, husband of Marcelina Vigil
103. MIGUEL MÁRQUEZ, 70, day laborer, father of Dionisio Márquez
104. CHILD, 5, son of Dionisio Márquez
105. CHILD, 9 months old, daughter of Dionisio Márquez
106. MARÍA ANSELMA MÁRQUEZ, 25, pregnant at time of death, daughter of Miguel Márquez
107. ARTURO GIDIO CHICAS, 39, day laborer, companion of Anselma Márquez

108. LUCÍA MÁRQUEZ, 14, daughter of María Anselma Márquez and Arturo Gidio Chicas
109. DORA MÁRQUEZ, 11, daughter of María Anselma Márquez and Arturo Gidio Chicas
110. CHILD, 7, daughter of María Anselma Márquez and Arturo Gidio Chicas
111. CHILD, 5, daughter of María Anselma Márquez and Arturo Gidio Chicas
112. CHILD, 1, son of María Anselma Márquez and Arturo Gidio Chicas
113. GIRL, 18, daughter of Miguel Márquez (victim #103)
114. CHILD, 2 days old, grandson of Miguel Márquez
115. MARTO VIGIL, 75, farmer, brother of Eugenio Vigil (victim #98)
116. PAULA DÍAZ, 75, wife of Marto Vigil
117. DOMINGA DÍAZ, 30, ward of Marto Vigil
118. CHILD, 5, daughter of Dominga Díaz
119. MAGDALENA DÍAZ, 60, sister of Paula Díaz
120. GIRL, 19, daughter of Magdalena Díaz
121. GIRL, 16, daughter of Magdalena Díaz
122. CESARIO MÁRQUEZ, 70, farmer
123. CLEMENTINA PEREIRA OR CLEMENTINA ARGUETA, 60, wife of Cesario Márquez
124. GIRL, 15, daughter of Cesario Márquez
125. GIRL, 14, daughter of Cesario Márquez
126. CHILD, 11, son of Cesario Márquez
127. HILDA MÁRQUEZ, 25, pregnant at time of death, daughter of Cesario Márquez
128. CHILD, 6, daughter of Hilda Márquez and Felipe Argueta
129. CHILD, 4, son of Hilda Márquez and Felipe Argueta
130. CHILD, 3, son of Hilda Márquez and Felipe Argueta
131. CHILD, 1, daughter of Hilda Márquez and Felipe Argueta
132. FILOMENA CLAROS, 50, daughter of Concepción Márquez (victim #17)
133. CHILD, 11, son of Filomena Claros
134. BOY, 18, day laborer, son of Filomena Claros
135. GIRL, 14, daughter of Filomena Claros
136. CHILD, 7, son of Filomena Claros
137. CHILD, 5, son of Filomena Claros
138. ASCENCIÓN MÁRQUEZ, 39, day laborer, brother of Concepción Márquez (victim #17)
139. SUSANA CLAROS, 48
140. EUGENIA CLAROS, 30, pregnant at time of death, daughter of Susana Claros and companion of Ascención Márquez
141. JESÚS CLAROS, 10, son of Ascención Márquez and Eugenia Claros

142. ROSITA CLAROS, 5, daughter of Ascención Márquez and Eugenia Claros
143. CHILD, 7, son of Ascención Márquez and Eugenia Claros
144. CHILD, 3, son of Ascención Márquez and Eugenia Claros
145. CHILD, 2, daughter of Ascención Márquez and Eugenia Claros
146. ANDREA DEL CID, 60
147. VICENTA DEL CID, 80, sister of Andrea Del Cid
148. ROSA DEL CID, 20, pregnant at time of death, daughter of Andrea Del Cid
149. EMELY DEL CID, 4, son of Rosa Del Cid
150. MAURICIO DEL CID, 9 months, son of Rosa Del Cid
151. ÁNGELA DEL CID, 5, daughter of Rosa Del Cid
152. LEONCIO DÍAZ, 105, a butcher in his youth
153. LEONCIA MÁRQUEZ, 100, companion of Leoncio Díaz
154. GILBERTO SORTO, 25, farmer
155. FELICITA VIGIL, 20, wife of Gilberto Sorto
156. ANACLETA SORTO, 65, mother of Gilberto Sorto
157. CHILD, 5, son of Gilberto Sorto and Felicita Vigil
158. CHILD, 3, son of Gilberto Sorto and Felicita Vigil
159. MARTINA ARGUETA, 35
160. CHILD, 12, daughter of Martina Argueta
161. CHILD, 9, son of Martina Argueta
162. CHILD, 7, son of Martina Argueta
163. CHILD, 2, daughter of Martina Argueta
164. ONOFRE ARGUETA, 19
165. CHILD, 11, daughter of Onofre Argueta
166. CHILD, 9, son of Onofre Argueta
167. CHILD, 7, son of Onofre Argueta
168. CHILD, 5, daughter of Onofre Argueta
169. CHILD, 3, son of Onofre Argueta
170. GERTRUDIS GUEVARA, 80, day laborer
171. MARCELINA MÁRQUEZ, 25, companion of Gertrudis Guevara
172. TOMÁS MÁRQUEZ, 5, son of Gertrudis Guevara and Marcelina Márquez
173. CHILD, 3 months old, daughter of Gertrudis Guevara and Marcelina Márquez
174. SEGUNDO CHICAS, 25, day laborer
175. SATURNINA ROMERO, 25, companion of Segundo Chicas
176. CHILD, 9 months old, daughter of Segundo Chicas and Saturnina Romero
177. CHILD, 10, son of Segundo Chicas and Saturnina Romero
178. CHILD, 7, son of Segundo Chicas and Saturnina Romero
179. CHILD, 5, son of Segundo Chicas and Saturnina Romero

180. FACUNDO CHICAS, 25, brother of Segundo Chicas
181. MELDA MÁRQUEZ CHICAS, 25, wife of Facundo Chicas
182. CHILD, 12, son of Facundo Chicas and Melda Márquez
183. CHILD, 10, son of Facundo Chicas and Melda Márquez
184. CHILD, 9, son of Facundo Chicas and Melda Márquez
185. CHILD, 7, son of Facundo Chicas and Melda Márquez
186. CHILD, 2, son of Facundo Chicas and Melda Márquez
187. ANSELMA dE MÁRQUEZ, 80
188. CHON MÁRQUEZ, 22, mentally retarded son of Anselma de Márquez
189. DOROTEO N., 60, day laborer
190. FERNANDO GUEVARA, 60, farmer
191. FLORINDA DEL CID DE GUEVARA, 58, an amputee (one leg), wife of Fernando Guevara and sister of Francisca Del Cid (victim #53)
192. MARÍA ROMERO, 45, merchant, a widow
193. LUCAS GUEVARA, 35, day laborer
194. ANDRÉS GUEVARA, 50, day laborer, father of Lucas Guevara
195. RUFINA ROMERO, 35, companion of Lucas Guevara
196. TELMA ROMERO, 12, daughter of Lucas Guevara and Rufina Romero
197. ROSITA ROMERO, 10, daughter of Lucas Guevara and Rufina Romero
198. CANDELARIA ROMERO, 6, daughter of Lucas Guevara and Rufina Romero
199. JOAQUÍN ROMERO, 7, son of Lucas Guevara and Rufina Romero
200. JOSÉ ROMERO, 6 months, son of Lucas Guevara and Rufina Romero
201. BENITO ROMERO, 30, day laborer, son of María Romero (victim #192)
202. FLORENTINA DEL CID, 25, companion of Benito Romero
203. LUCÍA DEL CID, 10, daughter of Benito Romero and Florentina Del Cid
204. CAMILO DEL CID, 7, son of Benito Romero and Florentina Del Cid
205. ROSITA DEL CID, 4, daughter of Benito Romero and Florentina Del Cid
206. CHILD, 1, daughter of Benito Romero and Florentina Del Cid
207. EDUARDO DÍAZ OR EDUARDO CLAROS, 30, day laborer
208. CARMEN CLAROS, 18, companion of Eduardo Claros
209. JUBENCIO DÍAZ, 10, son of Eduardo Díaz
210. CLICERIO DÍAZ, 3, son of Eduardo Díaz
211. JOSÉ DÍAZ, 5, son of Eduardo Díaz
212. DECIDERIO DÍAZ OR DECIDERIO CLAROS, 50, farmer, father of Eduardo Díaz
213. MARÍA MÁRQUEZ OR MARÍA GUEVARA, 40, companion of Deciderio Díaz

214. SANTOS MÁRQUEZ OR SANTOS GUEVARA, 20, daughter of María Márquez

215. ELADIO CLAROS, 25, day laborer, son of Deciderio Díaz and companion of Santos Márquez

216. DORIS CLAROS, 16, daughter of Eladio Claros and Santos Guevara

217. CHILD, 13, son of Eladio Claros and Santos Guevara

218. CHILD, 11, daughter of Eladio Claros and Santos Guevara

219. CHILD, 8, son of Eladio Claros and Santos Guevara

220. CHILD, 5, daughter of Eladio Claros and Santos Guevara

221. VIRGINIA CLAROS, 16, sister of Eduardo Claros (victim #207)

222. OLAYO CLAROS, 15, day laborer, brother of Eduardo Claros (victim #207)

223. MARTINA CLAROS, 15, pregnant at time of death, companion of Olayo Claros

224. FRANCISCA CLAROS, 18, sister of Eduardo Claros (victim #207)

225. IGNACIO GUEVARA, 60, farmer

226. PETO DÍAZ, 50, farmer

227. ANDREA MÁRQUEZ, 45, companion of Peto Díaz

228. VICTORIANA DÍAZ MÁRQUEZ, 30, daughter of Peto Díaz and Andrea Márquez

229. LOCADIO DÍAZ MÁRQUEZ, 18, son of Peto Díaz and Andrea Márquez

230. UGENIA DÍAZ MÁRQUEZ, 14, daughter of Peto Díaz and Andrea Márquez

231. CHILD, 4, son of Victoriana Díaz Márquez

232. CHILD, 1, son of Victoriana Díaz Márquez

233. SALOMÉ MÁRQUEZ, 25, day laborer

234. MARTA MÁRQUEZ VIGIL, 50

235. MARGARITA MÁRQUEZ CLAROS, 25, daughter of Marta Márquez

236. LIRIA MÁRQUEZ, 7, daughter of Margarita Márquez

237. DINORA MÁRQUEZ, 6, daughter of Margarita Márquez

238. AMPARO MÁRQUEZ, 4, daughter of Margarita Márquez

239. ROSITA MÁRQUEZ, 2, daughter of Margarita Márquez

240. MIRIAM MÁRQUEZ, 1, daughter of Margarita Márquez

241. CLEOTILDE MÁRQUEZ, 60, sister of Marta Márquez

242. COSME DÍAZ, 80, day laborer

243. JOSÉ MARCOS DÍAZ, 34, merchant

244. ROSA PEREIRA, 22, wife of José Marcos Díaz

245. IRMA YANET DÍAZ, 4, daughter of José Marcos Díaz and Rosa Pereira

246. LORENA PEREIRA, 3, daughter of José Marcos Díaz and Rosa Pereira

247. AMÍLCAR PEREIRA, 2 months, son of José Marcos Díaz and Rosa Pereira

248. MAURA PEREIRA, 10, student, goddaughter of José Marcos Díaz
249. ALEJANDRO DÍAZ, 60, merchant, father of José Marcos Díaz
250. MARÍA MÁRQUEZ, 50, companion of Alejandro Díaz
251. RAMÓN MÁRQUEZ DÍAZ, 18, merchant, son of Alejandro Díaz
252. SANTOS MÁRQUEZ, 40, farmer
253. AGUSTINA GARCÍA, 35, companion of Santos Márquez
254. RENE MÁRQUEZ, 11, student, son of Santos Márquez and Agustina García
255. EDI MÁRQUEZ, 5, daughter of Santos Márquez and Agustina García
256. CHILD, 2, daughter of Santos Márquez and Agustina García
257. FELIX DEL CID, 19, day laborer
258. ESTANISLAO CHICAS, 75, blind man
259. ANGÉLICA MÁRQUEZ, 45, seamstress, wife of Estanislao Chicas
260. CARLOS CHICAS, 25, blind, son of Estanislao Chicas and Angélica Márquez
261. NARCISA MÁRQUEZ, 20, companion of Carlos Chicas
262. CHILD, 5, daughter of Carlos Chicas and Narcisa Márquez
263. CHILD, 3, daughter of Carlos Chicas and Narcisa Márquez
264. CHILD, 2, daughter of Carlos Chicas and Narcisa Márquez
265. ANTONIO CHICAS, 15, student, brother of Carlos Chicas and son of Estanislao Chicas
266. HUMBERTO CHICAS, 13, son of Estanislao Chicas and Angélica Márquez
267. ESTANISLAO GUEVARA, 30, day laborer
268. FELIPA DÍAZ, 25, companion of Estanislao Guevara
269. CHILD, 8, son of Estanislao Guevara and Felipa Díaz
270. CHILD, 7, son of Estanislao Guevara and Felipa Díaz
271. CHILD, 6, son of Estanislao Guevara and Felipa Díaz
272. NATIVIDAD ARGUETA, 80
273. MARTINA DÍAZ, 65, maguey spinner, wife of Natividad Argueta
274. DANIEL ROMERO, 48, farmer
275. FLORENTINA PEREIRA, 42, wife of Daniel Romero
276. ANA MARÍA ROMERO, 16, daughter of Daniel Romero and Florentina Pereira
277. JESÚS SALVADOR ROMERO, 13, son of Daniel Romero and Florentina Pereira
278. ELMER NICOLÁS MÁRQUEZ, 2, ward of Daniel Romero
279. LEONCIO DÍAZ, 60, merchant
280. EDILFONZA DÍAZ, 68, wife of Leoncio Díaz
281. JOSÉ MARÍA MÁRQUEZ, 60, day laborer
282. DONATILA PEREIRA, 45, seamstress, companion of José María Márquez

283. SOFÍA MÁRQUEZ, 25, daughter of José María Márquez and Donatila Pereira

284. OSCAR MÁRQUEZ, 19 son of José María Márquez and Donatila Pereira

285. CHILD, 7, son of Sofía Márquez

286. CHILD, 3, son of Sofía Márquez

287. CHILD, 2, son of Sofía Márquez

288. EVENOR MÁRQUEZ, 17, day laborer, son of José María Márquez and Donatila Pereira

289. MARÍA FREDY MÁRQUEZ, 14, student, daughter of José María Márquez and Donatila Pereira

290. CHILD, 3, daughter of José María Márquez and Donatila Pereira

291. CAYETANO ARGUETA, 60, day laborer

292. MARÍA ÁNGELA GUEVARA, 50, companion of Cayetano Argueta

293. CHILD, 12, student, son of Cayetano Argueta and María Ángela Guevara

294. CHILD, 10, student, son of Cayetano Argueta and María Ángela Guevara

295. FLORENCIO ARGUETA DEL CID, 62, day laborer

296. MARÍA VALENTINA ARGUETA MÁRQUEZ, 30, daughter of Florencio Argueta Del Cid

297. AGUSTINA ARGUETA MÁRQUEZ, 22, daughter of Florencio Argueta Del Cid

298. MARÍA MÁRTIR ARGUETA MÁRQUEZ, 23, daughter of Florencio Argueta Del Cid

299. JUAN FRANCISCO ARGUETA MÁRQUEZ, 10, son of Florencio Argueta Del Cid

300. LUCIO MÁRQUEZ, 24, day laborer, husband of María Valentina Argueta Márquez (victim #296)

301. EVARISTO MÁRQUEZ ARGUETA, 8, son of María Valentina Argueta Márquez and Lucio Márquez

302. ANTONIO MÁRQUEZ ARGUETA, 5, son of María Valentina Argueta Márquez and Lucio Márquez

303. CRISTINO MÁRQUEZ ARGUETA, 2, son of María Valentina Argueta Márquez and Lucio Márquez

304. CELESTINO MÁRQUEZ ARGUETA, 1, son of María Valentina Argueta Márquez and Lucio Márquez

305. TIMOTEO ARGUETA MÁRQUEZ, 30, day laborer, husband of Agustina Argueta Márquez (victim #297)

306. SANTOS ARGUETA MÁRQUEZ, 9, student, son of Agustina Argueta Márquez and Timoteo Argueta Márquez

307. JESÚS ARGUETA MÁRQUEZ, 6, son of Agustina Argueta Márquez and Timoteo Argueta Márquez

308. ISABEL ARGUETA MÁRQUEZ, 4, daughter of Agustina Argueta Márquez and Timoteo Argueta Márquez
309. SANTOS CLAROS, 30, day laborer, companion of María Mártir Argueta Márquez (victim #298)
310. ARMANDO ARGUETA CLAROS, 8 months, son of María Mártir Argueta Márquez and Santos Claros
311. ANTONIO MÁRQUEZ, 35, day laborer
312. EDUVINA MÁRQUEZ, 25, sister of Antonio Márquez
313. MÓNICA DÍAZ, 80, murdered in the area of Tierra Colorada, jurisdiction of Arambala
314. LORENZO CLAROS, 7, grandson of Mónica Díaz
315. ROFELIA ORELLANA, 70, murdered in the area of Tierra Colorada, jurisdiction of Arambala
316. EDUARDO HERNÁNDEZ, 70, day laborer, murdered in the area of Tierra Colorada, jurisdiction of Arambala
317. SARA N., 75, companion of Eduardo Hernández, murdered in the area of Tierra Colorada, jurisdiction of Arambala
318. LUCITA CHICAS, 35, niece of Israel Márquez (victim #46)
319. EFRAÍN RAMOS OR EFRAÍN MÁRQUEZ, 40, merchant, husband of Lucita Chicas
320. CHILD, 2, son of Efraín Ramos
321. CHILD, 4, son of Efraín Ramos
322. CHILD, 12, son of Efraín Ramos
323. ANTONIA GUEVARA, 35
324. CHILD, 5, son of Antonia Guevara
325. CHILD, 10, student, niece of Antonia Guevara
326. CHILD, 8, student, nephew of Antonia Guevara
327. CHILD, 6, student, nephew of Antonia Guevara
328. CHILD, 3, student, nephew of Antonia Guevara
329. FLORINDA DÍAZ, 60
330. NEFTALÍ MÁRQUEZ, 40, day laborer, companion of Florinda Díaz
331. CHILD, 7, ward of Florinda Díaz and Neftalí Márquez
332. PERFECTO DÍAZ, 64, bricklayer
333. ANDREA MÁRQUEZ, 40, wife of Perfecto Díaz
334. EUGENIA DÍAZ MÁRQUEZ, 20, daughter of Perfecto Díaz and Andrea Márquez
335. CHILD, 3, daughter of Eugenia Díaz Márquez
336. MACARIO DÍAZ MÁRQUEZ, 15, day laborer, son of Perfecto Díaz and Andrea Márquez
337. VICTORINA DÍAZ MÁRQUEZ, 16, daughter of Perfecto Díaz and Andrea Márquez
338. CHILD, 3, daughter of Victorina Díaz Márquez and Francisco Argueta

339. CHILD, 2, daughter of Victorina Díaz Márquez and Francisco Argueta

340. JOSÉ RAUL DÍAZ, 14, day laborer, nephew of Perfecto Díaz

341. JOSÉ CAYETANO ARGUETA, 40, musician

342. MARÍA GUEVARA, 30, companion of José Cayetano Argueta

343. SALOMÉ ARGUETA, 18, day laborer, son of José Cayetano Argueta and María Guevara

344. JOSÉ ARGUETA, 14, day laborer, son of José Cayetano Argueta and María Guevara

345. CHILD, 12, day laborer, son of José Cayetano Argueta and María Guevara

346. LORENZO ARGUETA, 40, day laborer

347. WOMAN, 18, wife of José Argueta

348. SALVADOR MÁRQUEZ, 65, day laborer

349. MEDARDA DÍAZ, 60, wife of Salvador Márquez

350. CRISTINA MÁRQUEZ, 25, daughter of Salvador Márquez and Medarda Díaz

351. BARTOLOMÉ MÁRQUEZ OR SALOMÉ MÁRQUEZ, 40 son of Salvador Márquez and Medarda Díaz

352. RUFINO MÁRQUEZ, day laborer, son of Bartolomé Márquez

353. CLEMENTINA MÁRQUEZ OR PASITA DÍAZ, 26, wife of Rufino Márquez

354. WALTER MÁRQUEZ, 3, son of Rufino Márquez and Clementina Márquez

355. EDITH MÁRQUEZ, 12, daughter of Rufino Márquez and Clementina Márquez

356. GLORIA MÁRQUEZ, 10, daughter of Rufino Márquez and Clementina Márquez

357. NORBERTA DÍAZ, 60, wife of Eugenio Vigil

358. JOSÉ MARÍA MÁRQUEZ, 10, son of Leonardo Márquez (victim #51 and Orbelina Márquez (victim #54)

359. MARIO MÁRQUEZ, 6, son of Leonardo Márquez (victim #51 and Orbelina Márquez (victim #54)

360. MAXIMINO MÁRQUEZ, 4, son of Leonardo Márquez (victim #51 and Orbelina Márquez (victim #54)

361. VILMA YANET MÁRQUEZ, 1, daughter of Leonardo Márquez (victim #51 and Orbelina Márquez (victim #54)

362. MARÍA SANTOS PEREIRA ARGUETA, 25

363. MIRIAM RODRÍGUEZ PEREIRA, 9, daughter of María Santos Pereira Argueta

364. DOLORES RODRÍGUEZ PEREIRA, 7, daughter of María Santos Pereira Argueta

365. LILIÁN ELIZABETH RODRÍGUEZ PEREIRA, 6, daughter of María Santos Pereira Argueta

366. NILSON RODRÍGUEZ OR HERNÁN RODRÍGUEZ, 4, son of María Santos Pereira Argueta
367. EVELIO RODRÍGUEZ PEREIRA, 3, son of María Santos Pereira Argueta
368. CHILD, 10 months old, son of María Santos Pereira Argueta
369. ISABEL ARGUETA, 65, widow
370. MARGARITA REYNA MÁRQUEZ, 55

LA JOYA

371. MARÍA ROMERO MARTÍNEZ, 25
372. MARIBEL ROMERO, 5, daughter of María Romero Martínez
373. LUPITA ROMERO, 3, daughter of María Romero Martínez
374. ARNOLDO ROMERO, 6 months old, son of María Romero Martínez
375. MARÍA HERIBERTA MARTÍNEZ, 30, 9 months pregnant at time of death
376. ANASTACIO CHICAS ROMERO, age unknown, day laborer, companion of María Heriberta Martínez
377. DORÉ CHICAS MARTÍNEZ, 7, son of María Heriberta Martínez and Anastacio Chicas Romero
378. NUNCIACIÓN CHICAS MARTÍNEZ, 3, daughter of María Heriberta Martínez and Anastacio Chicas Romero
379. JUSTINIANO CHICAS MARTÍNEZ, 8, daughter of María Heriberta Martínez and Anastacio Chicas Romero
380. PEDRO CHICAS MARTÍNEZ, 12, daughter of María Heriberta Martínez and Anastacio Chicas Romero
381. MARINO CHICAS MARTÍNEZ, 14, daughter of María Heriberta Martínez and Anastacio Chicas Romero
382. DAVID CHICAS MARTÍNEZ, 1, son of María Heriberta Martínez and Anastacio Chicas Romero
383. FELIPA MARTÍNEZ, 60, mother of María Heriberta Martínez
384. VICENTA TORRES, 30
385. DORA TORRES MARTÍNEZ, 3, daughter of Vicenta Torres
386. CHILD, several months old, daughter of Vicenta Torres
387. CHILD, several months old, daughter of Vicenta Torres
388. VICTORINA CHICAS, 35, maguey spinner
389. LUCRECIA CHICAS, 5, daughter of Victorina Chicas
390. PETRONA CHICAS OR PETRONILA CHICAS, 40
391. CATALINA CHICAS, 8, daughter of Petrona Chicas
392. JUSTINA GUEVARA OR JUSTINIANA GUEVARA, 50, maguey spinner
393. JACINTA GUEVARA OR JACINTA DÍAZ, 25, maguey spinner, daughter of Justina Guevara

394. MARÍA GUEVARA OR MARÍA DÍAZ, 5, daughter of Jacinta Díaz and granddaughter of Justina Guevara
395. ROQUE GUEVARA OR ROQUE DÍAZ, 4, son of Jacinta Díaz and grandson of Justina Guevara
396. AMBROSIO GUEVARA, 1, son of Jacinta Díaz and grandson of Justina Guevara
397. JOSEFINA GUEVARA OR JOSEFINA HERNÁNDEZ, 50
398. HILARIA HERNÁNDEZ, 45, sister of Josefina Hernández
399. LORENZO VIGIL, 40, day laborer
400. AMINTA VIGIL ARGUETA, 19, daughter of Lorenzo Vigil
401. PEDRITO VIGIL ARGUETA, 10, son of Lorenzo Vigil
402. JOSÉ WILFREDO VIGIL, 2, son of Aminta Vigil Argueta and grandson of Lorenzo Vigil
403. CHILD, 3, son of Aminta Vigil Argueta and grandson of Lorenzo Vigil
404. MATEA VIGIL, 60, aunt of Lorenzo Vigil
405. CONCEPCIÓN VIGIL, 40, day laborer and maguey spinner, son of Matea Vigil
406. EUGENIA MARTÍNEZ, 25, companion of Concepción Vigil
407. LEONARDA MARTÍNEZ, 60, mother of Eugenia Martínez
408. MARÍA MARTÍNEZ, 6, daughter of Concepción Vigil and Eugenia Martínez
409. FEDERICO MARTÍNEZ, 4, son of Concepción Vigil and Eugenia Martínez
410. CHILD, 6 months old, daughter of Concepción Vigil and Eugenia Martínez
411. MARÍA ARGUETA, 30, sister of Eugenia Martínez
412. CHILD, age unknown, son of María Argueta
413. CHILD, age unknown, son of María Argueta
414. CHILD, age unknown, daughter of María Argueta
415. AQUILINO DÍAZ OR AQUILINO SÁENZ, 35, day laborer
416. FRANCISCA CHAVARRÍA, 40, companion of Aquilino Díaz
417. SANTOS CHAVARRÍA, 9, son of Aquilino Díaz and Francisca Chavarría
418. JOSÉ CHAVARRÍA, 8, son of Aquilino Díaz and Francisca Chavarría
419. CHILD, age unknown, daughter of Aquilino Díaz and Francisca Chavarría
420. CHILD, age unknown, daughter of Aquilino Díaz and Francisca Chavarría
421. ESTANISLAO DÍAZ, 65, farmer, father of Aquilino Díaz
422. TOMASA MARTÍNEZ, 70, wife of Estanislao Díaz and mother of Aquilino Díaz

423. DOMINGA CHAVARRÍA, 20
424. CHILD, age unknown, son of Dominga Chavarría
425. CHILD, age unknown, son of Dominga Chavarría
426. CHILD, age unknown, son of Dominga Chavarría
427. SEBASTIANA RAMOS, 35
428. PETRONA CHAVARRÍA, 50, aunt of Francisca Chavarría (victim #416)
429. TOMASA CHAVARRÍA, age unknown, mother of Francisca Chavarría (victim #416)
430. SANTOS CHAVARRÍA, 55, brother of Tomasa Chavarría, maguey spinner
431. FAUSTINA CHAVARRÍA LUNA, 15, daughter of Santos Chavarría
432. EUSTAQUIA CHAVARRÍA LUNA, 11, daughter of Santos Chavarría
433. SANTOS CHAVARRÍA LUNA, 5, daughter of Santos Chavarría
434. CHILD, 1, daughter of Santos Chavarría
435. REGINO CHAVARRÍA, 65, brother of Santos Chavarría
436. OTILIA HERNÁNDEZ, 30, daughter of Regino Chavarría
437. JOSÉ ROSARIO PÉREZ, 20, day laborer and maguey spinner, companion of Otilia Hernández
438. CHILD, age unknown, son of Otilia Hernández and José Rosario Pérez
439. CHILD, age unknown, son of Otilia Hernández and José Rosario Pérez
440. CHILD, age unknown, son of Otilia Hernández and José Rosario Pérez
441. CHILD, age unknown, son of Otilia Hernández and José Rosario Pérez
442. MARCIAL PÉREZ, 15, maguey spinner, brother of José Rosario Pérez
443. AGAPITO LUNA, 23, farmer
444. INÉS MARTÍNEZ, 45, day laborer
445. MARGARITA MARTÍNEZ OR MARGARITA ROMERO, 40, wife of Inés Martínez
446. CRISTINA MARTÍNEZ, 23, daughter of Margarita Romero and Inés Martínez
447. CRISTINITA MARTÍNEZ, 9 months old, daughter of Cristina Martínez
448. CHILD, 6, son of Cristina Martínez
449. FACUNDA ROMERO, 25, daughter of Margarita Romero and Inés Martínez
450. MARTA ROMERO, 10, daughter of Facunda Romero
451. CHILD, 8, son of Facunda Romero
452. CHILD, 6, son of Facunda Romero

453. MAN, 22, day laborer, son of Margarita Romero and Inés Martínez
454. BOY, 19, day laborer, son of Margarita Romero and Inés Martínez
455. JACINTO SÁNCHEZ, 80, day laborer
456. AMELIA SÁNCHEZ, 95, sister of Jacinto Sánchez
457. DOMINGA SÁNCHEZ, 30, daughter of Jacinto Sánchez
458. MELA SÁNCHEZ OR ANGÉLICA SÁNCHEZ, 14, daughter of Dominga Sánchez
459. JUANCITO SÁNCHEZ, 10, student, son of Dominga Sánchez
460. SANTOS SÁNCHEZ OR SANTOS ARGUETA DE SÁNCHEZ, 35, wife of José Sánchez
461. FIGENIA SÁNCHEZ, 13, daughter of José Sánchez and Santos Sánchez
462. IRMA SÁNCHEZ, 6, daughter of José Sánchez and Santos Sánchez
463. MARIANA SÁNCHEZ, 4, daughter of José Sánchez and Santos Sánchez
464. ESPENTACIÓN SÁNCHEZ OR PETIO SÁNCHEZ, 2, son of José Sánchez and Santos Sánchez
465. JACINTO SÁNCHEZ, 3, son of José Sánchez and Santos Sánchez
466. CONCEPCIÓN SÁNCHEZ, 3 days old, daughter of José Sánchez and Santos Sánchez
467. REYNELDA LÓPEZ OR REYNELDA ELIZABETH LÓPEZ, 32
468. ARNOLDO LÓPEZ, 10 daughter of Reynelda López
469. EDGAR MARÍN LÓPEZ, 8, daughter of Reynelda López
470. JOAQUÍN LÓPEZ, 6, daughter of Reynelda López
471. HERIBERTO LÓPEZ, 4, daughter of Reynelda López
472. JOSÉ DORE LÓPEZ, 2, daughter of Reynelda López
473. JOSÉ CLEOFÁS LÓPEZ, 8 months old, daughter of Reynelda López
474. FRANCISCA GÓMEZ OR FRANCISCA SÁNCHEZ, 75, wife of Ismael López
475. PRISCILA LÓPEZ, 22, daughter of Ismael López
476. CHILD, 7 months old, daughter of Priscila López
477. MARÍA INÉS MARTÍNEZ, 34
478. JESÚS MARTÍNEZ, 8, son of María Inés Martínez
479. TEODORO MARTÍNEZ, 5, son of María Inés Martínez
480. MÁXIMA MARTÍNEZ, 10, daughter of María Inés Martínez
481. CHILD, 4, son of María Inés Martínez
482. GREGORIA MARTÍNEZ, 24, cousin of María Inés Martínez
483. BERNARDA MARTÍNEZ OR CECILIA MARTÍNEZ, 12, daughter of Gregoria Martínez
484. ESTHER MARTÍNEZ, 9, daughter of Gregoria Martínez
485. CHILD, 5, daughter of Gregoria Martínez
486. CHILD, 3, daughter of Gregoria Martínez
487. CHILD, 9 months old, daughter of Gregoria Martínez
488. TEODORA RAMÍREZ, 45

489. TRÁNSITO RAMÍREZ, 22
490. RODOLFO RAMÍREZ, 8, son of Tránsito Ramírez
491. FLORITA RAMÍREZ, 3, daughter of Tránsito Ramírez
492. CECILIA RAMÍREZ, 85, aunt of Tránsito Ramírez
493. ALEJANDRA ROMERO, 75
494. CRISTINA GUEVARA, 25
495. CHILD, 3 months old, son of Cristina Guevara
496. SILVERIA MEJÍA ROMERO, 25, maguey spinner
497. JESÚS MEJÍA CHICAS, 10, son of Silveria Mejía Romero
498. MARÍA MARTA MEJÍA CHICAS, 8, daughter of Silveria Mejía Romero
499. JUANITA MEJÍA CHICAS, 6, daughter of Silveria Mejía Romero
500. JOSÉ LUCAS MEJÍA CHICAS, 3 son of Silveria Mejía Romero
501. CHILD, 2, son of Silveria Mejía Romero
502. CHILD, 3 months old, son of Silveria Mejía Romero
503. MARÍA MARCOS REYES, 20
504. JOSÉ FRANCISCO REYES LUNA, 5, son of María Marcos Reyes
505. MARÍA NELY REYES LUNA, 3, daughter of María Marcos Reyes
506. EVARISTO REYES LUNA, 6 months old, son of María Marcos Reyes
507. PRESENTACIÓN MÁRQUEZ, 41, day laborer
508. MARÍA MÁRTIR MÁRQUEZ, 38, wife of Presentación Márquez
509. GIRL, 14, daughter of Presentación Márquez and María Mártir Márquez
510. CHILD, 11, daughter of Presentación Márquez and María Mártir Márquez
511. CHILD, 9, son of Presentación Márquez and María Mártir Márquez
512. CHILD, 7, son of Presentación Márquez and María Mártir Márquez
513. CHILD, 4, son of Presentación Márquez and María Mártir Márquez
514. VICENTA MÁRQUEZ, 80, widow
515. ENEMESIO RODRÍGUEZ OR ENEMESIO GUEVARA, 38, day laborer
516. DONATILA CHICAS OR DOMITILA ORELLANA, 30, pregnant at time of death, companion of Enemesio Rodríguez
517. CHILD, 7, daughter of Enemesio Rodríguez and Donatila Chicas
518. CHILD, 5, daughter of Enemesio Rodríguez and Donatila Chicas
519. CHILD, 1, daughter of Enemesio Rodríguez and Donatila Chicas
520. CATARINO RODRÍGUEZ OR CATARINO GUEVARA, 70, day laborer, father of Enemesio Rodríguez
521. NARCISA MÁRQUEZ, 68, wife of Catarino Rodríguez
522. MÁXIMO RODRÍGUEZ, 40, day laborer, son of Catarino Rodríguez and Narcisa Márquez
523. LEONARDA MÁRQUEZ, 40, wife of Máximo Rodríguez
524. ELENA RODRÍGUEZ, 16, daughter of Máximo Rodríguez and Leonarda Márquez

525. HERMINIO RODRÍGUEZ, 14, son of Máximo Rodríguez and Leonarda Márquez
526. CAMILO RODRÍGUEZ, 12, son of Máximo Rodríguez and Leonarda Márquez
527. CHILD, 6, son of Máximo Rodríguez and Leonarda Márquez
528. CHILD, 4, son of Máximo Rodríguez and Leonarda Márquez
529. FÉLIX RODRÍGUEZ, 30, daughter of Catarino Rodríguez and Narcisa Márquez
530. CHILD, 10, daughter of Félix Rodríguez
531. CHILD, 8, son of Félix Rodríguez
532. CHILD, 6, daughter of Félix Rodríguez
533. CHILD, 4, son of Félix Rodríguez
534. PEDRO ARGUETA, 40, day laborer
535. PEDRO ARGUETA, 35, day laborer, brother of Pedro Argueta
536. JULIA DEL CID, 18, pregnant at time of death
537. HUMBERTO CHICAS, 19, day laborer, companion of Julia Del Cid
538. CHILD, 2, son of Julia Del Cid and Humberto Chicas
539. VICENTE MÁRQUEZ, 60, day laborer
540. SERVANDA MÁRQUEZ, 28, daughter of Vicente Márquez
541. SERGIO MÁRQUEZ OR SERSIDO MÁRQUEZ, 25, day laborer, son of Vicente Márquez
542. CHILD, 7, son of Servanda Márquez
543. CHILD, 3, son of Servanda Márquez
544. MONCHO MÁRQUEZ, 15, day laborer, husband of Mercedes Pereira, who was killed in Los Toriles
545. TERESA ARGUETA OR TERESA RODRÍGUEZ, 22
546. PEDRO CHICAS, 27, farmer, husband of Teresa Argueta
547. CHILD, age unknown, son of Pedro Chicas and Teresa Argueta
548. CHILD, age unknown, son of Pedro Chicas and Teresa Argueta
549. CHILD, age unknown, son of Pedro Chicas and Teresa Argueta
550. CHILD, age unknown, son of Pedro Chicas and Teresa Argueta
551. CHILD, 4, daughter of Pedro Chicas and Teresa Argueta
552. CARLOS CLAROS, 25, day laborer
553. LUCAS CHICAS, 20, companion of Carlos Claros
554. RUMALDO MÁRQUEZ, 30, day laborer
555. MÉLIDA CHICAS, 24, wife of Rumaldo Márquez
556. CHILD, 8 days old, son of Rumaldo Márquez and Mélida Chicas
557. CHILD, 2, son of Rumaldo Márquez and Mélida Chicas
558. CHILD, 11, daughter of Rumaldo Márquez and Mélida Chicas
559. CHILD, 8, daughter of Rumaldo Márquez and Mélida Chicas
560. CHILD, 6, daughter of Rumaldo Márquez and Mélida Chicas

LOS TORILES

561. NARCISO ARGUETA, 80, farmer, father of Felipe Argueta (killed in El Mozote)
562. ABILIO VIGIL, 43, farmer
563. SATURNINA ARGUETA, 45, companion of Abilio Vigil
564. ESTANISLAO ALVARENGA OR ESTANISLAO ARGUETA, 60, father of Abilio Vigil
565. JUSTINIANA N., 50, companion of Estanislao Alvarenga
566. SEFERINA VIGIL OR SEFERINA ARGUETA, 15 daughter of Abilio Vigil and Saturnina Argueta
567. FRANCISCO ARGUETA, 13, son of Abilio Vigil and Saturnina Argueta
568. MARÍA ANTONIA ARGUETA, 11, daughter of Abilio Vigil and Saturnina Argueta
569. MERCEDES ARGUETA, 9, daughter of Abilio Vigil and Saturnina Argueta
570. MARÍA SANTOS ARGUETA, 7, daughter of Abilio Vigil and Saturnina Argueta
571. CHILD, 5, daughter of Abilio Vigil and Saturnina Argueta
572. CHILD, 3, daughter of Abilio Vigil and Saturnina Argueta
573. CHILD, 1, daughter of Abilio Vigil and Saturnina Argueta
574. MANUEL ALVARENGA OR MANUEL SANTOS PEREIRA ARGUETA, 30, day laborer, companion of Adonisia Rodríguez (killed in El Mozote)
575. FLORENTINA PEREIRA, 70, mother of Manuel Santos Pereira Argueta
576. PETRONA MÁRQUEZ, 39
577. HERMINIO MÁRQUEZ, 41, day laborer, companion of Petrona Márquez
578. MARÍA ZOILA MÁRQUEZ, 17, day laborer, son of Petrona Márquez and Herminio Márquez
579. MARÍA CARMEN MÁRQUEZ, 15, daughter of Petrona Márquez and Herminio Márquez
580. JOSÉ SANTOS MÁRQUEZ, daughter of Petrona Márquez and Herminio Márquez
581. MARÍA JUANA MÁRQUEZ, 8, daughter of Petrona Márquez and Herminio Márquez
582. JUAN MÁRQUEZ, 5, son of Petrona Márquez and Herminio Márquez
583. NICOLASA MÁRQUEZ, 17 months old, daughter of Petrona Márquez and Herminio Márquez
584. CHILD, 8 days old, son of Petrona Márquez and Herminio Márquez

585. CRESCENCIO ARGUETA, 80, day laborer, stepfather of Orbelina Márquez (victim #54, killed in El Mozote)
586. GIRL, 14, daughter of Crescencio Argueta
587. CHILD, 12, daughter of Crescencio Argueta
588. CHILD, 8, son of Crescencio Argueta
589. NATALIA GUEVARA, 45
590. ROSA CÁNDIDA PEREIRA, 14, daughter of Natalia Guevara
591. JOSÉ MARIO PEREIRA, 10, son of Natalia Guevara
592. SIMEONA VIGIL, 90, mother-in-law of Natalia Guevara
593. BERTOLDINO PEREIRA, 70, farmer, son of Simeona Vigil
594. MARÍA MÁRQUEZ, 65, wife of Bertoldino Pereira
595. INÉS PEREIRA MÁRQUEZ, 18, day laborer, son of Bertoldino Pereira and María Márquez
596. CARMEN MÁRQUEZ, 17, companion of Inés Pereira Márquez
597. JOSÉ IGNACIO PEREIRA, 25, farmer, son of Bertoldino Pereira and María Márquez
598. MERCEDES PEREIRA, 16, daughter of Bertoldino Pereira and María Márquez
599. JESÚS PEREIRA, 13, son of Bertoldino Pereira and María Márquez
600. JUAN ANGEL PEREIRA, 55, day laborer, son of Simeona Vigil
601. NELIDA ROMERO, 10, granddaughter of Simeona Vigil
602. MARTO VIGIL, 25, day laborer
603. GUILLERMA MÁRQUEZ, 25, pregnant at time of death, wife of Marto Vigil
604. JOSÉ VIGIL, 8, son of Marto Vigil and Guillerma Márquez
605. MARÍA VIGIL, 7, daughter of Marto Vigil and Guillerma Márquez
606. ANGEL VIGIL MÁRQUEZ, 6, son of Marto Vigil and Guillerma Márquez
607. CHILD, 4, son of Marto Vigil and Guillerma Márquez
608. CHILD, 2, daughter of Marto Vigil and Guillerma Márquez
609. LUIS VIGIL, 50, day laborer, uncle of Marto Vigil
610. JOSÉ VIGIL, 30, farmer, cousin of Marto Vigil
611. BERNARDA MÁRQUEZ, 25, wife of José Vigil
612. CHILD, 7, son of José Vigil and Bernarda Márquez
613. CHILD, 5, son of José Vigil and Bernarda Márquez
614. CHILD, 1, son of José Vigil and Bernarda Márquez
615. AGUSTINA MÁRQUEZ, 46, mother of Bernarda Márquez
616. JOSÉ DANILO MÁRQUEZ, 35, farmer
617. MARTA CHICAS, 30, wife of Danilo Márquez
618. JOSÉ MÁRQUEZ, 10, son of Danilo Márquez and Marta Chicas
619. CHILD, 8, son of Danilo Márquez and Marta Chicas

620. CHILD, 12, son of Danilo Márquez and Marta Chicas
621. CHILD, 5, son of Danilo Márquez and Marta Chicas
622. CHILD, 1, son of Danilo Márquez and Marta Chicas

JOCOTE ARMIRILLO

623. CELESTINA VIGIL, 50, killed in El Mozote with her children, mother of Florentina Del Cid
624. FLORENTINA DEL CID VIGIL, 30, pregnant at time of death
625. CAMILO DEL CID, 12, son of Florentina Del Cid Vigil
626. JAZMÍN DEL CID, 8, son of Florentina Del Cid Vigil
627. CHILD, 3, daughter of Florentina Del Cid Vigil
628. GENOVEVA DÍAZ, 60
629. MODESTA N., 40
630. CHILD, 2 months old, son of Modesta N.
631. CHILD, 9, daughter of Modesta N.
632. CHILD, 6, daughter of Modesta N.
633. LORENZA MÁRQUEZ, 40
634. BENEDICTO MÁRQUEZ, 9, son of Lorenza Márquez
635. MODESTO MÁRQUEZ, 6, son of Lorenza Márquez
636. MARÍA BERNALDA MÁRQUEZ, 4, daughter of Lorenza Márquez
637. MARÍA ARGUETA, 35
638. SANTOS HERNÁNDEZ, 12, student, son of María Argueta
639. CHILD, 10 months old, son of María Argueta

CERRO PANDO

640. SATURNINA DÍAZ, 22
641. EUSEBIA DÍAZ, 10, daughter of Saturnina Díaz
642. ESTELA DÍAZ, 2, niece of Saturnina Díaz
643. CHILD, 20 days old, daughter of Saturnina Díaz
644. ANTOLÍN DÍAZ, 22, maguey spinner
645. TOMASA ARGUETA, 20, companion of Antolín Díaz
646. CHILD, 3, son of Antolín Díaz and Tomasa Argueta
647. CHILD, 2, son of Antolín Díaz and Tomasa Argueta
648. CHILD, 15 days old, daughter of Antolín Díaz and Tomasa Argueta
649. JUAN CHICAS, 29, maguey spinner
650. CIRIACA ARGUETA, 30, companion of Juan Chicas
651. LUCIANO CHICOS ARGUETA, 15, maguey spinner, son of Juan Chicas
652. GERVASIO CHICAS ARGUETA, 12, maguey spinner, son of Juan Chicas

653. TRÁNSITO CHICAS ARGUETA, 9, son of Juan Chicas
654. NICOLASA CHICAS ARGUETA, 6, daughter of Juan Chicas
655. DIONISIO ARGUETA OR LEONISIO ARGUETA, 32, maguey spinner
656. FÉLIX PORTILLO OR FÉLIX DÍAZ, 29, companion of Dionisio Argueta
657. CHILD, 10, daughter of Dionisio Argueta and Félix Portillo
658. CHILD, 7, daughter of Dionisio Argueta and Félix Portillo
659. REGINO ARGUETA, 40, maguey spinner, brother of Dionisio Argueta
660. MÁRTIR PORTILLO, 35, wife of Regino Argueta
661. MATILDE ARGUETA PORTILLO, 16, day laborer, son of Regino Argueta and Mártir Portillo
662. FILIBERTA CHICAS, 16, companion of Matilde Argueta
663. GERARDO ARGUETA, 29, maguey spinner
664. JUANA ARGUETA, 24, companion of Gerardo Argueta
665. CHILD, 9, daughter of Gerardo Argueta and Juana Argueta
666. MIGUEL ARGUETA, 25, maguey spinner
667. DOMINGA ARGUETA, 22, companion of Miguel Argueta
668. CHILD, 5, daughter of Miguel Argueta and Dominga Argueta
669. CHILD, 3, daughter of Miguel Argueta and Dominga Argueta
670. CHILD, 2, daughter of Miguel Argueta and Dominga Argueta
671. CATARINO ARGUETA, 65, maguey spinner, father of Ciriaca Argueta (victim #650)
672. FRANCISCA ARGUETA, 70, wife of Catarino Argueta
673. TIMOTEO ARGUETA, 28, artisan, son of Catarino Argueta and Francisca Argueta
674. ROMANA PEREIRA, 28, companion of Timoteo Argueta
675. GIRL, 15, daughter of Timoteo Argueta and Romana Pereira
676. CHILD, 8, son of Timoteo Argueta and Romana Pereira
677. CHILD, 5, son of Timoteo Argueta and Romana Pereira
678. JORGEN ARGUETA, 80, mother of Dionisio Argueta (victim #655)
679. GENARO ARGUETA, 82, farmer, companion of Jorgen Argueta
680. EDILFONZO ARGUETA, 51, farmer, son of Jorgen Argueta and Genaro Argueta
681. LOLA MARTÍNEZ, 20
682. CHILD, 8, daughter of Lola Martínez
683. LUCIO ARGUETA, 24, day laborer, son of Catarino Argueta (victim #671) and Francisca Argueta (victim #672)
684. WOMAN, 22, companion of Lucio Argueta
685. CHILD, 3, son of Lucio Argueta
686. CHILD, 2, son of Lucio Argueta
687. JUSTO MARTÍNEZ, 45, locksmith

688. ANGELA ARGUETA, 33, wife of Justo Martínez
689. TOMÁS MARTÍNEZ ARGUETA, 20, son of Justo Martínez and Angela Argueta
690. DIONISIA MARTÍNEZ, 18, companion of Tomás Martínez Argueta
691. CHILD, 2 months old, son of Tomás Martínez Argueta and Dionisia Martínez
692. ESTEBAN MARTÍNEZ ARGUETA, 16, son of Justo Martínez and Angela Argueta
693. BOY, 14, son of Justo Martínez and Angela Argueta
694. CHILD, 12, daughter of Justo Martínez and Angela Argueta
695. CHILD, 9, daughter of Justo Martínez and Angela Argueta
696. MÁXIMO ARGUETA, 30, maguey spinner, son of Catarino Argueta (victim #671)
697. HERIBERTA RAMOS, 28, companion of Máximo Argueta
698. BOY, 15, son of Máximo Argueta and Heriberta Ramos
699. BOY, 13, son of Máximo Argueta and Heriberta Ramos
700. CHILD, 10, son of Máximo Argueta and Heriberta Ramos
701. CHILD, 8, son of Máximo Argueta and Heriberta Ramos
702. MATEO LÓPEZ, 55, maguey spinner
703. AGUSTINA MARTÍNEZ, 30, wife of Mateo López
704. GIRL, 15, daughter of Mateo López and Agustina Martínez
705. CHILD, 12, daughter of Mateo López and Agustina Martínez
706. CHILD, 9, daughter of Mateo López and Agustina Martínez
707. CHILD, 6, son of Mateo López and Agustina Martínez
708. VITOR MARTÍNEZ, 60, mother of Agustina Martínez
709. JESÚS LUNA, 78, day laborer, companion of Vitor Martínez
710. CATARINO MARTÍNEZ, 26, maguey spinner, son of Vitor Martínez
711. FERMINA CHICAS, 24, companion of Catarino Martínez
712. CHILD, 10, son of Catarino Martínez and Fermina Chicas
713. CHILD, 7, son of Catarino Martínez and Fermina Chicas
714. CHILD, 5, son of Catarino Martínez and Fermina Chicas
715. MARTÍN MARTÍNEZ, 32, maguey spinner, brother of Catarino Martínez
716. FERMINA ARGUETA, 29, companion of Martín Martínez
717. CHILD, 10, daughter of Martín Martínez and Fermina Argueta
718. CHILD, 7, daughter of Martín Martínez and Fermina Argueta
719. CHILD, 5, son of Martín Martínez and Fermina Argueta
720. PABLO CHICAS, 28, maguey spinner
721. DIONISIA ARGUETA OR LEONISIA MEJÍA, 24, companion of Pablo Chicas
722. GIRL, 13, daughter of Pablo Chicas and Dionisia Argueta
723. ANDRÉS CHICAS ARGUETA, 11, son of Pablo Chicas and Dionisia Argueta

724. CHILD, 9, daughter of Pablo Chicas and Dionisia Argueta
725. CHILD, 6, son of Pablo Chicas and Dionisia Argueta
726. NASARIA ARGUETA, 70, mother of Dionisia Argueta
727. RAFAEL ARGUETA MEJÍA, 27, maguey spinner, son of Nasaria Argueta
728. LEONCIA ARGUETA, 24, companion of Rafael Argueta Mejía
729. CHILD, 5, son of Rafael Argueta Mejía and Leoncia Argueta
730. CHILD, 2, daughter of Rafael Argueta Mejía and Leoncia Argueta
731. TIBURCIO MEJÍA, 35, day laborer, son of Nasaria Argueta
732. ELOISA PORTILLO OR ARCADIA PORTILLO, 30, companion of Tiburcio Mejía
733. MARÍA MEJÍA, 29, daughter of Nasaria Argueta
734. ANDRÉS FLORES, 48, day laborer, companion of María Mejía
735. COLÁSTICO MEJÍA, 40, maguey spinner, cousin of María Mejía
736. BRUNA ARGUETA, 42, companion of Colástico Mejía and daughter of Jorgen Argueta (victim #678) and Genaro Argueta (victim #679)
737. GIRL, 15, daughter of Colástico Mejía and Bruna Argueta
738. CHILD, 12, daughter of Colástico Mejía and Bruna Argueta
739. CHILD, 9, daughter of Colástico Mejía and Bruna Argueta
740. SINFOROSO PEREIRA, 30, day laborer
741. EUGENIA DÍAZ, 28, companion of Sinforoso Pereira
742. CHILD, 8, son of Sinforoso Pereira and Eugenia Díaz
743. MARÍA RAMOS, 75, widow
744. PATRICIA ARGUETA, 75, artisan
745. MIGUEL ARGUETA, 58, farmer
746. EDILFONZA ARGUETA, 48, companion of Edilfonzo Argueta (victim #680)
747. AURELIA RAMÍREZ, 70
748. SUSANA RAMÍREZ, 32, daughter of Aurelia Ramírez
749. ENEMESIA LUNA, 75, widow
750. FELIPE CHICAS, 38, day laborer
751. CONCEPCIÓN PORTILLO, 35, bricklayer
752. DOMINGA PORTILLO, 28, seamstress, wife of Concepción Portillo

JOATECA

753. MÁXIMO PÉREZ, 28, catechist
754. BENEDICTO PÉREZ, 10, son of Máximo Pérez
755. ESTANISLASA PÉREZ, 8, daughter of Máximo Pérez
756. RÓMULO PÉREZ, 4, son of Máximo Pérez
757. AGUSTINA PÉREZ, 23
758. CHILD, 3 days old, daughter of Agustina Pérez

759. CRESCENCIA PÉREZ, 18, sister of Máximo Pérez
760. CARLOS ORTÍZ, 48, day laborer
761. TERESO DE JESÚS LUNA, 14, day laborer, deaf and mute
762. NATIVIDAD LUNA, 18, cousin of Tereso de Jesús Luna
763. OCTAVIANA LUNA, 8 months old, daughter of Natividad Luna
764. JULIA N., 12
765. WOMAN, 50
766. GIRL, 15, daughter of victim #765
767. GIRL, 13, daughter of victim #765